COMPLEXITY

Science and Technology Studies
Mario Bunge, Series Editor

NICHOLAS RESCHER

COMPLEXITY
A Philosophical Overview

Transaction Publishers
New Brunswick (U.S.A.) and London (U.K.)

This book is printed on acid-free paper that meets the American National Standard for Permanence of Paper for Printed Library Materials.

Library of Congress Catalog Number: 98–28312
ISBN: 1–56000–377–4
Printed in the United States of America

Library of Congress Cataloging-in-Publication Data

Rescher, Nicholas,
        Complexity : a philosophical overview / Nicholas Rescher.
        p.   cm. — (Science and technology studies)
        Includes bibliographical references and index.
        ISBN 1–56000–377–4 (alk. paper)
        1. Science—Philosophy.   2. Complexity (Philosophy)   I. Title.
    II. Series.
    Q175.R393324   1998
    501—dc21
                                                             98–28312
                                                                 CIP

For Roderick Chisholm
in cordial friendship

Contents

Preface

This book brings together ideas developed over many years in various seminars, lectures, and publications in an endeavor to clarify the concept of complexity and to illustrate its many-faceted impact. The unifying theme of the discussion is that the development of our knowledge in a complex world is critically shaped and conditioned by the incidence of that world's complexity and increasingly brings it to light. Life in a complex environment presents a difficult challenge to us, and although this may sound trite as an abstract thesis its detailed ramifications are replete with interesting and instructive perspectives.

I am a great believer in the idea that an author should make it easy for readers to see the forest for the trees. For this reason I have given a brief account of the book's aims at the beginning and a compact summary of its main theses at the end. Moreover, each chapter has been prefaced by a synopsis of its deliberations. The reader (or reviewer!) who is only after the general idea can save time and trouble by perusing these few pages. But this would be an ill-advised economy, since the value of the enterprise lies in its details.

The book was drafted in Pittsburgh during the 1995-96 academic year, completed in Oxford during the summer of 1996, and then polished over the ensuing academic year (1996-97). I am indebted to Mr. Jeffrey Knight for his editorial vetting of a draft and to Ms. Estelle Burris for her patient competence in preparing a publishable version on the word processor. I am also grateful to my friend, Professor Mario Bunge, for his supportive interest in the project.

Pittsburgh, PA
September 1997

Introduction
The Ramifications of Complexity

Complexity is at once at bane and a blessing—a blessing because it is the unavoidable accompaniment and indeed prerequisite of progress, and a bane because it is both a negativity in itself and a burden that impedes the smooth realization of further progress. The aim of this book will be to examine the nature of complexity and to consider its bearing on our understanding of the world and on the management of our affairs within it. It unfolds the sobering story of how an inherent impetus to complexity is at work throughout our efforts to enhance our knowledge and our technology so as to lead our lives in ways that we find cognitively and affectively satisfying. As beings of finite physical and intellectual powers living in a realm whose complexity is literally unlimited, the ramifications of this circumstance are both ubiquitous and inescapable.

The overall line of thought to be developed here runs as follows:

- Complexity is itself a complex notion that combines compositional, structural, and functional elements. (Chapter 1)
- Complexity is a profoundly characteristic feature of the real. The world we live in is an enormously complex system—so much so that nature's complexity is literally inexhaustible. This circumstance is reflected in the inherent limitedness of our knowledge of nature: the descriptive/explanatory project of natural science is ultimately incompletable. In fact, our recognition that reality is indefinitely complex—that its nature extends beyond the horizons that it can possibly know or even conjecture about—betokens the objective mind-independence of the real. (Chapter 2)
- Progress in scientific research as it unfolds over time requires a growth in technical sophistication that renders science itself increasingly complex. In the course of scientific and technological progress we build ourselves an ever higher tower of complexity, as it were. Accordingly, what we call *progress* has a darker side to it as well,

being a journey into regions of ever deeper difficulty. This ongoing complexification makes for an increasing sophistication, diversification—and indeed disintegration—of our science itself. (Chapter 3)

- On this basis, scientific progress is achieved only at the cost of a vast and ever increasing effort in the generation and processing of information. (Chapter 4)
- The ongoing development of natural science requires *technological escalation*—an ascent to ever higher levels of sophistication and power. Scientific progress is a technologically mediated struggle with unending complexity. (Chapter 5)
- The perfecting and completing of science is an impracticable idea. And in consequence we must understand that science affords a no more than imperfect picture of reality in its full complexity. (Chapter 6)
- Beings differently constituted from ourselves must be expected to develop a natural science very different from ours. The world's complexity means that science is limited by the very fact of being *our* science. (Chapter 7)
- Making rational decisions in a complex world is also an increasingly difficult and risky business. Here, reason faces the predicament that it must call on us to do that which, for aught we know, may in the end prove totally inappropriate. (Chapter 8)
- And this is no less true at the level of public policy making. The processes involved in human progress mean that the life-setting we create for ourselves—the world of human artifice—also grows increasingly complex. And this growing complexity also often inhibits the realization of our social goals through chaos and gridlock. (Chapter 9)
- The answer to the question of how to manage our human affairs in a complex world is: very carefully. Nevertheless, being the sort of creatures we are, the fact of our limitedness in a complex world is not an unqualified tragedy for us. (Chapter 10)

A human being inhabits different worlds. On the one hand there is the outer world, the real world of human experience. Here we encounter the realm of natural reality as it functions under the aegis of the laws of nature. Through investigation, inquiry, and the development of information we try continually to expand and deepen our knowledge of this realm, and manage to enlarge it by ever more extensive observation and experimentation. But even as its history after the big bang expands the physical universe, so our history after the evolutionary emergence of intelligence has seen an ongoing—and accelerating—expansion of the realm of human knowledge about this real world of ours. The explosive growth of the literature of science through journals, books, tapes, and records of various sorts attests to this virtually explosive process which renders the achievement of comprehensive knowledge effectively unattainable. Yet, nevertheless, complexity is not an unqualifiedly negative factor owing to the challenges it presents. A complex mind would not be able to take much interest—and could in fact not have emerged through evolution—in a world that lacks complexity.

Then there is also the inner world, the realm of human thought-artifice through the use of imagination. Here we deal with fictions, with self-created imagining rather than naturally encountered facts. We use thought to explore the domain of its own creation: the realm of possibility. Here we have not lawful order but a virtual chaos: it is pretty much a matter of anything goes. (Even the restraining claims of logical coherence and consistency can be thrown off.) In this realm we encounter the ongoing development of an ever larger and more complex domain as our imagination runs riot.

An irony comes to the fore in this connection. The development of the inner world of thought proceeds within the outer world of nature: intelligent beings are themselves part of nature. Our world of mental artifice is the work of imagination alright, but the imagination of a terrestrial mammal—a creature all of whose resources and capacities belong within and are shaped by the processes of nature. This means that despite its increasing complexity this chaotic-seeming realm is not, after all, totally chaotic. It has several modes (music, plastic arts, etc.) and genres, kinship groups that evolve along certain particular lines. While the realm of artifice seems to grow in ways whose inherent variety knows no limits, the painstaking student of its phenomena can nevertheless discern various patterns of order here. Cataloguers and taxonomists find work to do. Still, the fact remains that all of our different worlds growing increasingly large, diverse, and complex over time—alike our particular natural world as science reveals it, the thought would developed through creative artifice, and the social world of the structures and modalities of human interrelationship.

Of course, this social world—the realm of our interrelationships among fellow humans—is of particular significance for us. And here too specialization and division of labor everywhere characterizes the scene we confront,[1] creating an ever-increasing diversity of structured relationships that define our position vis-a-vis our fellows: as businessmen, fellow kinsmen, friends, fellow employees, professional associates, hobby-sharers, and so on. So here too complexity comes on the scene. The patterns of affinity interdependencies and social interrelations are enormously complex—and have become increasingly so in the course of history. Consider, for example, our circumambient everyday-life conditions. Even a casual look at the shopping areas of a modern city and its suburbs suffices to give a convincing demonstration of the extent to which modern life is growing more complex. And inspection of a bookstore or a news agents display would do much to reinforce this realization. The contemporary proliferation of products and services, of ideas and information is staggering. (The diversity of contemporary means of transportation and—even more—of communication afford another illustration.) But with enlarged opportunities there comes the need for ever more choices. Alternatives multiply in every direction: educational, professional, recreational, and so on. And this expansion of opportunity calls for ever greater discrimination—for deploying one's standards, criteria, priorities. The community confronts a situation of a profusion and variety that is to all interests and purposes chaotic but out of this chaos individuals must fashion a manageable order for themselves.

A common pattern of growing complexity thus confronts us on all sides. All of the different "projects" that are characteristic of the human condition—specifically including the cognitive, the productive, and the social—are embarked on a journey of increasing complexification. And this everywhere produces the same results: increased diversification and specialization, greater ranges of divorce, increased difficulty of operation. As doing particular things becomes easier in the course of "progress," the management of affairs-at-large becomes more laborious. For while the community in its collective totality can set off "in all directions at once," the individual must make delimiting decisions. Yet our resources are finite—especially as regards time and energy. And this points to the ever more urgent role of choice-guiding personal values and priorities in an increasingly complex operating environment.

If such a perspective is correct, then however undesirable this situation may be judged to be, the growing complexification that we see all about us is simply inevitable. It is something inherent in the very nature and structure of these human projects themselves, which throughout exhibit the shared feature of taking the simple as far as it will go and then having to accept more complexity in order to go further. And enhanced complexity management always calls for substantially greater efforts.

Such an account cannot expect to meet a ready welcome. We incline to prefer those who give answers to those who raise questions and indicate difficulties. People yearn for solutions—and the simpler the better. Few of us are pleased to hear that the problems that confront us may well prove too formidable for our limited powers—that frequently the best we can do is simply to muddle through in a spirit of hopeful determination. And yet there is good reason to think that the realities of a complex world are such that in the interests of realism we would do well to come to terms with our own limitations—alike in the cognitive, practical, and social domains. The school of bitter experience all too often confronts us with the disillusioning ramifications of complexity. Acknowledging and understanding this unwelcome phenomenon not only helps to avoid futile disappointments and pointless regrets, but also helps to point the way to a realistic recognition of the challenges that confront us in addressing our cognitive and our practical tasks. And in any case, it is the philosopher's job "to tell it like it is"—as best he can.

As a philosophical study, this book is an exercise in second-order reflection. The sciences endeavor to depict the world's complexities in themselves, directly as it were. The present, primarily philosophical deliberations are not concerned to describe the world but to provide orientation regarding the descriptions obtained elsewhere, and above all from science. They accordingly proceed at a remove from factual information and are correspondingly indirect, not elaborating the factual substance of science but seeking to assess its wider implications.

Some readers might thus be tempted to complain that the deliberations of the book are rather abstract. But this sort of complaint is not altogether warranted. There is a profound analogy between geographical and cognitive cartography. In both cases, one can depict the terrain at issue at very different levels of scale. On the one hand, one can depict it in microscopic detail; on the other, one can present just the big picture, as it were, drawn with a broader brush. And both approaches have their uses. For cognitive processing generally brings different sorts of information to view at different levels of scale so that different sorts of insights emerge there. To be sure, we live in an era where studies of microdetail predominate in fashion, but all the same it is instructive from time to time to step back and look at the big picture. Even when the individual trees are highly interesting and picturesque, it has its use to see what the forest looks like in the large. At any rate, the very nature of present concerns dictates that this will have to be our mode of approach here.

Note

1. It proves illuminating in this context to compare classificatory inventories of professions and specialties used in the nineteenth century with those of the twentieth.

1

The Ways of Complexity

(1) A system's complexity is a matter of the quantity and variety of its constituent elements and of the interrelational elaborateness of their organizational and operational make-up. (2) Ontological complexity accordingly has three main aspects: the compositional, the structural, and the functional. (3) As an item's complexity increases, so do the cognitive requisites for its adequate comprehension, although, of course, cognitive ineptitude and mismanagement can manage to complicate even simple issues. All the same, our best practical index of an item's complexity is the effort that has to be expended in coming to cognitive terms with it in matters of description and explanation. And this means that complexity can in principle make itself felt in any domain whatsoever.

1. What Complexity Involves

The world's complexity is a fact of life that has profound and far-reaching implications for us. Complexity is first and foremost a matter of the number and variety of an item's constituent elements and of the elaborateness of their interrelational structure, be it organizational or operational. Any sort of system or process—anything that is a structured whole consisting of interrelated parts—will be to some extent complex. Accordingly, all manner of things can be more or less complex: natural objects (plants or river systems), physical artifacts (watches or sailboats), mind-engendered processes (languages or instructions), bodies of knowledge, and so on. In greater or lesser degree, complexity is present throughout the domain of the real. And complexity appertains to the realm of fiction as well. Even as a "simple" person is

1

naive and unsophisticated, so a "complex" character in a novel or drama will be one whose actions are not easy to explain and whose described motivations are varied and convoluted.

Some writers identify complexity with chaos. But they are mistaken because there are other, equally effective routes to complexity. Take holistic systems, for example. In chaotic systems we cannot predict the properties of wholes on the basis of details relating to their constituents because (1) we cannot determine (observe) very fine-grained details, and (2) these fine-grained details matter crucially for the large-scale results that emerge from them. In holistic system, by contrast, we cannot determine the properties of units on the basis of the details relating to their constituents because the constituents do not determine the properties of those wholes—their features emerge in autonomous independence of the behavior of the parts.[1] Thus, for example, nothing in the psychology of individuals enables us to predict various features of the social aggregates they constitute—the suicide rate, for example, or the rate of money circulation. When such holistic principles concern us we must study the relevant whole at large; there is no prospect of deriving the large-scale parameters that interest us from information about the comportment of individuals. With both sorts of systems, problem solving at the larger details of scale becomes a project separate from and additional to that of problem solving at the lesser levels. Both sorts of systems accordingly take a step in the direction of greater operational complexity. For example, the complexity of stories is holistic. It resides in the volume of their events, the intricacy of their plots, and the interweaving of the relationships among their characters: chaos, as such, has nothing to do with it.

The salient fact of the matter is that the modes of complexity are multiple. The physicist Seth L. Loyal has computed an inventory of definitions of complexity—perhaps "standards" would be better. His list includes: information (Shannon); entropy (Gibbs, Boltzman); algorithmic complexity; algorithmic information; Renyi entropy; self-delimiting code length (Huffman, Shannon-Fano); error-correcting code length (Hamming); Chernoff information; minimum description length (Rissanen); number of parameters, or degrees of freedom, or dimensions; Lempel-Ziv complexity; mutual information, or channel capacity; algorithmic mutual information; correlation; stored information (Shaw); conditional information; conditional algorithmic information content; metric entropy; factual dimension; self-similarity; stochastic complexity (Rissanen); sophistication (Koppel, Atlan); topological machine size (Crutchfield); effective or ideal complexity (Gell-Mann); hierarchical complexity (Simon); tree subgraph diversity (Huberman, Hogg); homogeneous complexity (Teich, Mahler); time computations complexity; space computations complexity; information-based complexity (Traub); logical depth (Bennett); thermodynamic depth (Lloyd, Pagels); grammatical complexity (position in Chomsky hierarchy); Kullbach-Liebler information; distinguishability (Wooters, Caves, Fisher); Fisher distance; discriminability (Zee); information distance (Shannon); algorithmic information distance (Zurek); Hamming distance; long-range order; self-organization; complex adaptive systems; edge of chaos.[2] The possibilities are vast.

In a paper published more than a century ago, C. S. Peirce concluded "that there is probably in nature some agency by which the complexity and diversity of things can be increased."[3] For Peirce, this idea of the world's ever unfolding complexity was closely linked to nature's impetus to *novelty*: He held that as natural systems evolve they ongoingly develop new features that require ever more elaborate descriptive specification[4] —a condition of things exhibited in the emergence of new law levels in the course of cosmic evolution (as per the sequence of physics, chemistry, biology, sociology, etc.). And there is much to be said for such a view of the matter. In nature, certain factors—energy, matter, life, and complexity among them—appear to be self-potentiating: the more of them there is, the more powerful the impetus to the production of yet more. Left to its own devices without let or hindrance, such a tendency is liable to result in exponential growth,[5] a condition illustrated in the initial phase of a big bang universe and that of the expansion of life through biological evolution in the organic realm. This sort of thing holds for complexity also,[6] seeing that the operations of a complex system tend by their very nature to make for yet further complexity (whose management, cognitive or otherwise, becomes increasingly difficult[7]). Moreover, we encounter this phenomenon in the social realm as well as in the physical. One striking instance is the hypercomplexity of laws and regulations in the present era—an object of widespread complaint regarding which numerous proposals for remedy are astir, invariably to no avail.[8] And similarly, complexity growth also characterizes the domain of human creativity—in art and literature, for example, which knows virtually no limits.

But why is it that the realms of nature and of artifact are so complex?

Four principal modes of explanation have been proposed here: the intelligent design theory, the inherent teleology theory, the chance-plus-self-perpetuation theory, and the automatic self-potentiation theory. Each of them deserves at least brief consideration.

The Intelligent Design Theory effectively represents the standpoint of traditional theology. It sees complexity as the work of intelligence, and views the world as the theater of operation of a powerful intelligent agency—a creative world-mind or world-spirit, if one likes, but one might as well call it God. This agency guides the course of evolution—physical and biological alike—in the direction of increasing functional sophistication. Complexity enhancement is thus impressed upon nature "from on high" so the speak.

With regard to design in biological evolution, the most sophisticated current exponent of this sort of position is Michael J. Behe, whose recent book reasons essentially as follows: Complexity in nature—and in particular in the biological realm—is best accounted for (or perhaps even can *only* be accounted for) by supposing the operation of an intelligent designer.[9] A naturalistic developmental theory—such as Darwinian evolution by natural selection—encounters difficulties when it comes to explaining the development of the cell, seeing that many cellular systems are what can be characterized as "irreducibly complex." That is, such systems need several duly coordinated components before they can function properly. A mousetrap, for example, built of several pieces (platform, hammer, spring, and so on). Such a system probably cannot be put together in the Darwinian evolutionary manner of improving its function bit by bit, one piece at a time. One cannot catch a mouse with just the platform and then catch a few more by adding the spring. All the pieces have to be functioning well in their duly coordinated collaborative roles before the trap can catch any mice at all. Whenever we encounter such interactive systems, we can (and should) assume that they are the products of intelligent activity. And this reasoning—so it is contended—should be extended to cellular systems apart from intelligence. The thesis is that we simply know of no other mechanism, including Darwin's, which produces such operational complexity among collaborative components. Such, in essentials, is Behe's position with regard to intelligence's role in biological evolution. And the Intelligent Design Theory expands this position regarding the basis of complexity across a greater landscape.

The Inherent Teleology Theory sees nature itself as the bearer of an intrinsic, self-engendered penchant towards increasing complexity. The most dedicated philosophical exponent of this position is C. S. Peirce, who put the matter as follows in one of the many discussions on this theme:

> Evolution means nothing but *growth* in the widest sense of that word. Reproduction, of course, is merely one of the incidents of growth. And what is growth? Not mere increase. Spencer says it is the passage from the homogeneous to the heterogeneous—or, if we prefer English to Spencerese—*diversification*. That is certainly an important factor of it. Spencer further says that it is certainly an important factor of it. Spencer further says that it is a passage from the unorganized to the organized; but that part of the definition is so obscure that I will leave it aside for the present. But think what an astonishing idea this of *diversification* is! Is there such thing in nature as increase of variety? Were things simpler, was variety less in the original nebula from which the solar system is supposed to have grown than it is now when the land and sea swarms with animal and vegetable forms with their intricate anatomies and still more wonderful economies? It would seem as if there were an increase in variety, would it not? And yet mechanical law, which the scientific infallibilist tells us is the only agency of nature, mechanical law can never produce diversification. That is a mathematical truth—a proposition of analytical mechanics; and anybody can see without any algebraical apparatus that mechanical law out of like antecedence can only produce like consequents. It is the very idea of [mechanical] law. So if observed facts point to real growth, they point to another agency, to a spontaneity for which infallibilism provides no pigeonhole.[10]

On such a view, growth, diversification, and complexification are simply intrinsic developmental tendencies in nature. The physical universe is seen as autoteleological in this regard, propelling itself through its own resources into ever greater complexity.

The Chance-Plus-Self-Perpetuation Theory is a third major approach to the explanation of increasing complexity. It takes the line that (1) the merely chance fluctuation of things occasionally brings manifolds of greater-than-prevailing complexity into being, and that (2) complexity once present tends to be self-perpetuating. Such a situation makes for a drift towards an ever increasing complexity, on its basis chance ongoingly engenders new complexity which is henceforth continued through complexity's capacity to maintain its new gains over time. Such a view of complexity enhancement is entirely naturalistic and nonteleogical. It contemplates a supranatural intelligence nor an intranatural teleology to provide for its explanatory mechanism, but rests content with the purely natural processes of chance fluctuation and self-maintenance. (Perhaps the main obstacle that such an otherwise attractive theory faces is that of the question whether the actual historical course of complexity-enhancement in nature may not have been too rapid to be explained satisfactorily by the operations of mere chance.)

The Self-Potentiation Theory turns on the idea that complexity is in its own inherent nature self-propagating—that even as intelligence, for example, pushes itself to higher levels through the impetus of its own operation, so also does complexity. Complexity is by nature expansive; once present it clambers up upon itself to achieve yet higher levels of complexity. In this way, complexification can develop "from the bottom up." Sentences make up books, books make up libraries, and so on. But such productivity is a two-way street that also goes "from the top down." Where there are books, the production of further sentences is greatly facilitated. Where there are libraries, books come to multiply. (Indeed without libraries many sorts of books—catalogues, indices, citation indices, etc.—would not exist at all.) Even as increases in power in personal or institutional affairs set the stage for yet further increases in power—at any rate up to some point fixed by the context of the case—so increases in complexity function in an analogous manner. More complex systems generally not only permit but actually demand the addition of yet further complexities. As is illustrated by the evolution of organisms and of machines—be they mechanical or electronic—increases in complexity engender yet further increases.[11] And the theory of complexity self-potentiation sees this as a universal phenomenon.

These, then, are the principal approaches to the explanation of complexity enhancement in nature. But irrespective of the mechanism, the upshot is substandardly the same. Any process of this general sort means that the natural diversity emphasized by C. S. Peirce and the natural fertility insisted upon by Leibniz are at work in the scheme of things to bring about a natural expansion of complexity in nature.[12]

We need not here resolve the choice that these alternatives present. For present purposes the paramount consideration is simply *that* complexity enhancement is a fact of life in nature. The question *why* this should be so, however interesting and important it may be in the larger scheme of things, can safely remain unresolved within the confines of our present deliberations. What can and should be said, however, is that the bibliography of the subject attests that the emergence of complexity and its survival and propagation are issues of lively investigation in many sectors of contemporary science ranging from astrophysics to social science. And while explaining the *existence* of nature may conceivably call for some sort of supranatural expedient, explaining various *descriptive aspects* of its character—such as its complexity—is something that we should certainly expect to be able to manage without bringing supranatural agencies into it.[13]

While philosophers of science, in specific, have been unable to avoid the conception entirely, the fact remains that the idea of complexity is effectively absent from most metaphysical systems—save for a few honorable exceptions such as those of Leibniz, Peirce, and Whitehead. The very term is missing from the standard philosophical dictionaries and encyclopedias. Nevertheless, it is clear that the world's complexity has important implications and ramifications throughout the entire realm of our concerns—and actually not just in philosophy and in science, but also in everyday life. It impacts profoundly on our understanding of the world—as regards both our knowledge of its doings and the management of our affairs within it. The complexity of the things and situations we confront throughout our experience is one of reality's most significant and portentous aspects, affording both opportunities and prospects of frustration for us.

But be this matter of nature's increasing *ontological* complexity as it may, the situation as regards increasing *cognitive* complexity of our knowledge is more straightforward. Even if nature does not militate in this direction the progress of knowledge has the same functionally equivalent effect. Consider the series

ababababab. . .

Suppose that we become able to discriminate two sorts of a's, say *a* and **a**. The series may then transmute into

*ab*ababab**a**b . . .

And suppose that the same thing happens with the b's

*ab*ab*a*b**a**b . . .

As we introduce further discriminations—further distinctions—that initial easy pattern becomes increasingly complex. And this is a standard phenomenon: More refined distinction and difficulties never introduce more simplicity than there was before, they can only militate in the direction of greater complexity.

Our exploration of reality standardly takes us from the comparatively simple to the comparatively more complex. In every branch of science, the treatises and handbooks grow ever larger and more elaborate. New resources for experimentation and observation continually bring greater ranges of phenomena to view thereby destabilizing the primarily oversimple account and introducing an ever greater complexity. The rationale of this process resides in a simple mechanism, since rational beings for this very reason begin with the simple and introduce complications only insofar as the course of events requires. It is this natural dialectic of rational inquiry that carries us into ever greater depths of cognitive complexity.

And whenever present, complexity coordinates with difficulty in cognitive and operational management: the more complex something is the more difficulty we have in coming to grips with it and the greater the effort that must be expended for its cognitive and/or manipulative control and management. Complex statements are harder to understand; complex arguments harder to follow; complex machines harder to operate.

2. Modes of Complexity

There is no agreed upon definition of "complexity" any more than there is one of "chair." In both cases alike we are dealing with one of those things we can generally recognize when we see them, but cannot readily pin down with some straightforward adequate verbal formula. And while we can usually compare things of the same general sort in point of complexity, we certainly do not have anything like an across-the-board measure of complexity to compare the complexity, say, of stories and of machines. What we do know is that complexity is the inverse of simplicity. The latter is a matter of economy, the former of profusion. Simplicity represents economy and orderliness in a thing's make-up or operations; complexity, its elaborateness as reflected in the intricacy or even actual disharmony in these regards. As many writers see it, complexity is determined by the extent to which chance, randomness, and lack of lawful regularity in general is absent. But this cannot be the whole story, since law systems themselves can clearly be more or less complex.[14]

As Display 1.1 indicates, systems can be more or less complex in substantially different ways. And the distinctions at work show that complexity is itself a markedly complex idea. From the conceptual

DISPLAY 1.1
Modes of Complexity

Epistemic Modes

Formulaic Comlexity

1. *Descriptive Complexity*: Length of the account that must be given to provide an adequate description of the system at issue.
2. *Generative Complexity*: Length of the set of instructions that must be given to provide a recipe for producing the system at issue.
3. *Computational Complexity*: Amount of time and effort involved in resolving a problem.

Ontological Modes

Compositional Complexity

1. *Constitutional Complexity*: Number of constituent elements or components. (Compare, for example, tricycles, automobiles and jet aircraft.)
2. *Taxonomical Complexity (Heterogeneity)*: Variety of constituent elements: number of different *kinds* of components in their physical configurations. (Consider again of the preceding example, or compare the domain of physical elements which come in some 100-plus types with that of insects of which there are many thousands of species.)

Structural Complexity

3. *Organizational Complexity*: Variety of different possible ways of arranging components in different modes of interrelationship. (Compare jigsaw puzzles with their two-dimensional arrangements with LEGO blocks with their three-dimensional modes of assembly.)
4. *Hierarchical Complexity*: Elaborateness of subordination relationships in the modes of inclusion and subsumption. Organizational disaggregation into subsystems. (For example: particles, atoms, molecules, macrolevel physical objects, stars and planets, galaxies, galactic clusters, etc.; or again: molecules, cells organs, organisms, colonies, etc.) Here the higher-order units are, for this very reason, always more complex than the lower-order ones.

Functional Complexity

5. *Operational Complexity*: Variety of modes of operation or types of functioning. (Primates have a more complex lifestyle than mollusks. The processual structure of chess is vastly more elaborate than that of checkers.)
6. *Nomic Complexity*: Elaborateness and intricacy of the laws governing the phenomena at issue. (Steam engines are more complex in this manner than pulleys.)

point of view, the concept fuses and integrates a plurality of distinct elements into an elaborately articulated coordination.[15]

Descriptive complexity is perhaps its most fundamental form. The idea was first explicated by C. S. Peirce, who construed the complexity of a physical system in terms of the number of distinct factors that must be specified for its complete description.[16] Clearly, complexity is the inverse of simplicity, and the more elaborate the description of one item in comparison to another, the more complex it is. Complex flavors, say or complex plots, or complex characters all require comparatively greater descriptive elaboration. On this basis the sequence:

121212121212121212 . . .

is descriptively rather less complex than:

123456123456123456 . . .

And this is so in both compositional and structural regards. For the first group has only two components (1, 2), the second has six (1, 2, . . . , 6). And moreover, the two preceding groups also differ in their generative complexity, since the first group of twenty-one entries can be reproduced by rather simpler instructions than the second. ("Ceaselessly repeat the group 1-2" vs. "Ceaselessly repeat the group 1-2-3-4-5-6"). Or again, contrast two series:

- A randomly generated series of 0's and 1's.
- A series of integers whose n'th place is occupied by the n'th integer after the decimal point in the decimal representation of the n'th root of n.

The first series may well be easier to produce than the second—just flip a coin. But the first can only be identified by presentation *in toto*, while the second is fully identified by that indicated two-line formula. From the descriptive point of view, the second sequence is by far the simpler. With this sort of thing in mind, the Russian mathematician Andrei Kolmogorov proposed to measure generative complexity by the minimal length of an instruction-program for generating a sequence (by use of a standardized process such as a universal Turing machine).[17] This idea elegantly articulates at least one sort of formulaic complexity. On its basis, random structures such as the "snow" on TV screens or the pure noise of radio static are far more complex than any of their more orderly congeners, since in describing a strictly random series one has to make a separate specification for each and every component involved.

The computational approach to complexity has interesting larger ramifications. From the computational point of view, time is money, and so the complexity of an issue, question, or problem can effectively be answered by the sum total of resource cost incurred resolving it. Computational complexity is a matter of operational/functional complexity with regard to information management in the particular domain of problem solving. With this mode of complexity we have $C = P \times t$ where P is a measure of the power of the information-processor at issue and t is the time required for its successful deployment in the problem-solving context at hand. An issue that can be resolved with a few minutes of paper-and-pencil work is thus rather simple, while one that requires many hours in a supercomputer is vastly more complex. As is pretty generally the case, complexity here comes down to the demands of cognitive management.

Constitutional complexity is perhaps the generic conception's most striking form. It is hard to overlook it and to fail to be impressed by it in the context of machines. A modern spaceship, for example, has many millions of constituent parts, all of which must be subject to engineering assessments during NASA's flight-readiness review. (Investigation after the *Challenger* disaster brought to light that all of this spaceship's components passed this review with flying colors.) Constitutional complexity also arises as the world of artifice. A play with ten interacting characters will be more complex than one with three when other things are anything like equal.

Biologists are particularly attached to taxonomical complexity or heterogeneity of composition. J. T. Bonner, for example, has it that organic complexity is to be measured simply as the number of different cell types in an organism.[18] And in general terms it seems natural to construe the complexity of an issue in terms of the ramifications of the taxonomy that relevantly revolves about it.

Organizational and hierarchical complexity are also pervasive versions of the phenomenon. A complex system that embodies subsystems can be organized either *hierarchically* through the subordination relations among its elements or *coordinatively* through their reciprocal interrelationships. An army or a government department is an example of the former type, a single biological organism or an economic system illustrates the latter. The organizational charts for human institutions of the flow diagrams for process-characterization render this sort of complexity graphic. Fractal structures are particularly interesting from the angle of organizational complexity. Notwithstanding their intricacy, they have but a single mode of organization repeated ad infinitum at different levels of scale. Such a system's organizational complexity is minimal while its hierarchical complexity is endless.

Highly complex systems generally tend to exhibit an hierarchical structure because this conduces to the coherence of their make-up. They will consist of subsectors which themselves will in turn have subsectors of their own. Geography has regions that have subregions; automobiles have components that have parts; books have chapters that have sections that have paragraphs. Such hierarchical organization will not necessarily be functional—though it frequently is—but it will in any case be structural.[19] With a hierarchical complex there is a sequence of domain relationships, whereas with mere coordination there is mutual adjustment with reciprocal interaction, lacking any unified overall control. It is thus generally easier to get a cognitive grip on a hierarchical system because mastery of the controlling element will in large measure provide the key to unlocking the whole. Hierarchical organization serves to make complexity manageable by furnishing the bonding glue that enables enduring complex structures to be realized and preserved. After all, complexity generally does not exist all at once, it requires building blocks. For all-out complexity is unstable—with increasing size it tends to fall apart like a house of cards. Hierarchically complex structures, on the other hand, can be realized, though by small complexes of small complexes of small complexes, and so on, and such structuring facilitates stability.

Functional complexity takes two forms; it can be either *operational*, displaying dynamical complexity in the temporal unfolding of its processes (as with the forming of an oil slick on water), or *nomic*, displaying a timeless complexity in the working interrelationships of its elements (as with a lawfully complex mathematical manifold). As regards operational complexity, the more degrees of freedom a system exhibits in its make-up and operations—the more versatile it is—the more operationally complex it is inevitably going to be.[20] An automobile's movement, for example, has two degrees of freedom (direction and speed as controlled by the steering wheel and the break-accelerator complex, respectively). An aircraft with its ability to change altitude introduces a third degree of freedom. And so it goes without saying that the latter requires ampler information for its comprehension and more elaborate controls for its operation.

Operational complexity is thus closely bound up with complexity of other sorts. In particular, the management of increasing constitutional complexity makes for new operational challenges. With increasingly complex machines, for example, we require a larger manuals when it comes to construction and maintenance. And the operating manual for increasingly complex organisms will exhibit the same feature. One has to be able to do a wider variety of things to qualify as a mouse than one does to qualify as a paramecium.[21] But does greater capacity really require greater complexity? Is a word processor not a great deal easier to use than a manual typewriter? Perhaps so—but only because it is a part of a vastly more complex system of process. It is easier to drive one's automobile on an errand than to latch up Old Dobbin to the shay. But the overall support systems for the two vehicles are of very different orders of magnitude.

One recent author suggests that complexity is the same as suspense and impredictability.[22] But this is an exaggeration. The most that can be said is that complexity has the tendency to make for a destabilization that tends toward potentially surprising results. Still, one of the principal ways in which operational complexity can manifest itself is by way of impredictability. The crux is that of the extent to which a system is disorderly in that its future states are impredictable and chance precludes foresight. Here the entropy of the system will serve as a prime indicator. A system whose few possible states are of comparatively high probability (i.e., a low entropy system) will have to count as operationally simple, while a system with many states, all of which have low probability (i.e., high entropy systems) will have to count as operationally more complex.

As regards nomic complexity, it is clear that the more complex a system, the more elaborate its law structure. And here chaos represents an extreme. For chaos (unlike anarchy) is not an absence of laws but involves a mode of lawfulness so elaborate as to render a system's phenomenology cognitively unmanageable in matters of prediction and explanation.

It deserves note that a process characterized by very simple operating principles can yield a very complex product, even as a river that simply "follows the path of least resistance" can trace out a meandering path that continually twists back upon itself, or as crystals can grow into vastly elaborate structures. Thus consider the rule: "Add 1 to the number at hand and multiply the result by itself." When we confront this straightforward rule of operation with the number 2 it proceeds to generate the sequence:

$$2, (2 + 1)^2 = 9, (9 + 1)^2 = 100, (100 + 1)^2 = 10{,}201, \ldots$$

The result is clearly a series of substantial constitutional complexity, generated though it is by a functionally rather simple rule.[23]

Accordingly, the different modes of complexity do not necessarily stand together; in theory, at least, they can go their separate ways. For example, a human corpse is structurally complex but functionally simple—i.e., inert. On the other hand, *functional* complexity does not necessarily require *compositional* complexity. A typewriter with a modest number of keys can produce an infinite variety of texts. The examples of games like chess or go, of axiom systems in logic and mathematics, or of languages whose compact dictionaries can give rise to vast multivolume libraries, all serve to indicate that systems whose constitutional complexity is relatively modest can in their operations engender products whose structural and operational complexity is very great. Moreover, even a world that is finite in the structural complexity of its physical constituents may well exhibit a functional complexity that involves a "hierarchy of nomic orders" in its lawful operations, with an ongoing sequence of levels of ever higher-order laws.

The world's nomic complexity has implications for its compositional complexity as well. A *natural kind* of thing is based on a fundamental uniformity of lawful comportment. With humans, *mother* is a natural kind, since mothers will here have to be mature human females, while *neighbor* is not, since neighbors can be of any age, any sex; *fish* is a natural kind in view of a sameness of lifestyle and reproductive process, while *sea product* is not since what is at issue can be animal, vegetable, or mineral. The principle of limited variety has it that there is a finite number of natural kinds in the world. Yet in nature as in chess different modes of process—different ways of moving—indicate different kinds of objects (or pieces), and this renders that so-called principle a very doubtful proposition.[24]

We, of course, try to conduct our affairs with the least possible complication.[25] But nature is not generally so obliging. And it frequently raises the stakes by increasing one sort of complexity along with the other. To function effectively, systems of greater compositional complexity generally exhibit greater structural complexity (mammals have a more complexly elaborated manifold of subsystems than amoebae). And systems of greater structural complexity are generally more complex in point of their operational modalities. Technologically more sophisticated systems are not only usually bigger (compare the Wright Brothers' airplane with the present-day Boeing 747 or the brain of a chimpanzee with that of a human), but they also manifest more elaborate operating principles. It is not just that the parts inventory for a 1990s auto is thicker than that of a Ford Model-T, but its operator's manual is also much larger. In general, complexity of one sort consorts with that of another.

Thus while separable in theory, the different modes of complexity do tend to run together in practice. For example, systems that exhibit compositional and structural complexity will also generally exhibit functional complexity. When they are goal directed at all in their modus operandi, it is generally towards a plurality of potentially competing goals. Man does not live by bread alone—nor is speed the only desideratum for automobiles without safety, fuel economy, etc., entering into the issue.

Complexity cannot arise in a situation of total anarchy, the absence of any and all lawful order—the ultimate of cognitive defeators. Its emergence and stabilization require order. By contrast, chaos exhibits a high degree of order, albeit order of a particular and distinctly stochastic sort. Here complexity not only can emerge but is indeed even bound to do so. For the very presence of randomness will bring distinctive forms of order in its wake.[26] The fact is that complexity is congenial to the minor atom of order, since complex units will interrelate or interact in ways that were not heretofore available: the physics of element-complexes yields chemistry; the compilation of books generates libraries. In particular, it is only natural that biological systems should develop increasing complexity over time—at any rate insofar as they exist in an ever changing environment. For whenever change destabilizes the achieved balance between a system's modus operandi and its environmental conditions, then new modes of behavior are called for. And these new modes of functioning will engender new structures to enable greater efficiency and effectiveness. In biological evolution structural complexity will thus sail in the wake of the enhanced functional complexity demanded by changing circumstances. (The development of the brain with the evolution of intelligence is only one example of this.[27])

It may on first thought that *order* is an enemy of complexity. But the fact of the matter is that order itself is something that admits of levels. Principles of order can themselves exhibit higher levels of order—or of disorder. Second-order order, for example, is a very real phenomenon—and disorder is a prospect here too. Suppose we have a random series of 0's and 1's. But let it be that every time three 1's occur in succession we change the next two 0's to 1's. The result will no longer be a random mix of 0's and 1's; it has fewer 0's than a random series would. But it nevertheless exhibits no order whatever—no discernible pattern.[28] Complexity is certainly no a lack of order as such, seeing that any order be it lawful or taxonomic or structural, or whatever—is itself something that can be more or less complex. Order is not the enemy of complexity but, potentially at least, its co-conspirator.

All in all, then, the best overall index we have of a system's complexity is the extent to which resources (of time, energy, ingenuity) must be expanded on its cognitive domestication. Accordingly, complexity is in general not something that is purely ontological or purely epistemic, but involves both sides. It hinges on the relationship of minds and of things—on the ways in which the former can come to terms with the latter.

3. The Cognitive Aspect

All sorts of things can be more or less complex, but the situation is particularly notable with respect to bodies of knowledge. In fact, complexity, like simplicity, pertains in the first instance to cognitive artifacts: descriptions, explanations, accounts. But this is not without its ontological repercussions. For whenever no satisfactory account of system A manages to be as simple as one that we have of system B, then we have little choice but to say that A is more complex than B. Exactly because cognition is an instrumentality of order-detection, this linkage between complexity and order means that ontological complexity issues an open invitation to cognitive complexity. For ontologically complex systems—not so much by definition as by consequence of that very complexity—are of a character that cannot be modeled adequately by simple conceptual means. Trying to represent a complex system by models that have the conceptual rigidity required for convenient management and manipulation is like trying to wrap a ball with an inflexible board: we simply cannot achieve the necessary fit.

As creatures of limited capacity, cognitive complexity is of course of particular concern for us humans. Our scientific endeavor to gain understanding of the phenomena of nature confronts the challenges of complexity on every side. And reality's systemic structure means that every field of knowledge is surrounded by others: the history of China stands alongside the history of Japan, the literature of France stands alongside that of the literature of Germany. Wherever there is causal interaction, the idea of effecting a neat separation in understanding the phenomena is obviously impracticable. But even where there is no *interaction* there is nevertheless *interrelation.* Comparisons and contrasts can be drawn on each side that illuminate the phenomena of the other—and indeed that bring a whole new manifold of phenomena to view. Comparative literature, comparative linguistics, and the like, develop via relationships of similarity and contrast a set of issues that simply does not exist on either side alone. And with such high-order studies we always reach new levels of sophistication and complexity in our comprehension of the world's facts.[29]

To be sure, complication is something rather different from complexity. "To complicate" as a verb represents a matter of process and procedure generality by treating matters so as to render more complex something that is comparatively less so—introducing an *imputed* complexity that is actually absent. Thus cognitive incompetence can issue in perceived complexity; it can certainly complicate matters. For example, in the case of that perfectly regular sequence of alternating, 1's, and 2's, if you have difficulty in discriminating between them and frequently mistake a 1 for a 2 (or conversely) you will confront a sequence that is pervaded by randomness and thus exhibits a great deal of complexity. But, of course, the reverse can happen as well. If you cannot discriminate 1 from 2 at all, a random series of 1's and 2's will (or may) look to you a uniform series, XXXXXX . . . , which is simplicity itself. In general, however, cognitive difficulty reflects rather than creates complexity. As a rule, an item's complexity is indicated by the extent to which we encounter difficulty in coming to adequate cognitive terms with it.[30] By and large, the amount of effort that must be expended in describing and understanding the make-up and workings of a system is our best practical indicator complexity, and its inverse is our best practical indicator of simplicity.

Some writers see complication as having the field to itself. They dismiss complexity as something that lies wholly in the eyes of the beholder. For them, nothing of a realistically objective nature is involved. Thus K. R. Popper wrote:

> To begin with, I shall exclude from our discussion the application of the term "simplicity" to anything like a presentation or an exposition. It is sometimes said of two expositions of one and the same mathematical proof that the one is simpler or more elegant than the other. This is a distinction which has little interest from the point of view of the theory of knowledge; it does not fall within the province of logic, but merely indicates a preference of an *aesthetic or pragmatic* character. The situation is similar when people say that one task may be "carried out by simpler means" than another, meaning that it can be done more easily or that, in order to do it, less training or less knowledge is needed. In all such cases the word "simple" can be easily eliminated; its use is extra-logical.[31]

Popper accordingly saw simplicity as a matter of mind-projected preferences.

But this sort of subjectivism seems quite wrong. The fact that a particular process or procedure is more efficient and effective than another in creating a certain product or in performing a certain task can be and generally is an important fact about that product or task itself. It is emphatically not a mere matter of what we happen to wish or value.[32] The capacity and the time that a computing machine requires to resolve its problems are perfectly objective matters. Even a cognitively all-powerful God, who has no difficulty whatsoever in managing information, will nevertheless recognize that one object of understanding is more complex than another—the make-up (say) of children's stories as compared with Shakespearean plays—or one line of reasoning more intricate than another. Complexity is to all appearances a real and pervasive feature of things.

Moreover, complexity pervades not just the realm of nature but that of artifice as well. When a range of information is too vast for comprehensive item-by-item mastery, we can survey it by way of selective sampling. And then the possibility of bias can never be eliminated. Different people are going to see different parts of the terrain. Their judgment of what is typical, normal, exotic, central, peripheral, important, and impartial are bound to disagree in consequence. (Think of the story of the seven wise men and the elephant.) Dissensus, diversity of opinion, and communal disagreement will eventually ensue. The geography of thought, opinion, and appraisal of any large and sophisticated community is inevitably going to depict a complex terrain.

The progress of human endeavor, alike in the cognitive and practical domains as in that of artifice, represents an ever greater involvement with complexity. Consider the fine arts, for example. Not long ago, art museums displayed paintings and sculptures, period. But nowadays they display artifacts of many different sorts, both static and dynamic, and both in stable and in changeable environments. Consider just painting. In its initial history, it was not only representational but thematic. At first there were only religious and mythological themes, then historical tableaux emerged, and later portraiture became prominent, followed by natural and civic and domestic vistas. Subsequently there evolved a proliferation of topics that ultimately burst beyond the limits of thematic bonds altogether, first focusing on process rather than product ("impressionism") and ultimately bursting outside the domain of thematic and representational concerns altogether.

But is it really true that human artifice is growing more complex. For example, has art—say painting—been growing more complex? Compare a painting of Brueghel's with one by Mondrian or Klee. Surely the latter is simplicity itself by comparison. True enough! But while those individual paintings may indeed be simpler this is certainly not true for painting-at-large. There is no question that painting, collectively considered, has been even more diversified, variegated, and complex. Here, as elsewhere, local simplicity has been riding on the back of globally systemic complexity. As graphic art in the natural course of its development metamorphosed from a project in the representation of visible reality to an exploration of imaginable possibility, it set out along a road where the prospect of unending complexification is ever unfolding before it. The agenda of "approaches" in present day art is so variegated that it to all intents and purposes outruns the prospect of a workable inventory.

The same phenomenon is at work in enhancing the complexity of knowledge. Consider, for example, the issues that our books deal with. To indicate "what the book is about" we might say that it is a treatise on nineteenth-century French domestic furniture design. Consider the various taxonomic factors that come into play here:

> *Place*: countries, geographic areas, etc.
> *Time*: decades, centuries, eras, etc.
> *Subject matter*: geography, politics, history

Each admits of substantial elaboration. Spatiotemporal characterizations can of course be made ongoingly refined and convoluted—divided and reassembled in increasingly intricate patterns. And subject matter is open to virtually endless complexification. Given any two substantive themes or topics, a variety of relationships come to the fore that lay the groundwork for an expansion of our knowledge. Thus once we have arrived at the history and philosophy and economics, we can set out on such further concatentative elaborations as:

- history of philosophy of economics
- economics of philosophizing about history

The potential for compounding is endless. Thematic refocusing—the superposition of a certain problem-perspective upon the interests of a particular subject-matter domain—is something capable of virtually endless complexification.

The natural sciences study the world of nature, the humanities study the world of human artifice And even as the Hubble expansion of the universe proceeding in the wake of the Big Bang ongoingly enlarges the realm of the former, so the Gutenberg explosion of the printing presses ongoingly enlarges that of the latter. The Sunday *New York Times* contains more information than people in a primitive tribal society deal with in a lifetime. The present-day growth of our libraries beyond the bursting point is thus deeply symbolic. The complexity of the domain of information is vividly indicated by the volume of publication. Some 50,000 titles are published annually in the U.S. alone, more than two-thirds of them in matters of knowledge rather than entertainment.[33]

Complexity is something that we always have to reckon with as we try to come to cognitive terms with the world.[34] Since reality is indeed complex, we shall inevitably encounter difficulty with it—which is to say that more time, effort, energy, etc. will have to be expended in its cognitive domestication. The mathematics, the science, the theology, and the legal systems of medieval times were vastly more complex than their predecessors in classical antiquity. And ours are vastly—almost immeasurably—more complex yet.

As our proceedings in this domain of cognitive development unfold, new sorts of facts always come to light and things get increasingly complicated. And those cognitive complications clearly reveal—rather than create!—the complexities that characterize the subject matter at hand. Here again cognitive complexity, properly handled, becomes an index of ontological complexity. From this point of view it can be argued that computational complexity with regard to problem solving will generally provide our best-available measure for complexity in general, in that any sort of complexity as reflected at the epistemic level in the cognitive difficulty in reasoning an adequate understanding of the system at issue.

One of the most fundamental principles of epistemology is that a less powerful intelligence is bound to be baffled by the ways of a more powerful one. There can be no adequate comprehension here: a child of seven cannot grasp what the adult mathematics expert is talking about. The later, more sophisticated stages of knowledge, capable of more amply accommodating the complexity of things, are imponderable from the vantage point of their less sophisticated predecessors. And the progress of science also exhibits this phenomenon. A person equipped with the scientific state of the art of Aristotle's day cannot read with pleasure and profit the treatises of present-day physics or cosmology. As science takes us into ever deeper thickets of complexity, we face limitations of such a sort that the question of overcoming them in the future is an imponderable for us. Complexity, in sum, creates challenges for us in every area of human endeavor, serious and frivolous alike.[35]

Notes

1. We are not talking here about the "downwards causation" which transpires when the properties of wholes causally determine those of parts. It is simply the absence of "upwards explicability" that is at issue here.
2. Quoted in John Horgan, *The End of Science* (Reading, MA: Addison Wesley, 1996), p. 288. Names indicate the main originators of the definition.
3. In the second of four papers on "The Doctrine of Necessity," which appeared in *The Monist*, vol. 2 (1892), pp. 321-37. Reprinted in Charles Sanders Peirce, *Collected Papers*, eight vols. (Cambridge, MA: Harvard University Press, 1931-1958); see vol. 6 (1935), sect. 6.58.
4. "But think what an astonishing idea this of *diversification* is! Is there such thing in nature as increase of variety? Were things simpler, was variety less in the original nebula from which the solar system is supposed to have grown that it is now when the land and sea swarms with animal and vegetable forms with their intricate anatomies and still more wonderful economies? It would seem as if there were an increase in variety, would it not?" Charles Sanders Peirce, *Collected Papers* (op. cit.),vol. 1, sect. 1.174; compare also vol. 6, sect. 6.50.
5. This occurs whenever F grows proportionately with F's already attained size. For then we have: $\Delta F(t) \approx F(t)$. And when this is so, then $\Delta F(t)/F(t) \approx$ const, so that:
   $\int dF(t)/F(t) \approx \log F(t) = t$.
   In consequence: $F(t) \approx e^t$. Q. E. D.
6. On the process in general see John H. Holland, *Hidden Order: How Adaptation*

Builds Complexity (Reading, MA: Addison Wesley, 1995). Regarding the specifically evolutionary aspect of the process see Robert N. Brandon, *Adaptation and Environment* (Princeton, NJ: Princeton University Press, 1990).

7. Be it in biological evolution through fitness or in cognitive explanation through adequacy, the exploration of any rugged (random) parametric landscape is such that with every step one takes uphill, the number of directions leading yet higher is continually diminished. When this reduction by a constant fraction (say one-half), then as one climbs higher, it becomes not just harder but exponentially more so to effect further improvements. On these issues see Stuart Kaufmann, *At Home in the Universe* (New York and Oxford: Oxford University Press, 1998), pp. 169-80.

8. See, for example, Richard A. Epstein, *Simple Rules for a Complex World* (Cambridge, MA: Harvard University Press, 1995). There are few more imposing monuments to administrative complexity than the U.S. tax code. When the Internal Revenue Service was launched in 1913, federal tax regulations ran to 400 pages; by 1993 there was 80,000 of them—a two hundred-fold increase in eighty years that betokens a growth industry of awesome proportions. (In one of his election campaign infomercials, Ross Perot noted that Americans dedicate over five billion man-hours annually to preparing income tax forms—more than to the production of automobiles.)

9. See Michael J. Behe, *Darwin's Black Box: The Biochemical Challenge to Evolution* (New York: Free Press, 1996).

10. Charles Sanders Peirce, *Collected Papers*, vol. 1 (op. cit.), sect. 1.174.

11. The question arises as to how this phenomenon of complexity escalation squares with entropy enhancement as reflected in the second law of thermodynamics—that is, with nature's penchant for the path of least resistance in the road-system of probabilistic transitions. In the final analysis the answer here lies in the capacity of simple laws to engender products of great complexity in ways entirely consistent with entropic principles. An accessible discussion of the issues is given in P.W. Atkins, *The Second Law* (New York: Scientific American Library, 1984).

12. An excellent overview of this theme in its wider systems-theoretic and specifically scientific setting is Klaus Mainzer, *Thinking in Complexity: The Complex Dynamics of Matter, Mind, and Material* (Berlin: Springer Verlag, 1994).

13. On these issues compare the author's *The Riddle of Existence* (Lanham, MD: University Press of America, 1984).

14. Many writers on the subject of complexity do not trouble to define the phenomenon at issue. One striking example is Herbert A. Simon's stumbling essay on "The Architecture of Complexity," *Proceeding of the American Philosophical Society*, vol. 106 (December 1962), pp. 467-82, reprinted in his *The Science of the Artificial* (Cambridge, MA: MIT Press, 1969; 2nd ed. 1981). Simon here characterizes a complex system as being "rightly" one such that "given the properties of the parts and the terms of their interaction, it is not a trivial matter to infer the properties of the whole" (1981, p. 195). Since few whole from atoms to galaxies or from human cells to entire societies seem exempt from this principle it is not as helpful as it might be.

15. For further substantiation of this point see Charles H. Bennett, "How to Define Complexity in Physics, and Why," in W. H. Zurck (ed.), *Complexity, Entropy and the Physics of Information:SFI Studies in the Science of Complexity* (New York: Addison Wesley, 1990).

16. C. S. Peirce, *Collected Papers*, vol. 6 (op. cit.), sect. 6.56.

17. This means that a high rate of program redundancy—as with the repetitive parts

of the so-called junk DNA represented by the large proportion of chromosomes that can be discounted—makes for diminished complexity. For an authoritative and accessible introduction to issues of computational complexity see John von Neumann, "The General and Logical Theory of Automata," in J.R. Newman (ed.), *The World of Mathematics*, vol. 4 (New York: Simon and Schuster, 1956), pp. 2070-98.

18. John Tyler Bonner, *The Evolution of Complexity* (Princeton, NJ: Princeton University Press, 1988).
19. Compare H. A. Simon, *Science of the Artificial*, 2nd ed. (Cambridge, MA: MIT Press, 1981), pp. 116-17 and 195 ff.
20. Compare K. R. Popper, *The Logic of Scientific Discovery* (New York: Basic Books, 1959), pp. 139-40.
21. Interestingly, the complexity of the assembly code of an organism as encapsulated in its DNA is not reflected in the mere length of that DNA. Some decades ago, biologists sought to compare the complexity of different organisms by measuring the length of their DNA strands, but arrived at results drastically at odds with our intuitions. For example, among vertebrates, it is amphibians (not mammals!) that have the most DNA per cell. Even more striking, the cells of onions have five times more DNA than those of humans, and those of tulips have ten times as much.
22. See John L. Casti, *Complexification* (New York: Harper Collins, 1994), pp. 269-78.
23. On the mathematical side, the most developed part of our subject is the theory of computational complexity, focusing on such issues as the length of programs and the duration of computations. The subject is abstruse but relevant to our topic in its larger dimension. I know of no good elementary and popularly accessible introduction to the topic. Informative but highly technical (and now somewhat dated) is: J. Hartmann and J. E. Hopcroft, "An Overview of the Theory of Computational Complexity," *Journal of the Association for Computing Machinery*, vol. 18 (1971), pp. 444-75.
24. On this issue see p. xyz below.
25. And according to Leibniz, God makes his decision to acknowledge one of the innumerable alternative possible worlds on exactly this principle. See Nicholas Rescher, *Leibniz's Philosophy of Nature* (Dordrecht: D. Reidel, 1981).
26. See Stuart Kauffman, *At Home in the Universe: The Search for Laws of Self-Organization and Complexity* (New York and Oxford: Oxford University Press, 1995), and also see John Barrow and Frank J. Tipler, *The Anthropic Cosmological Principle* (Oxford: Clarendon Press, 1968), p. 256.
27. On these issues see Peter Godfrey-Smith, *Complexity and the Function of Mind in Nature* (Cambridge: Cambridge University Press, 1996).
28. Thus if the die tosses yield 2, 3, 6, 6, 1, 4, 6 the series will begin 1, 1, 2, 3, 1, 4, 5.
29. The treatment of complex processes through a combinatory fusion of simple ones is the standard cognitive strategy of artificial intelligence research and cognitive heuristics generally. The literature is vast, but a good start can be made with William Bechtel and Robert C. Richardson, *Discovering Complexity* (Princeton, NJ: Princeton University Press, 1993).
30. This circumstance establishes the connection that obtains between our present topic of simplicity/complexity and that of cognitive economy which I have discussed in such earlier books as: *Scientific Progress* (Oxford: Blackwell, 1978), *Cognitive Economy* (Pittsburgh, PA: University of Pittsburgh Press, 1989), and *Priceless Knowledge?* (Lanham, MD: University Press of America, 1996). *Scien-*

tific Progress is also available in translation: German trans., *Wissenschaftlicher Fortschritt* (Berlin: De Gruyter, 1982); French trans., *Le Progrès scientifique* (Paris: Presses Universitaire de France, 1994).

31. Karl R. Popper, *The Logic of Scientific Discovery* (op. cit.), p. 137.

32. Compare Moritz Schlick: "Simplicity is . . . a concept indicative of preferences which are partly pragmatic, partly aesthetic in character" (*Die Naturwissenschaften*, vol. 19 [1931], p. 148).

33. See *The Bowker Annual: Library and Book Trade Almanac*, 40th edition (New Providence, NJ: P. R. Bowker, 1995).

34. For a challenging modern articulation of the nineteenth-century idea that the impetus behind the evolution of mind is to enable its processes to cope ever more effectively with the complexity of their functional environment see Peter Godfrey-Smith, *Complexity and the Function of Mind in Nature* (Cambridge: Cambridge University Press—Studies in the Philosophy of Biology, 1996).

35. The range of choice with which modern technology confronts us in the entertainment sphere is truly staggering. The same tapes, cassettes, diskettes that make for an information glut also practice an entertainment glut. Along with hundreds of cable TV channels in operation, the magic of electronics puts thousands of films and tens of thousands of CDs at our fingertips. (Anyone who thinks that modern technology makes life simpler is living on another planet.)

2

The Complexity of the Real

(1) The world's descriptive complexity is literally limitless: the descriptive truths that can be articulated about reality never manage to exhaust the range of actual fact. Moreover, the operation of a "Law of Natural Complexity" means that any real particular belongs to more than any finite number of natural kinds, a circumstance that clearly blocks a Keynesian principle of limited variety. (2) Even a world whose physical constitution *does not exhibit an unending complexity can nevertheless engender a range of* phenomena *that is unendingly diverse. And this means that reality is bound to be cognitively opaque— we cannot see all the way through it. (3) Since concrete particulars always have more properties than they can bring to actual manifestation, we can never make a complete inventory of the facts about real things. Our descriptive knowledge about them is always incomplete. (4) Accordingly, our conception of reality must always be seen as provisional and subject to change. The scientific investigation of nature is a process that involves not only ongoing additions but also replacements. Such a dynamism means that the complexity of nature is cognitively inexhaustible. (5) And this holds not only for nature's things but for its laws as well. Thus our scientific exploration of an immensely complex world imposes upon us a cognitive task of potential endlessness—one that literally knows no limits. (6) There is, accordingly, no real prospect of perfecting our knowledge of this unendingly complex world, seeing that our knowledge can always be improved but cannot be completed.*

1. The Descriptive Inexhaustibility of Things: The Law of Natural Complexity

Much can be said for the dictum that "Truth is stranger than fiction." And the reason for this is straightforward. The human intellect's capacity for complexity management is limited. Nature is vastly more complex than the human brain—if only because we ourselves are merely a minor constituent of nature itself. The states of affairs that our minds can envision are vastly fewer and simpler than those that nature can present. To give just one rather obvious example, we cannot even begin to conceive the facts and phenomena that will figure on the agenda of the science of the future. On a map of the U.S., Chicago is but a dot. But when we go to a map of Illinois it begins to take on some substance, and on a map of Cook County it presents a substantial and characteristic shape. But matters do not end there. We could, in theory, go on to map it block by block, house by house, room by room, dish by pitcher. And with increasing detail new and different features constantly emerge. Science is like that. Where does the process stop? Not with atoms, certainly—for the impenetrable and unchanging atoms of the ancient Greeks have become increasingly dematerialized and ethereal composed of automatically smaller processes. As we increase the power of our particle accelerators, our view of the makeup of the substance realm becomes not only ever different but also ever stranger. There is, as best we can tell, no limit to the world's ever increasing complexity that comes to view with our ever increasing grasp of its detail.

It is important for the world's modus operandi—and for our understanding of it—that the details often do not matter to the particular issue on the agenda—that fine-grained differences produce no large consequences here. What you as an individual decide to do—whether to buy that umbrella or not—makes no difference to the American economy; its money supply, inflation rate, balance of trade, etc. all remain unaffected. But not every sort of system is like that. Natural systems can be classified into two types: the linear and the nonlinear. Linear systems admit of approximation. If we oversimplify them we change nothing essential: the results we obtain by working with their simplified models will appropriate the condition of their more complex counterparts in the real world. Small-scale departures from reality will make no big difference. But nonlinear systems behave otherwise.

Here small variations—even undetectably small ones—can make big differences. Accordingly, simplification—let alone oversimplification—can prove fatal: even the smallest miss can prove to be as good as a mile as far as outcomes are concerned. The idea of a difference between an essential core and a negligible periphery is beyond implementation here. Every detail matters—none is "irrelevant" or "negligible." Simplified models will accordingly be of no help at all—with nonlinearity it is a matter of all or nothing. And so, perhaps the most fundamental question that can be asked of any natural system is: Is it linear of nonlinear? Everything turns on this, since nonlinear systems must be studied holistically and comprehensively. And a system whose formative subsystems are to any appreciable extent nonlinear becomes for that very reason the more complex. Just here lies the reason why intricately convoluted complex systems such as biological evolution or human history or electoral politics—processes where seemingly haphazard and "external" events can substantially effect outcomes—are so complex that the questions they pose for us defy calculation and foreclose the prospect of computational problem solving. The machinations of a deranged assassin can make an enormous difference for the entire nation whose leader is his victim. Nonlinear systems are always far less tractable, be it operationally or cognitively. And nature is nonlinear to an extent greater than we like to think.

To be sure, from a *methodological* point of view we do well to struggle against such complexity, inclining to the assumption that the systems we confront are cognitively tractable—that we can (over) simplify and "get away with it." Methodological simplificationism—the *presumption of simplicity*—is an important, common, and legitimate instrumentality of inquiry. But it is, as we well know, no more than that—a mere *presumption*. And we recognize full well that the realities of a difficult world will often fail to humor us in this regard. Often, but fortunately not predominantly—let alone always. For intelligence could not emerge and make its evolutionary way in a world where it could get no purchase-hold where its effects increasingly proved abortive.

C. S. Peirce never tired of emphasizing nature's inherent tendency to complexity proliferation. He wrote:

Evolution means nothing but *growth* in the widest sense of that word. Reproduction, of course, is merely one of the incidents of growth. And what is growth? Not mere increase. Spencer says it is the passage from the homogeneous to the heterogeneous—or, if we prefer English to Spencerese—*diversification*. That is certainly an important factor of it. Spencer further says that it is a passage from the unorganized to the organized; but that part of the definition is so obscure that I will leave it aside for present. But think what an astonishing idea this of *diversification* is! Is there such thing in nature as increase of variety? Were things simpler, was variety less in the original nebula from which the solar system is supposed to have grown than it is now when the land and the sea swarms with animal and vegetable forms with their intricate anatomies and still more wonderful economies? It would seem as if there were an increase in variety, would it not?[1]

The fact is that complexity is self-potentiating. Complex systems generally function so as to engender further principles of order that possibilize additional complexities. Complex organisms militate towards complex societies, complex machines towards complex industries, complex armaments towards complex armies. And the world's complexity means that there is, now and always, more to reality than our science—or for that matter our speculation and our philosophy—is able to dream of.

In particular, the world's descriptive complexity is literally limitless. Ever since the days of Locke and Leibniz in the seventeenth century, theorists have endorsed the conception that new ideas can always be generalized by recombinations of the old. And once this sort of process gets under way, there is no reason or principle why it should ever have to come to a stop. For it is clear that the number of true descriptive remarks that can be made about a thing—about any concrete element of existence, and, in specific, any particular physical object—is theoretically inexhaustible. Take a stone for example. Consider its physical features: its shape, its surface texture, its chemistry, and so on. And then consider its causal background: its genesis and subsequent history. And then consider its functional aspects as reflected in its uses by the stonemason, or the architect, or the landscape decorator, and so on. There is, in principle, no end to the different lines of consideration available to yield descriptive truths, so that the totality of potentially available facts about a thing—about any real thing whatever—is bottomless. John Maynard Keynes' principle of limited variety is simply wrong: there is no inherent limit to the number of distinct descriptive kinds or categories to which the things of this world can belong. As best we can possibly tell, natural reality has an infinite descriptive depth. It confronts us with a law of natural complexity: *There is no limit to the number of natural kinds to which any concrete particular belongs.*

It is helpful to introduce a distinction at this stage. On the standard conception of the matter, a "truth" is something to be understood in *linguistic* terms—the representation of a fact through its statement in some actual language. Any correct statement in some actual language formulates a truth. (And the converse obtains as well: a truth must be encapsulated in a statement, and cannot exist without linguistic embodiment.) A "fact," on the other hand, is not a linguistic entity at all, but an actual circumstance or state of affairs—a condition of things existing in the world. Anything that is correctly characterizable in some *possible* language constitutes a fact.[2]

Every truth must state a fact, but it is not only possible but indeed to be expected that there will be facts that cannot be stated in any actually available language— and which thus fail to be captured as truths. Facts afford *potential* truths whose actualization hinges on the availability of appropriate linguistic machinery for their formulation. Truths involve a one-parameter possibilization: they include whatever can be currently stated in some (actual) language. But facts make a two-parameter possibilization: they constitute what ever *can* be stated truly in some *possible* language. Truths are *actualistically* language-correlative, while facts are *possibilistically* language-correlative.[3] Accordingly, it must be presumed that there are facts that we cannot manage to formulate as truths, though it will obviously be impossible to give concrete examples of this phenomenon.[4]

Now there will always be more facts about a thing than we can ever manage to capture through the truths that we can formulate about it. One reason for this is the fundamentally progressive nature of knowledge in a world domain of potentially ongoing discovery. But another, deeper reason, lies in the self-potentiation of fact inherent in the circumstance that any n facts give rise to $n!$ fact combinations that themselves represent further facts.

To be sure, it is in principle possible to have latent or implicit knowledge of an infinite domain through deductive systematization. After all, the finite set of axioms of a formal system will yield infinitely many theorems. And so, it would seem that when we shift from overt or explicit to implicit or tacit fact-assertion we secure the prospect of capturing an infinitely manifold of facts by implicit containment within a finite *explicit* linguistic basis through recourse to deductive systematization.

The matter is not, however, quite so convenient. The totality of the deductive consequences that can be derived from any finite set of axioms is itself always denumerable. The most we can ever hope to encompass by any sort of *deductively* implicit containment within a finite basis of truths is a *denumerably infinite* manifold of truths. And thus as long as implicit containment remains a recursive process, it too can never hope to transcend the range of the denumerable, and therefore cannot hope to encompass the whole of the transdenumerable range of descriptive facts about a thing. (After all, even within the denumerable realm, our attempt at deductive systematization runs into difficulties: as is known from Kurt Gödel's work, one cannot even hope to certify—by any recursive, axiomatic process—all of the inherently denumerable truths of arithmetic.[5] One of the deepest lessons of modern mathematics is that we cannot claim that if there is a matter of fact in this domain, then we can encompass it within the deductive means at our disposal.)

At this point, the following objection may well arise:

> One single suitably general truth can encapsulate infinitely many descriptive facts—even a transdenumerable infinity of them. For example, in saying of a particular spring that it obeys Hooke's law (over a certain range)—assigning it the infinitely rich disposition to displace proportionally with imposed weights—I have implicitly provided for a transdenumerable infinity of descriptive consequences by means of the continuous parameter at issue. Accordingly, while it is true that the actual deductions which one can carry out from an axiomatic basis are denumerable, they can certainly manage to "cover"—at a certain level of implicitness—a transdenumerable range of descriptive fact.

But of course the process envisioned here allows for only one very limited sort of infinitude: the positing of a particular value within one and the same non-finite range of determination—the fixing of a special case within a prespecified spectrum. The objection is thus transcended when one recalls the law of natural complexity's contention that there is in principle no theoretical limit to the lines of consideration available to provide descriptive perspectives upon a thing—that the range of descriptive spectra can always, in principle, be extended. The limitless descriptive complexity of the world's concrete things establishes the need for acknowledging a clear contrast between the manifold of the *discerned properties* of things as we have established them to date (always a finite collection) and their *actual properties* (which are potentially limitless).

To be sure we can always oversimplify: The limitlessness of the world's descriptive complexity does not mean that we cannot say how things stand by way of a "reasonable approximation." We can, for example, specify how things normally and usually comport themselves within the range of our observation. And so, while we cannot present the full details, we can provide a somewhat approximate account of the real via a characterization of the usual and ordinary course of events. But, of course, it is an inevitable fact of life that the *actual* course of events is not always and everywhere normality-conforming: in the real world matters all too often eventuate in ways that depart from what we see as the usual course. It is exactly because reality is too complicated to be captured by our facile generalizations—is too full of vagaries and quirks—that we must constantly resort to qualifying locutions such as "generally," "standardly," and the like. If we insisted on "telling it exactly as it is," then we couldn't get there from here.

Nature's complexity means that the "fundamental laws" of natural science as we do—or can—ever actually established are inevitably inadequate to explain by themselves the phenomena as we actually observe them. Our "models of reality" are no more than rough approximations.[6]

2. Descriptive Incompleteness

Endlessly many true descriptive remarks can be made about any actual physical object. Take a stone, for example. Consider its physical features: its shape, its surface texture, its chemistry, and so on. And then consider its causal background, its subsequent genesis and history. Then consider its functional aspects as relevant to its uses by the stonemason, or the architect, or the landscape decorator. Again, the botanist, herbiculturist landscape gardener, farmer, painter, and real estate appraiser will operate from different cognitive "points of view" in describing one selfsame vegetable garden. There is, after all, no end to the perspectives of consideration that we can bring to bear on things. (Think of the law of natural complexity once more.)

And this of course means that there is a need for different disciplines in the study of a complex world. All epistemology is local (as all politics is said to be): our proper modus operandi in matters of inquiry must always allow for the local conditions that prevail in the particular public area at issue. There is no single, unique way of organizing our interests here: physicists, chemists, biologists, economists, etc., all have different ranges of concern—none have a monopoly on the study of nature. The prospect of proliferating disciplines is inherent in that of a multiplication of the perspectives of consideration we ourselves bring to the cognitive domestication of the real.[7]

Our characterization of real things can accordingly become more *extensive* without thereby becoming more *complete*. New descriptive features ongoingly come into view with the progress of knowledge. (Caesar not only did not, but in the existing state of knowledge could not have known that his sword contained tungsten.) Real things are— and by their very nature must be—such that their actual nature outruns any particular description of it that we might venture. From this angle too it is clear that the realm of reality-appertaining fact inevitably outruns the reach of our descriptive information.

Accordingly, there is reason to think that once things are so complex that further new facts about them can always be found out, then there can be no complete inventory of the facts about something even if we are prepared to contemplate listings of infinite length. For let us assume that such a supposedly complete enumeration existed, as per

$F_1(a), F_2(a), F_3(a), \ldots$

where all the $F_i(a)$ are facts, so that $(\forall i)F_i(a)$ is a fact as well. Then by the hypothesis of enumerative completeness we would have it that every fact is contentially contained in some member of the list:

(C) $(\forall F)[F(a) \rightarrow (\exists i)(F_i(a) \rightarrow F(a))]$

And by the hypothesis of ongoing novelty we would have it that what is informatively given up to my particular point never encompasses what is yet to come:

(N) $(\forall i) \sim ([F_1(a) \& F_2(a) \& \ldots \& F_i(a)] \rightarrow F_{i+1}(a))$

But now consider $F^*(a) = (\forall i)F_i(a)$. In view of its truth we will have it by (C) that:

$(\exists i)(F_i(a) \rightarrow F^*(a))$

Let the so-guaranteed value of i be k. Then by supposition $F_k(a) \rightarrow F^*(a)$. But since by the definition of F^* we have $F^*(a) \rightarrow F_{k+1}(a)$, we also have $F_k(a) \rightarrow F_{k+1}(a)$. And this contradicts (N).

What we actually have here is the demonstration of aporetic inconsistency among three theses:

1. omnifactuality as per $(\forall i)F_i(a)$
2. enumerative completeness as per (C)
3. unending novelty as per (N)

This chain of inconsistency is best broken at its weakest link. But since 1 and 3 are pretty much unavoidably subject to the assumptions at issue, it emerges that the prospect of enumerative completeness should be abandoned. And with it one must also abandon the idea that our linguistic resources can—at least in the theoretical long run—fully characterize the descriptive nature of the real.

One possible way of trying to avert this conclusion is to exclude F^* from the range of the F-quantifier that is at issue in (C), thus disqualifying such complex "facts" as that at issue with F^* from counting as genuine facts.[8] But notwithstanding that some philosophers have indeed taken such a line, it is little more than an artificial and highly problematic expedient. For convenience aside, there is no really convincing reason why the structural complexity of propositions should constitute an impediment to facticity.

It follows from these considerations that we can never justifiably claim to be in a position to articulate all the facts about a real thing; the domain of thing-characterizing fact inevitably transcends the limits of our capacity to *express* it, and *a fortiori* those of our capacity to canvas completely. In the description of concrete particulars we are caught up in an inexhaustible detail: There are always bound to be more descriptive facts about things than we are able to capture explicitly with our linguistic machinery.

The upshot is clear. *The descriptions that we can ever actually provide for real particulars are never complete.* The detail of the real is bound to outrun our descriptive accomplishments. We have every reason to presume reality to be cognitively inexhaustible. A precommitment to description-transcending features—no matter how far description is pushed—is essential to our conception of what it is to be a real, concrete object.

3. The Dynamic Aspect of Descriptive Inexhaustibility: The Instability of Knowledge

The preceding considerations regarding the descriptive complexity of things relate to the limits of knowledge that can be rationalized on *a fixed and given* conceptual basis—a fully formed and developed language. But in real life languages are never full-formed, and a conceptual basis is never "fixed and given." Even with such familiar items as birds, trees, and clouds, we are involved in a constant reconceptualization in the course of progress in genetics, evolutionary theory, aerodynamics, and thermodynamics. With the ongoing development of science we can—and do—ongoingly change our mind as to the make-up and functioning of nature's furnishings. Our conceptions of things always present a *moving* rather than a *fixed* object of consideration, and this historical dimension must also be reckoned with. It is thus not only instructive but ultimately essential to view our knowledge of the properties of things in a temporal perspective.

The prospect of change can never be eliminated in this cognitive domain since the properties of anything real are literally open-ended so that we can always discover more of them. Even if we were (surely mistakenly) to view the word's descriptive nature as inherently finitistic—espousing that mistaken Keynesian principle of limited variety to the effect that nature can be portrayed descriptively with the materials of a finite taxonomic scheme—there will still be no a priori guarantee that the progress of science will not lead ad indefinitum to changes of mind regarding this finite register of descriptive materials. This conforms exactly to our expectation in these matters. Be the items in question elm trees, volcanoes, or quarks, we have every expectation that in the course of future scientific progress people will come to view their origins and their properties differently from the way we do at this juncture. For where the real things of the world are concerned, we not only expect to learn more about them in the course of scientific inquiry, *we expect to have to change our minds about their nature and modes of comportment.*

The diachronic aspect is crucial here. Where the phenomena we address are sufficiently complex, we will ongoingly encounter novelty in the course of experiential exploration of the domain—that is, meet with phenomena that destabilize our existing theories by affording new data that simply do not fit the patterns established on the basis of the heretofore available observations. And so, as ample experience shows, novelties almost inevitably arise as we push our scientific efforts beyond the limits of heretofore available experience. And there is no sufficient reason of general principle why such scientific innovation need ever come to a stop. For even with respect to a finitely complex object there is always the prospect of an ongoing change of mind and opinion: variability can arise here from the side of the subject rather than the object of cognition. Only if we lived in a Nietzschean world of eternal recurrence—a world whose fixed patterns of experienced occurrence reiterated themselves in a vast periodicity of unchanging repetition—could the prospect of ongoing scientific innovation be decisively abolished. And there is obviously no reason whatsoever to regard this prospect as even remotely plausible.

Any adequate theory of inquiry must recognize that the ongoing process of information enhancement in scientific inquiry is a process of *conceptual* innovation that always leaves certain facts about things wholly outside the cognitive range of the inquirers of any particular period. Caesar did not know—and in the then existing state of the cognitive art could not have known—that his sword contained tungsten and carbon. There will always be facts about a thing that we do not *know* because we cannot even *conceive* of them within the prevailing conceptual order of things. To grasp such a fact would call for taking a perspective of consideration that as yet we simply do not have, since the state of knowledge (or purported knowledge) has not and indeed cannot yet reach a point at which such a consideration is feasible.

The language of emergence can perhaps be deployed usefully to make the point. But here emergence is not one of the features of things, but one of our unfolding information about them. Blood circulated in the human body well before Harvey; substances containing uranium were radioactive before Becquerel. The emergence at issue relates to our cognitive mechanisms of conceptualization, not to the *objects* of our consideration in and of themselves. Real-world objects must be conceived of realistically, as antecedent to any cognitive interaction, as being there right along—"pregiven" as Edmund Husserl put it. Those cognitive changes or innovations are to be conceptualized as something that occurs on *our* side of the cognitive transaction, rather than on the side of the *objects* with which we deal.

Accordingly, one of the most striking and characteristic features of reality in general—and indeed of anything in particular that is real—is its complexity. As G. W. Leibniz already stressed in the seventeenth century (see section 37 of his *Monadology*), real existence is always involved in an unending elaborateness of *detail*. Anything that exists in this world exhibits an infinite descriptive depth. No account of it can come to the end of the line. None can ever manage to tell us everything there is to know about something real—none can say all there is to be said. And this means that our knowledge of reality is incomplete—and invariably so, now or ever. The real has an inner complexity that is humanly inexhaustible and the range of fact inevitably outruns that of articulable truth.

4. The Cognitive Opacity of the Real

Ontological objectivity has to do with the things that exist; cognitive objectivity with the nature of our knowledge or, at any rate, our belief about things. The one deals with reality, the other with our views about it. How are the two related?

The issue posed here is unquestionably complex and carries us deep into the philosophical themes that have revolved around the topic of scepticism. But the crucial fact is that a particular sort of cognitive stance towards *ontological* objectivity lies at the base of our commitment to *cognitive* objectivity.[9] The pursuit of cognitive objectivity—with its injunction to align our own thought with our best judgment of the demands of reason—calls for a commitment to ontological objectivity, requiring the supposition of real-world objects whose true character is independent of what any of us happen to think. The task of the present chapter is to unfold the rather intricate tale of how this is so.

The quest for objective knowledge will, in theory, beckon us onwards to the infinite. From finitely many axioms, reason can generate a potential infinity of theorems; from finitely many words, thought can exfoliate a potential infinity of sentences; from finitely many data, reflection can extract a potential infinity of items of information. Even with respect to a world of finitely many object, the process of reflecting upon these objects can, in principle, go on unendingly. One can inquire about their features, the features of those features, and so on. Or again, one can consider their relations, the relations among those relations, and so on. Thought—abstraction, reflection, analysis—is an inherently ampliative process. As in physical reflection in which mirror-images can reflect one another indefinitely, so mental reflection can go on and on. Given a start, however modest, thought can advance ad indefinitum into new conceptual domains. The circumstance of its starting out from a finite basis does *not* mean that it need ever run out of impetus (as the example of Shakespearean scholarship seems to illustrate).

Any adequate theory of inquiry must recognize that the ongoing process of information acquisition at issue in science is a process of *conceptual* innovation, which always leaves certain facts about things wholly outside the cognitive range of the inquirers of any particular period. Caesar did not know—and in the then extant state of the cognitive art could not have known—that his sword contained tungsten and carbon. There will always be facts (or plausible candidate facts) about a thing that we do not *know* because we cannot even *conceive* of them in a prevailing order of things. To grasp such a fact means adopting a perspective of consideration which holds that we do not have a definitive and complete view of the item at hand since the state of knowledge is not yet advanced to a point at which finality and definitiveness can reasonably be claimed. Any adequate worldview must recognize that the ongoing progress of scientific inquiry is a process of *conceptual* innovation that always leaves various facts about the things of this world wholly outside the cognitive range of the inquirers of any particular period.

The prospect of change can never be eliminated in the cognitive domain. The properties of a thing are literally open-ended: we can always discover more of them. Even if we were (surely mistakenly) to view the world as descriptively finitistic—espousing the Keynesian principle of "limited variety" to the effect that nature can be portrayed with the materials of a finite taxonomic scheme—there will still be no a priori guarantee that the progress of science will not lead *ad indefinitum* to changes of mind regarding this finite register of descriptive materials. And this conforms exactly to our expectation in these matters. For where the real things of the world are concerned, we not only expect to learn more about them in the course of further scientific inquiry, *we expect to have to change our minds about their nature and modes of comportment.* Be the item at issue elm trees, or volcanoes, or quarks, we have every expectation that in the course of future scientific progress people will come to think about their origin and their properties differently from the way we do at this juncture. In sum, real things—actually existing physical objects—have a cognitive depth whose bottom we cannot possibly plumb.

It is worthwhile to examine more closely the considerations that indicate the inherent imperfection of our knowledge to things.

To begin with, it is clear that, as we standardly think about things within the conceptual framework of our fact-oriented thought and discourse, *any* real physical object has more facets than it will ever actually manifest in experience. For every objective property of a real thing has consequences of a dispositional character and these are never surveyable *in toto* because the dispositions which particular concrete things inevitably have endow them with an infinitistic aspect that cannot be comprehended within experience.[10] This desk, for example, has a limitless manifold of phenomenal features of the type: "having a certain appearance from a particular point of view." It is perfectly clear that most of these will never be actualized in experience. Moreover, a thing *is* what it *does*: entity and lawfulness are coordinated correlates—a good Kantian point. And this fact that real things involve lawful comportment means that the finitude of experience precludes any prospect of the *exhaustive* manifestation of the descriptive facets of real things.[11]

Physical things not only have more properties than they ever will overtly manifest, but they have more than they possibly can ever manifest. This is so because the dispositional properties of things always involve what might be characterized as *mutually preemptive* conditions of realization. This cube of sugar, for example, has the dispositional property of reacting in a particular way if subjected to a temperature of 10,000°C and of reaching in a certain way if emplaced for one hundred hours in a large, turbulent body of water. But if either of these conditions is ever realized, it will destroy the lump of sugar as a lump of sugar, and thus block the prospect of *its* ever bringing the other property to manifestation. The perfectly possible realization of various dispositions may fail to be mutually *compossible*, and so the dispositional properties of a thing cannot ever be manifested completely—not just in practice, but in principle. Our objective claims about real things always commit us to more than we can actually ever determine about them.

The existence of this latent (hidden, occult) sector is a crucial feature of our conception of a real thing. Neither in fact nor in thought can we ever simply put it away. To say of the apple that its only features are those it actually manifests is to run afoul of our conception of an apple. To deny—or even merely to refuse to be committed to the claim—that it *would* manifest particular features *if* certain conditions came about (for example, that it would have such-and-such a taste if eaten) is to be driven to withdrawing the claim that it is an apple. The process of corroborating the implicit contents of our objective factual claims about something real is potentially endless, and such judgments are thus "non-terminating" in C. I. Lewis' sense.[12] This cognitive depth of our objective factual claims is inherent in the fact that their *content* will always outrun the evidence for making them and means that the endorsement of any such claim always involves some element of evidence-transcending conjecture.

The very concepts at issue—namely "experience" and "manifestation"—are such that we can only ever *experience* those features of a real thing that it actually *manifests*. But the preceding considerations show that real things always have more experientially manifestable properties than they can ever actually manifest in experience. The experienced portion of a thing is like the part of the iceberg that shows above water. All real things are necessarily thought of as having hidden depths that extend beyond the limits, not only of experience, but also of experientiability. To say of something that it is an apple or a stone or a tree is to become committed to claims about it that go beyond the data we have—and even beyond those which we can, in the nature of things, ever actually acquire. The "meaning" inherent in the assertoric commitments of our factual statements is never exhausted by its verification. Real things are cognitively opaque—we cannot see to the bottom of them. Our knowledge of such things can thus become more *extensive* without thereby becoming more *complete*.

This cognitive opacity of real things means that we are not—and will never be—in a position to evade or abolish the contrast between "things as we think them to be" and things as the actual and complete truth of the matter maintains them to be, that is, "things as they actually and truly are." Their susceptibility to further elaborative detail— and to changes of mind regarding this further elaborative detail—is built into our very conception of a "real thing." To be a real thing is to be something regarding which we can always, in principle, acquire more and possibly discordant information. This view of the situation is supported rather than impeded once we abandon the naive cumulativist/ preservationist view of knowledge acquisition in recognizing that new discoveries need not *supplement* but can *displace* the old. We realize that people will come to think differently about things from the way we do—even when thoroughly familiar things are at issue—seeing that scientific progress generally entails fundamental changes of mind about how things work in the world. The complications arising in the characterization of reality are fathomless.

In view of the cognitive opacity of real things, we must never pretend to a cognitive monopoly or cognitive finality. This emphasis on the *tentative* (rather than definitive) nature of our information what things—its provisional rather than definitive nature which makes our knowledge of things into no more than merely purported knowledge—lead Kant to contrast the empirical/experiential objects that features in our knowledge with "something = X, of which we *know*, and with the present constitution of our understanding can *know*, nothing whatsoever."[13] This recognition of incomplete information is inherent in the very nature of our conception of a "real thing." It is a crucial facet of our epistemic stance towards the real world to recognize that every part and parcel of it has features lying beyond our present cognitive reach—at *any* "present" whatsoever.

Much the same story holds when our concern is not with physical things, but with *types* of such things. To say that something is copper or magnetic is to say more than that it has the properties we think copper or magnetic things have, and to say more than that it meets our test conditions for being copper (or being magnetic). It is to say that this thing *is* copper or magnetic. And this is an issue regarding which we are prepared at least to contemplate the prospect that we have got it wrong.

It is, of course, imaginable that natural science will come to a stop, not in the trivial sense of a cessation of intelligent life, but rather in Charles Sanders Peirce's more interesting sense of eventually reaching a condition after which even indefinitely ongoing effort at inquiry will not—and indeed actually *cannot*—produce any significant change. Such a position is, in theory, possible. But we can never *know*—be it in practice or in principle—that it is actually realized. We can never establish that science has attained such an omega-condition of final completion: the possibility of further change lying "just around the corner" can never be ruled out finally and decisively. We thus have no alternative but to *presume* that our science is still imperfect and incomplete, that no matter how far we have pushed our inquiries in any direction, regions of terra incognita yet lie beyond. And this means that to be realistic we must take the stance that our conception of real things, no matter how elaborately developed, will always be provisional and corrigible. Reality has hidden reserves; it is "deeper" than our knowledge of it ever is—or can be—at any particular juncture.

In this connection it is instructive to contemplate some of the great discoveries of twentieth century formal and empirical science:

- Gödel's incompleteness theorem and such of its cousins as Turing's halting problem and various noncomputability results

- the proliferation of logical, geometric, and mathematical systems
- the development of quantum physics with its statisticization of all nature (the cognitive domain included)
- the rise of scientific epistemology with its idea that theories are bound to be underdetermined by evidence.

These developments combine to convey and substantiate an important lesson. They surpass the general-principle argumentation of traditional skepticism in providing detailed substantive grounds for acknowledging that our knowledge of things is incomplete and incompleteable, imperfect and imperfectable. All we can do at this—or any—stage of inquiry is to project the best estimates for resolving our questions about the world that are achievable in the existing state of the art.[14] Our science represents not the definitive truth of things, but only our best currently attainable effort in this direction. The inescapable fact of the matter is that reality everywhere outruns our knowledge of it. As the history of science amply shows, for the impact of later, fuller knowledge, shows that matters are always more complex than we currently think them to be.

5. Nomic, or Operational Complexity

The preceding discussion has focused on the world's compositional complexity both in its synchronous and in its temporal dimension. We shall now turn to the question of its nomic and operational complexity.

Our ability to describe, explain, and predict the world's eventuations is geared to the state of the art regarding our grasp of nature's laws— or at any rate its putative laws. And throughout this domain we are in the presence of an ever unfolding complexity. It is instructive to explore the ramifications and implications of this circumstance.

A far-reaching principle is at work in this context of nomic complexity. In a law-hierarchy, any particular law is potentially a member of a wider family that will itself exhibit various lawful characteristics and thus be subject to synthesis under still "higher" laws. We thus move from first-order laws governing phenomena to second-order laws governing such laws, and so on, ascending to new levels of sophistication and comparative complexity as we move along. No matter what law may be at issue, there arise new questions about it that demand an answer in emergently new lawful terms. It becomes crucial in this context that higher-level patterns are not necessarily derivable from lower-level ones. The statistical frequency with which the individual letters A and T occur in a text fails to determine the frequency with which a combination like AT occurs. (Note that the groups ATATATAT and AATTAATT both have a 50 percent frequency of A's and of T's, yet the pair AT occurs four times in the first group but only twice in the second.)

On the other hand, lower level patterns may also become lost in higher level ones. Consider, for instance, the sequence of 0's and 1's projected according to the rule that $x_i = 1$ if a certain physical situation obtains (or is exemplified) on occasion number i, and $x_i = 0$ if not. Whenever two different features generate such sequences, say

0100110100 . . .

1001011010 . . .

we can introduce the corresponding *matching sequence* —namely 0010010001 . . .—such that its i-th position is 1 if the two base sequences *agree* at their respective i-th positions, and 0 if they *disagree*. Such matching sequences will have a life of their own. And even if two base sequences are entirely random, their matching sequence need not be—for example when those base sequences simply exchange 0's and 1's. (Even random phenomena can be related by laws of coordination.)

Note, moreover, that one can always regard matching sequences themselves as further base sequences, so as to yield "second-order" phenomena, as it were. One can then proceed to examine the relationships between them—or between them and other base sequences. This process yields a potential hierarchy of "laws of coordination"—at level $i + 1$ we have the laws of coordination between sequences at level i. Such a perspective illustrates how simple base phenomena can ramify to bring more and more grist to the mill of study and analysis. Increasingly sophisticated mechanisms of conceptual coordination can lead us to regard the same phenomena in the light of different complexity levels.

These considerations indicate that quite different regularities and laws can emerge at different law levels. Suppose, for example, a natural system to be such that for essentially technical reasons a certain parameter p cannot be evaluated by us at the precise time-point t, but only on average over an interval around t. In such a case, the system can be very simple indeed—it need contain *no* complexities apart from those at issue in the preceding assumptions—and yet the prospect of endless cognitive progress is nevertheless available. For as our capacity to make p-determinations down to smaller and smaller time-intervals increases from minutes to seconds to milliseconds to micro-seconds, and so on, we can obtain an increasingly comprehensive insight into the *modus operandi* of the system and thus obtain ever fuller information about it that could not have been predetermined on the basis of earlier knowledge. Since averages at larger levels of scale do not determine those at smaller ones, quite different modes of comportment—and thus laws—can manifest themselves with the new phenomena that arise at different levels.[15]

Or, consider a somewhat different illustration. Suppose a totally random sequence of 2's and 3's, on the order of 2 3 2 2 3. . . . And suppose further a transformation that substitutes the pair 10 for 2 and 11 for 3 so as to yield:

10 11 10 10 11 . . .

We are now in a position to ascertain such "laws" as:

1. The sequence of *even-numbered* positions 01001 . . . will be a random mix of 0's and 1's (which simply mirrors the initial random sequence of 2's and 3's).
2. All the *odd-numbered* positions are filled by 1's.

We confront a peculiar mixture of randomness with regularity here. But of course it is only by studying *pairs* in that initial zero-one sequence that we can discern its code. Only by bringing appropriate coordination *concepts* to bear can we discern the laws at issue. And no matter how far we push forward along such lines into even more elaborate configurations the prospect of *further* structural laws can never be eliminated—nor downplayed by claiming that such laws are inherently less significant than the rest.

And there is no reason why this sort of nomic novelty cannot continue to occur *ad infinitum*. For a particular system can always exhibit new patterns of phenomenal order in its operations over time, and so there is always more to be learned about it. There is no end to the new levels of functional complexity of operation that can be investigated with such a system. Coordination phenomena have a life of their own. In principle, it will always be possible to discern yet further levels of lawfully structured relationship.[16] When we change the purview of our conceptual horizons, there is always in principle more to be learned—novelties of order that could not have been predicted from earlier, lower-level information. And this means, interestingly enough, that once the world is sufficiently complex in the operational mode to impose limits upon our cognitive interaction with it, then it certainly need not be infinitely complex in the compositional mode to provide for the prospect of indefinite scientific progress.

To be sure, it could, in theory, possibly occur that just the same relationship-patterns simply recur from level to level—that the patterns of phenomena that we encounter at level $i + 1$ simply reduplicate those already met with at level i. (This is the functional equivalent at the nomic level of the recurrence of physical pattern at different levels of scale characterizing the "fractal" structures made prominent by E. Mandelbrot.) However, this is a very special case that need not and will not obtain across the board. Science as we have it in all its branches indicates that there is no good reason to think that our world is fractal in the structure of its natural processes.

Even when dealing with the same species of object (e.g., symbols), and the same basic laws (e.g., combination-rules or grammars), we can nevertheless always in principle deepen our understanding by introducing increasingly powerful means of analysis to secure new sorts of data. Consider an analogy. The chess master and the beginner make exactly the same sorts of moves—the individual pieces behave exactly alike for each of them. At this level their realms "are governed by exactly the same laws." An observer exclaims: "I know all about chess. For I have now discovered the rules according to which those pieces move." Splendid! But also naive, since this business of "the basic rules of the game" is of course merely step one, with principles of tactics and strategy yet in the offering. It is in virtue of the complexity of their governing principles that masters and beginners differ decisively. The game can be played—and its operational phenomena thus studied—at very different levels of depth or sophistication.

As the analogy of chess makes clear, it is radically mistaken to think that we have come to the end of the road when we merely grasp nature's basic physical laws. The question of what sort of game she is playing by those rules—those *basic* laws—still remains an open issue. Even though nature might be of finite physical and nomic complexity as regards its physical structure and its basic procedural laws, nevertheless it could be infinitely diverse in the unfolding operational complexity of its phenomenal products over time. To understand the world about us we need departments of biology and economics as well as departments of physics.

6. The Imperfectibility of Knowledge in a Complex World

Whatever the known character of a series of phenomena that we examine may be, we can never rule out the possibility that yet further patterns of relationship exist. For there will be patterns of phenomena, and patterns of such patterns, and patterns of patterns of such patterns—and on and on. We can study letter sequences as such, or move on to the level of words, and thence to sentences, and thence to paragraphs, and so to chapters, to books, to book categories, to book systems (as with French vs. Chinese literature), etc. Every new level of consideration will afford phenomena of its own that will themselves admit of further study and analysis. Confronted with repetitive phenomena of any description, inquiry will always in principle find new grist for its mill among the phenomena arising at higher levels of productive operation.

After all, even a system that is finitely complex *both* in its physical makeup *and* in its basic law structure might nevertheless yet be infinitely complex in its *productive operations* over time. A limited producer might well engender unlimited products. (There is no end to the different games of chess that can be played with the same pieces and the same rules.) Even were the number of constituents of nature to be small, the ways in which they can be combined to yield products in space-time might yet be infinitely varied. Think here of the examples of letters/syllables/words/ sentences/paragraphs/books/genres (novels, reference books, etc.)/libraries/library systems. Even an otherwise finite nature can, like a typewriter with a limited keyboard, yield an endlessly varied text over time. It can produce a steady stream of new phenomena—"new" not necessarily in kind but in their functional interrelationships and thereby in their implications for theory, so that our knowledge of nature's operations can continually be enhanced and deepened. Even a world that is relatively simple in point of basic operations may well exhibit an effectively infinite *cognitive* depth when one proceeds to broaden one's notion of a natural phenomenon to include not just the processes themselves and the products that they produce, but also the *relationships* among them.

And there is no warrant for assuming an end to such a sequence of levels of integrative complexity of phenomenal order. Each successive level of operational or functional complexity can in principle exhibit a characteristic order of its own. The phenomena we attain at the *n*th level here can have features whose investigation takes us to the (n + 1)th. New phenomena and new laws can in theory arise at every level of integrative order. The different facets of nature can generate conceptually new strata of productive operation to yield a potentially unending sequence of levels, each giving rise to its own characteristic principles of organization, themselves quite unpredictable from the standpoint of the other levels.

With such an unending exfoliation of law-levels, our knowledge of the world's lawful order becomes self-potentiating and new combinations can always spring up to exploit the interrelations among old disciplines. Given chemistry and biology we can develop biochemistry; given mathematics and astronomy, we can develop the mathematics of astronomical relationships. On every such front, new insights into lawful processes can be expected. And it is clear that such an infinite proliferation of laws would also serve to block any prospect of completing science. There is accordingly no need to suppose that the *physical* complexity of nature need be unlimited for nature to have an unlimited *cognitive* depth.[17] After all, the prime task of science lies in discovering the levels of lawful order of nature, and the ongoing law-complexity of nature suffices for our present purposes of providing for potentially endless discovery.

We must thus come to terms with the fact that we cannot realistically expect that our science will ever—at *any* given stage of its actual development—be in a position to afford us more than a very partial and incomplete representation of a highly complex nature. After all, the achievement of cognitive control over nature requires not only intellectual instrumentalities (concepts, ideas, theories, knowledge) but also, and no less importantly, the deployment of physical resources (technology and "power"), since our knowledge of nature's processes calls for interacting with her. Given that we can only learn about nature by interacting with it, Newton's third law of countervailing action and reaction becomes a fundamental principle of epistemology. Everything depends on just how *and how hard* we can push against nature in situations of observational and detectional interaction. And we cannot "get to the bottom of it" where nature is concerned; in this regard nature always has hidden reserves of power. And the physical resources at our disposal are restricted and finite. It follows that our capacity to effect control is bound to remain imperfect and incomplete, with much in the realm of the doable always remaining undone.

We shall never be able to travel down this route as far we might like to go.

The Danish historian of science A. G. Drachmann closed his fine book *The Mechanical Technology of Greek and Roman Antiquity*[18] with the following observation: "I should prefer not to seek the cause of the failure of an invention in the social conditions till I was quite sure that it was to be found in the technical possibilities of the time." The history of *science*, as well as that of *technology*, is crucially conditioned by the limited nature of "the technical possibilities of the time." And this is as true for us as it was of the ancients.

In scientific inquiry into nature, *technological dependency sets technological limits*, first to data acquisition and then to theory projection. Every successive level of technical capability in point of observation and experimentation has its limitation through limits whose overcoming opens up yet another more sophisticated operational level of the technological state of the art. There will always be more to be done. The accessible pressures and temperatures can in theory always be increased, the low-temperature experiments brought closer to absolute zero, the particles accelerated closer to the speed of light, and so on. And complex experience teaches that any such enhancement of practical mastery brings new phenomena to view—and thereby provides an enhanced capability to test yet further hypotheses and discriminate between alternative theories conducive to deepening our knowledge of nature.[19]

Limitations of physical capacity and capability spell *cognitive* limitations for empirical science. Where there are inaccessible phenomena, there must be cognitive inadequacy as well. To this extent, at any rate, the empiricists were surely right. Only the most fanatical rationalist could uphold the capacity of sheer intellect to compensate for the lack of data. The existence of unobserved phenomena means that our theoretical systematizations may well be (and presumably are) incomplete. Insofar as certain phenomena are not just undetected but by their very nature inaccessible (even if only for the merely economic reasons suggested above), our theoretical knowledge of nature must be presumed imperfect. Fundamental features inherent in the structure of man's interactive inquiry into the ways of the world thus conspire to ensure the incompleteness of our knowledge—and moreover, will do so at any particular stage of the game.

There will always be yet unrealized interactions with nature on so great a scale (as measured in energy, pressure, temperature, particle-velocities, etc.) that their realization would require greater resources than we can commit. And where there are interactions to which we have no access, there are (presumably) phenomena that we cannot discern. It would be very unreasonable to expect nature to confine the distribution of cognitively significant phenomena to those ranges that lie conveniently within out reach. But while there is always more to be discovered, the doing of it becomes increasingly difficult as we move into the increasingly remote regions of parametric space. And since our material resources are limited, these limits inexorably circumscribe our cognitive access to the real world.

We can plausibly estimate the amount of gold or oil yet to be discovered, because we know the earth's extent and can thus establish a proportion between what we have explored and what we have not. But we cannot comparably estimate the amount of knowledge yet to be discovered, because we have and can have no way of relating what we know to what we do not. At best, we can consider the proportion of currently envisioned questions we can in fact resolve; and this is an unsatisfactory procedure. For the very idea of cognitive limits has a paradoxical air. It suggests that we claim knowledge about something outside knowledge. But (to hark back to Hegel), with respect to the realm of knowledge, we are not in a position to draw a line between what lies inside and what lies outside—seeing that, *ex hypothesi*, we have no cognitive access to the latter. One cannot make a survey of the relative extent of our knowledge or ignorance about nature except by basing it on some overall picture or model of nature that is already in hand via prevailing science. But this is clearly an inadequate procedure. This process of judging the adequacy of our science on its own telling may be the best we can do, but it remains an essentially circular and consequently inconclusive way of proceeding. The long and short of it is that there is no cognitively satisfactory basis for maintaining the completeness of science in a rationally cogent way. For while we can confidently anticipate that our scientific technology will see ongoing improvement in response to continued expenditure of effort, we cannot expect it ever to attain perfection. There is no reason to think that we ever will, or indeed can, reach "the end of the line."

The finitude of actual knowledge in the face of the unlimited cognitive depth imposed by nature's complexity means not only that our science is always incomplete but also that it is always of questionable correctness. The description and explanation of the real as best we are able to achieve it can never actually exhaust reality: adequately describing or explaining the world is a matter of aspiration and never of achievable accomplishment.

The cognitive project like the moral project is a matter of doing the best we can in the face of a sobering realization of ultimate inadequacy. And in science as in the moral life, we can function perfectly well in the realization that perfection is unattainable. No doubt here and there a scientist may nurse the secret hope of attaining some fixed and final definitive result that will stand, untouchable and changeless, through all subsequent ages, but such unrealistic aspirations are by no means essential to the scientific enterprise as such. Here, as elsewhere, in the realm of human endeavor it is a matter of doing the best we can with the tools that come to hand.

As far as we can ever tell there is no limit of theoretical principle—let alone of cognitive practice—to the complexity of the real. The things that populate the real world are always—both individually and in the aggregate—of an inner complexity so deep that inquiry and cognition cannot get to the bottom of it. There is always more to be done—and to be said about it. Complexity as a definitive and unavoidable feature of the real and as such has far reaching—and profoundly humbling—implications for the nature of our knowledge.[20]

To be sure, the circumstance that *perfection* is unattainable does nothing to countervail against the no less real fact that *improvement* is realizable—that progress is possible. The undeniable prospect of realizable progress—of overcoming genuine defects and deficiencies that we find in the work of our predecessors—affords ample impetus to scientific innovation. Scientific progress is not only motivated *a fronte* by the pull of an unattainable ideal; it is also stimulated *a tergo* by the push of dissatisfaction with the deficiencies of achieved positions. The labors of science are doubtless sometimes pulled forward by the mirage of (unattainable) perfection. But they are less vigorously pushed onward by the (perfectly realizable) wish to do better than our predecessors in the enterprise.

There are two ways of looking at progress: as a movement away from the start, or as a movement towards the goal. On the one hand, there is advancement-progress, defined in terms of increasing distance from the starting point. On the other hand, there is destination-progress, defined in terms of decreasing distance from the goal (the "destination.") With any finitely distant goal these two are equivalent—as with a foot-race, for example. But when the goal is infinitely removed, they are very different. Consider this picture:

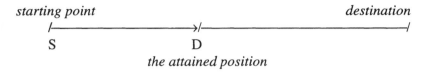

starting point   *destination*

/————————————————→/————————————————————/

S   D

the attained position

Here we obviously increase the distance travels from *S* in exactly the same amount as we decrease the distance remaining to a definite destination *D*: each step further from *S* is a step just exactly that much closer to *D*. But if there is no attainable destination—if we are engaged on a journey that is, for all we know, literally endless and has no determinable destination, or only one that is "infinitely distant"— then we just cannot manage to decrease our distance from it. We can move further from *S* but this takes us no nearer to that now unattainable destination. Where arrival at a definite destination is impossible, all we can then ever do is to make advancement-progress—to make still further improvements on the already attained position. The idea of approaching an ultimate goal becomes impossible here.

* * *

The present chapter's line of thought has unfolded as follows:

- Nature is unfathomably complex: The properties and features of the world's concrete particulars have no limit (law of natural complexity).
- For this reason among others, real things cannot bring all of their properties to manifestation. Their discerned features are only the part of the iceberg that reality manifests above the water of imperceptibility.
- And this hold for nature's laws as well, for its law-structure too is sufficiently complex that new operational features can always come to light.
- Our knowledge of things is bound to be developmental: its progress involves amplification but does so in such a way that cognitive amplification also means cognitive modification, i.e., changes of mind.
- There is no end of the road here—science is imperfectible.

The upshot of such deliberations is straightforward. The idea of ongoingly *improving* our science can be implemented without difficulty, since we can clearly improve our performance as regards its goals of prediction, control, and explanatory comprehensiveness. But the idea of *perfecting* our science cannot be implemented in an unfathomably complex world. We can not and never will warrantedly be able to regard the attained position of science (as it exists here and now) as something finished and complete. Our cognitive positioning in an immensely complex world imposes upon us a cognitive task of potential endlessness—one that literally knows no limits. The complexity of the real outreaches our cognitive grasp of it. But while the domain of what is (theoretically and potentially) knowable is thus infinite, the realm of what is known is finite. The ratio of knowledge to fact—of what is (presumably) known to what is in principle knowable—is accordingly always zero. All of us stand with Newton at the seashore. Our cognitive positioning in an immensely complex world imposes upon us cognitive task of potential endlessness—one that literally knows no limits.

There is wisdom in Hamlet's dictum: "There are more things in heaven and earth, Horatio . . ." The limits of our knowledge may be the limits of *our* world, but they are not the limits of *the* world. We do and must recognize the limitations or our cognition. We cannot justifiably equate reality with what can, in principle, be known by us, nor equate reality with what can, in principle, be expressed by our language. And what is true here for our sort of mind is true for any other sort of finite mind as well. Any physically realizable sort of cognizing being can only know a part or aspect of the real.

The complexity of the real manifests itself at the descriptive level with respect to the constitution of individuals and at the functional level with respect to their comportment. And this complexity is not static but an account of its self-potentiation is ever increasing. This dynamism makes for the complexity and complexification of science. It means that there is always more to be said here—that the complexity of the real as science reveals it to us is ultimately unfathomable.

The fact that reality has a cognitive depth that is, in effect, unfathomable has significant implications for realism, the philosophical doctrine that in the development of knowledge the mind at best models reality rather than creates it. For the inherent and unavoidable imperfection of our knowledge means that the limits of *our* world—the world of our belief and of our information—cannot be claimed to be the limits of *the* world. It is the very limitation of our knowledge of things—our recognition that reality extends beyond the horizons of what we can possibly know or even conjecture about—that most effectively betokens the mind-independence of the real. A world that is inexhaustible by our minds cannot easily be seen to be a product of their operations. The best possible argument for a realism which holds that reality outruns the reach of man's mind is provided by the fact that knowledge always changes—that in the complex world we inhabit it is never definitive but always destabilized in the course of scientific progress. If a realism-rejecting idealism is to be maintained then the mind whose operations are to bear the burden of reality-generation must clearly be a super-mind of the sort envisioned by absolute idealists such as F. H. Bradley, T. H. Green, B. Bosanquet, and A. S. Pringle Pattison. The finite human minds we ourselves possess and know are all too clearly unfitted to the task.[21]

Notes

1. Charles S. Peirce, *Collected Papers*, vol. I (Cambridge, MA: Harvard University Press, 1931), sect. 1.174.
2. Our position can come to terms with P. F. Strawson's precept that "facts are what statements (when true) state". ("Truth", *Proceedings of the Aristotelian Society*, supplementary volume 24 [1950], pp. 129-56; see p. 136.) Difficulty would ensue only if an "only" were inserted.
3. But can any sense be made of the idea of *merely* possible (i.e., possible but nonactual) languages? Of course it can! Once we have a generalized conception (or definition) of a certain kind of thing—be it a language or a caterpillar—then we are inevitably in a position to suppose the prospect of things meeting these conditions are over and above those that in fact do so. The prospect of mooting certain "mere" possibilities cannot be denied—that, after all, is just what possibilities are all about.
4. Note, however, that if a Davidsonian translation argument to the effect that "if it's sayable at all, then, it's sayable in *our* language" were to succeed—which it does not—then the matter would stand on a different footing. For it would then follow that any possible language can state no more than what can be stated in our own (actual) language. And then the realm of facts (i.e., what is [correctly] statable in some *possible* language) and that of truths (i.e., what is [correctly] statable in some *actual* language) would necessarily coincide. Accordingly, our thesis that the range of facts is larger than that of truths hinges crucially upon a failure of such a translation argument. And, of course, find it does. (See Donald Davidson, "The Very Ideas of a Conceptual Scheme," *Proceedings and Addresses of the American Philosophical Association*, vol. 47, 1973-1974, pp. 5-20, and also the critique of his position in chapter II of the author's *Empirical Inquiry* [Totowa, NJ: Rowman & Littlefield, 1982]).
5. Gödel demonstrated in 1931 that even elementary arithmetic is so complex that the totality of its truths cannot be captured with the resources of a deductively rigorous system. His ground-breaking paper is available in English translation; Kurt Gödel, *On Formally UndecidablePropositions of Principia Mathematica*

and Related Systems, tr. by B. Meltzer (Edinburgh and London: Oliver & Boyd, 1962).

6. On these issues see Nancy Cartwright, *How the Laws of Physics Lie* (Oxford: Clarendon Press, 1983).

7. On this theme see John Dupré, *The Disorder of Things* (Cambridge, MA: Harvard University Press, 1993).

8. Thus, if *facts* have be reflected in irreducibly "atomic" proportions, complex "facts"—disjunctive or conjunctive ones, for example—cannot qualify as such. And if indeed "facts belong to the objective world" (as Bertrand Russell's *The Philosophy of Logic Atomism* [LaSalle, IL: Open Court, 1985] has it on p. 183) or if facts encompass "everything that there is in the world" (as Russell says in *Human Knowledge* on p. 143) then disjunctive and general facts are in trouble, to say nothing of *infinitely* conjunctive ones. (Note Bertrand Russell's struggles with these conceptions in *Human Knowledge*, pp. 126-44.) But such gyrations carry us nowhere save deep into the tendentious technicalities of a problematic doctrine.

9. This, to be sure, is only a limited aspect of the topic. For others, see the author's *Scepticism* (Oxford: Blackwell, 1980) and *Scientific Realism* (Dordrecht: Reidel, 1987).

10. To be sure, *abstract* things, such as colors or numbers, will not have dispositional properties. For being divisible by four is not a *dispositional* of sixteen. Plato got the matter right in Book VII of the *Republic*. In the realm of *abstracta*, such as those of mathematics, there are not genuine *processes*—and process is a requisite of dispositions. Of course, there may be dispositional truths in which numbers (or colors, etc.) figure that do not issue in any dispositional properties of these numbers (or colors, etc.) themselves—a truth, for example, such as my predilection for odd numbers. But if a truth (or supposed truth) does no more than to convey how someone *thinks* about a thing, then it does not indicate any property of the thing itself. In any case, however, the subsequent discussion will focus on *realia* in contrast to *fictionalia* and *concreta* in contrast to *abstracta*. (Fictional things, however, *can* have dispositions: Sherlock Holmes was addicted to cocaine, for example. Their difference from *realia* is dealt with below).

11. This aspect of objectivity was justly stressed in the "Second Analogy" of Kant's *Critique of Pure Reason*, whose discussion rests on ideas already contemplated by Leibniz, *Philosophische Schriften*, edited by C. I. Gerhardt, vol. VII (op. cit.), pp. 319 ff.

12. See C. I. Lewis, *An Analysis of Knowledge and Valuation*, (La Salle, IL: Open Court, 1962), pp. 180-81.

13. Immanuel Kant, *Critique of Pure Reason*, A 250.

14. For variations on this theme see the author's *Satisfying Reason* (Dordrecht: Kluwer, 1995).

15. The variation of modes of comportment at different levels means that the descriptive taxonomies at those levels will differ also, and may well be conceptually disjoint from one another. For variations on this theme see John Dupré, *The Disorder of Things* (Cambridge, MA: Harvard University Press, 1993).

16. On issues of complexity in science see the works of Mario Bunge, especially *The Myth of Simplicity* (Englewood Cliffs, NJ: Prentice-Hall, 1963) and *Scientific Research* (New York: Springer, 1967; 2 vols.).

17. For an interesting and suggestive analysis of "the architecture of complexity," see Herbert A. Simon, *The Sciences of the Artificial* (Cambridge, MA: MIT Press, 1969).

18. Madison and Copenhagen: University of Wisconsin Press, 1963.

19. On the implausibility of seeing physics as a unified and closed mathematical system see Edoardo Amaldi, "The Unity of Physics," *Physics Today*, vol. 261 (Sept., 1973), pp. 23-29.
20. For other aspects of this situation see the author's *Scientific Progress* (Oxford: Blackwell, 1976).
21. On further aspects of some of this chapter's contentions see the author's *Limits of Science* (Berkeley and Los Angeles: University of California Press, 1985).

3

Cognitive Progress in a Complex World: Destabilization and Complexification

(1) In a complex world, the natural dynamics of rational inquiry will inevitably exhibit a tropism towards increasing complexity. (2) To be sure, a penchant for simplicity is built into the inductive process of scientific method. But this procedurally methodological *commitment does not prejudge or prejudice the substantively* ontological *issue of the complexity of nature. Our inductive commitment to simplicity is a matter of the procedural principle of least effort—an inseparable aspect of pragmatic rationality. (3) Scientific theorizing is an inductive projection from the* available *data. But data-availability is bound to improve with the changing state of the technological art—engendering a dynamism that ongoingly destabilizes the existing state of science so as to engender greater sophistication. The increasing complexity of our world picture is a striking phenomenon throughout this process. It is so marked, in fact, that natural science has in recent years been virtually disintegrating before our very eyes. (4) And this phenomenon characterizes all of science—the human sciences included. Indeed, complexification and its concomitant destabilization are by no means phenomena confined to the domain of science—they pervade the entire range of our knowledge.*

1. Spencer's Law: The Dynamics of Cognitive Complexity

Be it at the level of cosmological development, of biological evolution, or of technological invention, every major innovation in the world opens up a new "range of possibilities" which soon gets exploited in the natural course of things. But as this exploitation proceeds, there comes into operation a process of selection—be it natural or rational—that soon reduces the possibilities to a greatly diminished subgroup of survivors. With every step of this innovation-proliferation-selection cycle, the realized products are more complex than what existed before, more closely attuned to the needs of new conditions and circumstances.

We naturally adopt throughout rational inquiry—and accordingly throughout natural science—the methodological principle of rational economy to "try the simplest solutions first" and then make this do as long as it can. And this means that *historically* the course of inquiry moves in the direction of ever increasing complexity. The developmental tendency of our intellectual enterprises—natural science among them—is generally in the direction of greater complication and sophistication.

In a complex world, the natural dynamics of the cognitive process exhibits an inherent tropism towards increasing complexity. Herbert Spencer argued long ago that evolution is characterized by von Baer's law of development "from the homogeneous to the heterogeneous" and thereby produces an ever increasing definition of detail and complexity of articulation.[1] As Spencer saw it, organic species in the course of their development confront a successive series of environmental obstacles, and with each successful turning along the maze of developmental challenges the organism becomes selectively more highly specialized in its bio-design, and thereby more tightly attuned to the particular features of its ecological context.[2] Now this view of the developmental process may or may not be correct for *biological* evolution, but there can be little question about its holding for *cognitive* evolution. For rational beings will of course try simple things first and thereafter be driven step by step towards an ever enhanced complexification. In the course of rational inquiry we try the simple solutions first, and only thereafter, if and when they cease to work—when they are ruled out by further findings (by some further influx of coordinating information)—do we move on to the more complex. Things go along smoothly until an oversimple solution becomes destabilized by enlarged experience. For a time we get by with the comparatively simpler options—until the expanding information about the world's *modus operandi* made possible by enhanced new means of observation and experimentation insists otherwise. And with the expansion of knowledge those new accessions make ever increasing demands. And so evolution, be it natural or rational—whether of animal species or of literary genres—ongoingly confronts us with products of greater and greater complexity.[3]

Rational inquiry is a process of optimization—that is, maximization under constraints. In particular, it strives for comprehensiveness: we require enough amplitude to take synoptic account of the whole range of available experience. But, subject to this limitation, we seek the simplest, the most economical theory framework that is conveniently available to resolve our explanatory questions. We want, in sum, to find the most economical theory-accommodation for the amplest body of currently available experience. Induction—here short for "the scientific method" in general—proceeds by way of constructing the most straightforward and economical structures able to house the available data comfortably while yet affording answers to our questions.[4] Accordingly, economy and simplicity serve as cardinal directives for inductive reasoning, whose procedure is that of the precept: "Resolve your cognitive problems in the simplest, most economical way that is compatible with a sensible exploitation of the information at your disposal." In the course of resolving our cognitive problems we honor—and generally hold—the calls for implementing the general idea of rational economy. But we always encounter limits here.

Our cognitive efforts manifest a Manichaean-style struggle between complexity and simplicity—between the impetus to comprehensiveness (amplitude) and the impetus to system (economy). We want our theories to be as extensive and all-encompassing as possible and at the same time to be elegant and economical. The first desideratum pulls in one direction, the second in the other. And the accommodation reached here is never actually stable. As our experience expands in the quest for greater adequacy and comprehensiveness, the old theory structures become destabilized—the old theories no longer fit the full range of available fact. And so the theoretician goes back to the old drawing board. What he comes up with there is—and in the circumstances must be—something more elaborate, more *complex* than what was able to do the job before those new complications arose (though we do, of course, sometimes achieve local simplifications within an overall global complexification). We make do with the simple, but only up to the point when the demands of adequacy force additional complications upon us. An inner tropism towards increasing complexity is thus built into the very nature of the scientific project as we have it.

And the same is true also for technological evolution, with *cognitive* technology emphatically included. Be it in cognitive or in practical matters, the processes and resources of yesteryear are rarely, if ever, up to the demands of the present. In consequence, the life-environment we create for ourselves grows increasingly complex. The Occam's razor injunction, "Never introduce complications unless and until you actually require them," accordingly represents a defining principle of practical reason that is at work within the cognitive project as well. And because we try the simplest solutions first, making simple solutions do until circumstances force one to do otherwise, it transpires that in the development of knowledge—as elsewhere in the domain of human artifice—progress is always a matter of complexpification. An inherent impetus towards greater complexity pervades the entire realm of human creative effort. We find it in art; we find it in technology; and we certainly find it in the cognitive domain as well.[5]

2. The Principle of Least Effort and the Methodological Status of Simplicity-Preference in Science

An eminent philosopher of science has maintained that "in cases of inductive simplicity it is not economy which determines our choice. . . . We make the assumption that the simplest theory furnishes the best predictions. This assumption cannot be justified by convenience; it has a truth character and demands a justification within the theory of probability and induction."[6] This perspective is gravely misleading. What sort of consideration could possibly justify the supposition that "the simplest theory furnishes the best prediction"? Any such belief is surely unwarranted and inappropriate. There is simply no cogent rationale for firm confidence in the simplicity of nature. To claim the ontological simplicity of the real is somewhere between the hyperbolic and absurd.

The matter becomes far less problematic, however, once one approaches it from a methodological rather than a substantive point of view. For considerations of rational economy and convenience of operation obviously militate for inductive systematicity. Seeing that the simplest answer is (*eo ipso*) the most economical one to work with, rationality creates a natural pressure towards economy—towards simplicity insofar as other things are equal. Our eminent theorist has things upside down here: it is in fact methodology that is at issue rather than among any factual presumption.

Suppose, for example, that we are asked to supply the next member of a series of the format 1, 2, 3, 4,.... We shall straightaway respond with 5, supposing the series to be simply that of the integers. Of course, the actual series might well be 1, 2, 3, 4, 11, 12, 13, 14, 101, 102, 103, 104, . . . , with the correct answer thus eventuating as 11 rather than 5. But while we cannot rule such possibilities out, they do not for an instant deter our inductive proceedings. For the inductively appropriate course lies with the production rule that is the simplest issue-resolving answer—the simplest resolution that meets the conditions of the problem. And we take this line not because we know a priori that this simplest resolution will prove to be correct. (We know no such thing!) Rather we adopt this answer, provisionally at least, exactly because it is the least cumbersome and most economical way of providing a resolution that does justice to the facts and demands of the situation. We recognize that other possibilities of resolution exist but ignore them until further notice, exactly because there is no cogent reason for giving them favorable treatment *at this stage*. (After all, once we leave the safe harbor of simplicity behind there are always innumerable possibilities for complexification, and we lack any guidance in moving one way rather than another.)

Throughout inductive inquiry in general, and scientific inquiry in particular, we seek to provide a descriptive and explanatory account that provides the simplest, least complex way of accommodating the data that experience (experimentation and observation) has put at our disposal. When something simple accomplishes the cognitive tasks in hand, as well as some more complex alternative, it is foolish to adopt the latter. After all, we need not presuppose that the world is somehow systematic (simple, uniform, and the like) to validate our penchant for the systematicity of our cognitive commitments.

Henri Poincaré has remarked that:

> [Even] those who do not believe that natural laws must be simple, are still often obliged to act as if they did believe it. They cannot entirely dispense with this necessity without making all generalization, and therefore all science, impossible. It is clear that any fact can be generalised in an infinite number of ways, and it is a question of choice. The choice can only be guided by considerations of simplicity. . . . To sum up, in most cases every law is held to be simple until the contrary is proved.[7]

These observations are wholly in the right spirit. As cognitive possibilities proliferate in the course of theory-building inquiry, a principle of choice and selection becomes requisite. And here economy—along with its other systematic congeners, simplicity, and uniformity, and the like—are the natural guideposts. We subscribe to the inductive presumption in favor of simplicity, uniformity, normality,[8] etc., not because we know or believe that matters always stand on a basis that is simple, uniform, normal, etc.—surely we know no such thing!—but because it is on this basis alone that we can conduct our cognitive business in the most advantageous, the most *economical* way. In scientific induction we exploit the information at hand so as to answer our questions in the most straightforward, the most economical way.

Throughout inductive situations, our objective factual claims outreach the available evidence. Here we are invariably called on to answer questions whose resolution is beyond the secure reach of information at hand. And to accomplish this we develop our problem resolutions along the lines of least resistance, seeking to economize our cognitive effort by using the most direct workable means to our ends. Whenever possible, we analogize the present case to other similar ones, because the introduction of new patterns complicates our cognitive repertoire. And we use the least cumbersome viable formulations because they are easier to remember and more convenient to use. The rationale of the other-things-equal preferability of simpler solutions over more complex ones is obvious enough. Simpler solutions are less cumbersome to store, easier to take hold of, and less difficult to work with. It is indeed economy and convenience that determine our regulative predilection for simplicity and systematicity in general. Our prime motivation is to get by with a minimum of complication, to adopt strategies of question-resolution that enable us among other things: (1) to continue with existing solutions unless and until the epistemic circumstances compel us to introduce changes (uniformity) be; (2) to make the same processes do insofar as possible (generality); and (3) to keep to the simplest process that will do the job (simplicity). Such a perspective combines the commonsensical precept, "Try the simplest thing first," with a principle of burden of proof: "Maintain your cognitive commitments until there is good reason to abandon them."

When other things are anything like equal, simpler theories are bound to be operationally more advantageous. We avoid needless complications whenever possible, because this is the course of an economy of effort. It is the general practice in scientific theory construction to give preference to

- one-dimensional rather than multidimensional modes of description,
- quantitative rather than qualitative characterizations,
- lower- rather than higher-order polynomials,
- linear rather than nonlinear differential equations.

The comparatively simpler is for this very reason easier to work with. In sum, we favor uniformity, analogy, simplicity, and the like because they ease our cognitive labor. On such a perspective, simplicity is a concept of the practical order, pivoting on being more economical to use—that is, less demanding of resources.

As a fundamentally inductive endeavor, scientific theorizing accordingly involves the search for, or the construction of, the least complex and most straightforward theory-structure capable of resolving our questions while also adequately accommodating the currently available data. The key principle is that of the rational economy of means for the realization of given cognitive ends, of getting the most effective answer we can with the least complication. Complexities cannot be ruled out, but they must always pay their way in terms of increased systemic adequacy! It is thus methodology and not metaphysics that grounds our commitment to simplicity and systematicity.

The rational economy of process is the crux here. And this methodological commitment to rational process does not prejudge or prejudice the substantively *ontological* issue of the complexity of nature. Natural science is emphatically *not* bound to a principle of simplicity in nature. There really are no adequate grounds for supposing the "simplicity" of the world's make-up. Instead, the so-called "principle of simplicity" is really a principle of complexity-management: "Feel free to introduce complexity in your efforts to describe and explain nature's ways. But only when and where it is really needed. Insofar as possible 'keep it simple!' Only introduce as much complexity as you really need for your scientific purposes of description, explanation, prediction, and control." Such an approach is eminently sensible. But of course such a principle is no more than a methodological rule of procedure for managing our cognitive affairs. Nothing entitles us to transmute this methodological precept into a descriptive/ontological claim to the effect that nature is simple—let alone of finite complexity.

Our systematizing procedures in science pivot on the injunction always to adopt the most economical (simple, general, straightforward, etc.) solution that meets the demands of the situation. This penchant for inductive systematicity reflected in the conduct of inquiry is simply a matter of striving for rational economy. It is based on methodological considerations that are governed by an analogue of Occam's razor—a principle of parsimony to the effect that needless complexity is to be avoided *complicationes non multiplicandae sunt praeter necessitatem*. Given that the inductive method, viewed in its practical and methodological aspect, aims at the most efficient and effective means of question-resolution, it is only natural that our inductive precepts should direct us always to begin with the most systematic, and thereby economical, device that can actually do the job at hand.[9]

It clearly makes eminent sense to move onwards from the simplest (least complex) available solution to introduce further complexities when and as—but *only* when and as—they are forced upon us. Simpler (more systematic) answers are more easily codified, taught, learned, used, investigated, and so on. The regulative principles of convenience and economy in learning and inquiry suffice to provide a rational basis for systematicity-preference. Our preference for simplicity, uniformity, and systematicity in general, is now not a matter of a substantive theory regarding the nature of the world, but one of search strategy—of cognitive methodology. In sum, we opt for simplicity (and systematicity in general) in inquiry not because it is truth-indicative, but because it is teleologically more effective in conducing to the efficient realization of the goals of inquiry. We look for the dropped coin in the lightest spots nearby, not because this is—in the circumstances—the most probable location but because it represents the most sensible strategy of search: if it is not there, then we just cannot find it at all.

To be sure, only time will tell to what extent we can successfully move in the direction in which systematicity and implicity point. This is something that "remains to be seen." (This is where the importance of ultimate experiential retrovalidation comes in to supplement our commitment to methodological convenience.) But they clearly afford the most natural and promising starting point. The systematically smoothest resolution of our questions is patently that which must be allowed to prevail—at any rate *pro tem*, until such time as its untenability becomes manifest. Where a simple solution will accommodate the data at hand, there is no good reason for turning elsewhere. It is a fundamental principle of rational procedure, operative just as much in the cognitive domain as anywhere else, that from among various alternatives that are anything like equally well qualified in other regards we should adopt the one that is the simplest, the most economical—in whatever modes of simplicity and economy are relevant. In such a perspective, induction is seen as a fundamentally regulative and procedural resource in the domain of inquiry, proceeding in implementation of the injunction: "Do all you reasonably come to enhance the extent to which your cognitive commitments are simple and smoothly systematic." In the absence of such a principle—or some functional equivalent of it—the venture of rational inquiry could not get under way at all.

On such a view, inductive systematicity with its penchant for simplicity comes to be seen as an aspect, not of *reality* as such, but of our procedures for its conceptualization and accordingly of *our conception* of it, or, to be more precise, of our manner of conceptualizing it. Simplicity-preference (for example) is based on the strictly method-oriented practical consideration that the simple hypotheses are the most convenient and advantageous for us to put to use in the context of our purposes. There is thus no recourse to a substantive (or descriptively constitutive) postulate of the simplicity of nature; it suffices to have recourse to a regulative (or practical) precept of economy of means. And in its turn, the pursuit of cognitive systematicity is ontologically neutral: it is a matter of conducting our question-resolving endeavors with the greatest economy. The principle of least effort is in control here—the process is one of maximally economic means to the attainment of chosen ends. This amounts to a *theoretical* defense of inductive systematicity that in fact rests on *practical* considerations relating to the efficiencies of method. Accordingly, inductive systematicity is best approached with reference, not to reality as such—or even merely our conception of it—but to the ways and means we employ in conceptualizing it. It is noncommittal on matters of substance, representing no more than a determination to conduct our question-resolving endeavors with the greatest economy. For in inquiry, as elsewhere, rationality enjoins us to employ the maximally economic means to the attainment of chosen ends.

It is thus important to distinguish between substantive and methodological considerations and separate economy of means from substantive economy. For process is one things and product another. Simple tools or methods can, suitably used, create complicated results. A simple cognitive method, such as trial and error, can ultimately yield complex answers to difficult questions. Conversely, simple results are sometimes brought about in complicated ways; complicated methods of inquiry or problem solving might arrive at simple and uncomplicated solutions. Our commitment to simplicity in scientific inquiry accordingly does not, in the end, prevent us from discovering whatever complexities are actually there.

Of course, our theories regarding nature should not *oversimplify*— they should not picture the world as simpler, more uniform, etc., than it indeed is. But the striving for cognitive systematicity in its various forms can and should persist even in the face of complex phenomena. The ontological systematicity of nature is thus ultimately irrelevant for our procedurally regulative concerns: the commitment to inductive systematicity in our account of the world remains a methodological desideratum regardless of how complex or untidy that world may ultimately turn out to be.

3. Complexification and the Disintegration of Science

It is worthwhile to examine somewhat more closely the ramifications of complexity in the domain of cognition, now focusing upon science in particular. Progress in natural science is a matter of dialogue or debate in a reciprocal interaction between theoreticians and experimentalists. The experimentalists probe nature to discern its reactions, to seek out phenomena. And the theoreticians take the resultant data and weave about them a fabric of hypotheses that is able to resolve our questions. Seeking to devise a framework of rational understanding, they construct their explanatory models to accommodate the findings that the experimentalists put at their disposal. Thereafter, once the theoreticians have had their say, the ball returns to the experimentalists' court. Employing new, more powerful means for probing nature, they bring new phenomena to view, new data for accommodation. Precisely because these data are new and inherently unpredictable on the basis of earlier knowledge, they often fail to fit the old theories. Theory extrapolations from the old data could not encompass them; the old theories do not accommodate them. A disequilibrium thus arises between available theory and novel data, and at this stage, the ball reenters the theoreticians' court. New theories must be devised to accommodate the new, nonconforming data. Accordingly, the theoreticians set about weaving a new theoretical structure to accommodate the new data. They endeavor to restore the equilibrium between theory and data once more. And when they succeed, the ball returns to the experimentalists' court, and the whole process starts over again.

Scientific theory-formation is, in general, a matter of spotting a local regularity of phenomena in parametric space and then projecting it "across the board," maintaining it globally. But the theoretical claims of science are themselves never small-scale and local—they are not spatiotemporally localized and they are not parametrically localized either. They stipulate—quite ambitiously—how things are always and everywhere. But with the enhancement of investigative technology, the "window" through which we can look out upon nature's parametric space becomes constantly enlarged. In developing natural science we use this window of capability to scrutinize parametric space, continually augmenting our database and then generalizing upon what we see. What we have here is not a lunar landscape where once we have seen one sector we have seen it all, and where theory-projections from lesser data generally remain in place when further data comes our way. Instead it does not require a sophisticated knowledge of the history of science to realize that our worst fears are usually realized—that our theories seldom if ever survive intact in the wake of substantial extensions in our cognitive access to new sectors of nature's parametric space. The history of science is a sequence of episodes of leaping to the wrong conclusions because new observational findings indicate matters are not quite so simple as heretofore thought. As ample experience indicates, our ideas about nature are subject to constant and often radical change-demanding stresses as we "explore" parametric space more extensively. The technologically mediated entry into new regions of parametric space constantly destabilizes the attained equilibrium between data and theory. Physical nature can exhibit a very different aspect when viewed from the vantage point of different levels of sophistication in the technology of nature-investigator interaction. The possibility of change is ever present. The ongoing destabilization of scientific theories is the price we pay for operating a simplicity-geared cognitive methodology in an actually complex world.

The methodology of science thus embodies an inherent dialectic that moves steadily from the simpler to the more complex, and the developmental route of technology sails on the same course. We are driven in the direction of ever greater complexity by the principle that the potential of the simple is soon exhausted and that high capacity demands more elaborate and powerful processes and procedures. The simpler procedures of the past are but rarely adequate to the needs of the present—had they been so today's questions would have been resolved long ago and the issues at stake would not have survived to figure on the present agenda. Scientific progress is of a nature that inherently involves an inexorable tendency to complexification in both its cognitive and its ideational dimension. What we discover in investigating nature always must in some degree reflect the character of our technology of observation. It is always something that depends on the mechanisms with which we search.[10]

Induction with respect to the history of science itself—a constant series of errors of oversimplification—soon undermines our confidence that nature operates in the way we would deem the simpler. On the contrary, the history of science is an endlessly repetitive story of simple theories giving way to more complicated and sophisticated ones. The Greeks had four elements; in the nineteenth century Mendeleev had some sixty; by the 1900s this had gone to eighty, and nowadays we have a vast series of elemental stability states. Aristotle's cosmos had only spheres; Ptolemy's added epicycles; ours has a virtually endless proliferation of complex orbits that only supercomputers can approximate. Greek science was contained on a single shelf of books; that of the Newtonian age required a roomful; ours requires vast storage structures filled not only with books and journals but with photographs, tapes, floppy disks, and so on. Of the quantities currently recognized as the fundamental constants of physics, only one was contemplated in Newton's physics: the universal gravitational constant. A second was added in the nineteenth century, Avogadro's constant. The remaining six are all creatures of twentieth-century physics: the speed of light (the velocity of electromagnetic radiation in free space), the elementary charge, the rest mass of the electron, the rest mass of the proton, Planck's constant, and Boltzmann's constant.[11] It would be naive—and quite wrong—to think that the course of scientific progress is one of increasing simplicity. The very reverse is the case: scientific progress is a matter of complexification because oversimple theories invariably prove untenable in a complex world. The natural dialectic of scientific inquiry ongoingly impels us into ever deeper levels of sophistication.[12] In this regard our commitment to simplicity and systematicity, though methodologically necessary, is ontologically unavailing. And more sophisticated searches invariably engender changes of mind moving in the direction of an ever more complex picture of the world. Our methodological commitment to simplicity should not and does not preclude the substantive discovery of complexity.

The explosive growth of information of itself countervails against its exploitation for the sake of knowledge-enhancement. The problem of coping with the proliferation of printed material affords a striking example of this phenomenon. One is forced to ever higher levels of aggregation, compression, and abstraction. In seeking for the needle in the haystack we must push our search processes to ever greater depths.

Consider the books and documents that outfit our libraries. At the base level there are topical materials, novels, say, or mathematical treatises, or biographical works. At the next level of aggregation we have such things as collective plot summaries, comparative critical studies, synthetic monographs, and collective author biographies. This in turn leads to the next level of reference works: bibliographies, encyclopedias, topical dictionaries, citation studies, and the like. And then there remains the yet higher level of catalogues, document indices, and the like. Such a hierarchical structuring betokens our unavoidable but also unwinnable struggle for cognitive unity.

The ongoing refinement in the division of cognitive labor that an information explosion necessitates issues in a literal dis-integration of knowledge. The "progress of knowledge" is marked by an ever continuing proliferation of ever more restructured specialties marked by the unavoidable circumstance that the any given specialty cell cannot know exactly what is going on even next door—let alone at the significant remove. Our understanding of matters outside our immediate bailiwick is bound to become superficial. At home base one knows the details, nearby one has an understanding of generalities, but at a greater remove one can be no more than an informed amateur.

This disintegration of knowledge is also manifolded vividly in the fact that our cognitive taxonomies are bursting at the seams. Consider the example of taxonomic structure of physics. We may assume a three-layer taxonomy: the field as a whole, the branches thereof, and the sub-branches of the branches. The taxonomic situation prevailing towards the beginning of this century is given in table 3.1.

TABLE 3.1
The Taxonomy of Physics in the Eleventh Edition of
the *Encyclopedia Britannica* (1911)

Astronomy
 —Astrophysics
 —Celestial Mechanics
Acoustics
Optics
 —Theoretical Optics
 —Spectroscopy
Mechanics
Heat
 —Calorimetry
 —Theory of Radiation
 —Thermodynamics
 —Thermometry
Electricity and Magnetism
 —Electonchemistry
 —Electrokinetics
 —Electrometallurgy
 —Electrometallurgy
 —Electrostatics
 —Thermoelectricity
 —Diamagnetism
 —Electromagnetism
Pneumatics
Energetics
Instrumentation

Note: Adapted from the Classified List of Articles at the end of vol. XXIX (index volume).

It is interesting to contrast this picture of the taxonomic situation in physics with the picture of the situation in subsequent decades as given in table 3.2.

These tables tell a significant story. In the eleventh (1911) edition of the *Encyclopedia Britannica*, physics is described as a discipline composed of nine constituent branches (e.g., "Acoustics" or "Electricity and Magnetism") which were themselves partitioned into twenty further specialties (e.g., "Thermo-electricity" or "Celestial Mechanics"). The fifteenth (1974) version of the *Britannica* divides physics into twelve branches whose subfields are—seemingly—too numerous for listing. (However the fourteenth 1960s edition carried a special article entitled "Physics, Articles on " which surveyed more than 130 special topics in the field.) When the National Science Foundation launched its inventory of physical specialties with the National Register of Scientific and Technical Personnel in 1954, it divided physics

TABLE 3.2
Physics Specialties in the *National Register of Scientific and Technical Personnel* for 1954 and 1970

1954	1970
Astronomy (16 specialties)	Astronomy
Acoustics (7 specialties)	—Solar-Planetary Relationships
Optics (8 specialties	9 specialties)
Mechanics and Heat (13 specialties)	—Planetology (6 specialties)
Electromagnetism (6 specialties)	—11 Further Astrophysical
Solid State (8 specialties)	Specialties
Atomic and Molecular Physics	Acoustics (9 specialties)
(5 specialties)	Optics (10 specialties)
Nuclear Physics (9 specialties)	Mechanics (10 specialties)
Theoretical Physics: Quantum Physics	Thermal Physics (9 specialties)
(4 specialties) (= Elementary	Electromagnetism (8 specialties)
Particles and Fields)	Solids (25 specialties)
Theoretical Physics: Classical	Fluids (9 specialties)
3 specialties)	Atmospheric Structure and Dynamics
Electronics (7 specialties)	(16 specialties)
Instrumentation and Miscellaneous	Atoms and Molecules (10 specialties)
(4 specialties)	Nuclei (3 specialties)
	Elementary Particles and Fields
	(6 specialties)
	Physical Chemistry (25 specialties)
	Biophysics (6 specialties)
	Solid Earth Geographics (10 specialties)
	Instrumentation (28 specialties)

Data from American Science Manpower: 1954-1956 (Washington, DC: National Science Foundation Publications, 1961) and "Specialties List for Use with 1970 National Register of Scientific and Technical Personnel" (Washington, DC: National Science Foundation Publications, 1970).

into twelve areas with ninety specialties. By 1970 these figures had increased to sixteen and 210, respectively. And the process continues unabated to the point where people are increasingly reluctant to embark on this classifying project at all.

Substantially the same story can be told for every field of science. The emergence of new disciplines, branches, and specialties is manifest everywhere. And as though to negate this tendency and maintain unity, one finds an ongoing evolution of interdisciplinary syntheses— physical chemistry, astrophysics, biochemistry, and so on. The very attempt to counteract fragmentation produces new fragments. Indeed, the phenomenology of this domain is nowadays so complex that some writers urge that the idea of a "natural taxonomy of science" must be abandoned altogether.[13] The expansion of the scientific literature is in fact such that natural science has in recent years been disintegrating before our very eyes. An ever larger number of ever more refined specialties has made it ever more difficult for experts in a given branch of science to achieve a thorough understanding about what is going on in the specialty next door.

It is, of course, possible that the development of physics may eventually carry us to theoretical unification where everything that we class among the "laws of nature" belongs to one grand, unified theory— one all-encompassing deductive systematization integrated even more tightly than that of Newton's *Principia Mathematica*.[14] But the covers of this elegantly contrived "book of nature" will have to encompass a mass of ever more elaborate diversity and variety. Like a tricky mathematical series, it will have to generate ever more dissimilar constituents which, despite their abstract linkage are concretely as different as can be. And the integration at issue at the pinnacle of a pyramid will cover further down an endlessly expansive range encompassing the most variegated components. It will be an abstract unity uniting a concrete mishmash of incredible variety and diversity. The "unity of science" to which many theorists aspire may indeed come to be realized at the level of concepts and theories shared between different sciences—that is, at the level of ideational overlaps. But for every conceptual commonality and shared element there will emerge a dozen differentiations. The increasing complexity of our world picture is a striking phenomenon throughout the development of modern science.

The lesson of such considerations is clear. Scientific knowledge grows not just in extent but also in complexity, so that science presents us with a scene of ever increasing intricacy. It is thus fair to say that modern science confronts us with a cognitive manifold that involves an ever more extensive specialization and division of labor. The years of apprenticeship that separate master from novice grow ever greater. A science that moves continually from an oversimple picture of the world to one that is more complex calls for ever more elaborate processes for its effective cultivation. And as the scientific enterprise itself grows more extensive, the greater elaborateness of its productions requires an ever more intricate intellectual structure for its accommodation. The complexification of scientific process and product escalate hand and hand. And the process of complexity amplification that Peirce took to be revealed in nature through science is unquestionably manifested in the cognitive domain of scientific inquiry itself. The regulative ideal of science is to integrate our knowledge of the world's modus operandi into a coherent and cohesive unifying system. Nevertheless, the world's complexity means that this will be an aspiration rather than an accomplished fact. It represents a goal towards which we may be able to make progress but which we will never be able to attain.[15]

Yet complexity is not a unqualified negative. It is an unavoidable concomitant of progress. We could not extend our cognitive or our practical grasp of the world without taking its complexification in stride. Throughout the realm of human artifice—cognitive artifice included—further complexity is part and parcel of extending the frontiers of progress. The struggle with complexity that we encounter throughout our cognitive efforts is an inherent and unavoidable aspect of the human condition's progressive impetus to doing more and doing it better.[16]

4. Complexity and the Human Sciences

The complexity of the world as we know it also reflects back upon ourselves. The mind of a being able to achieve knowledge of a complex object can hardly be simpler than that object whose complexities it must encompass. The psyche of beings able to internalize cognitively the operations of a complex world and respond in due resonance with these complexities must itself be an elaborate manifold of unified elements. To whatever extent we can achieve mental adequation to a complex environment we ourselves must be intellectually complex beings.

And this state of affairs at the level of individual psychology is also narrowed at the level of human interaction that constitutes the domain of subject-matter concern for the social sciences.

Nineteenth-century German theorists (Dilthey, Rickert, etc.) maintained that there are fundamental differences between the natural and the human sciences in that the former can discover natural laws that provide for the explanation and prediction of its phenomena and the latter cannot, but must, instead, satisfy themselves with such weaker aims as insight and understanding. And in the twentieth century, thinkers of the Austrian school, such as Friedrich Hayek[17] and Karl Popper[18] have argued that just the same sort of difference exists between the natural and the social sciences. It is, so they insist, impossible and thus an in-principle hopeless venture to seek to discover rigid scientific laws for social phenomena.

Now one of the key reasons generally adduced for this infeasibility is the supposedly greater complexity of the phenomena at issue in the social domain.[19] And so, recent theorists such as May Brodbeck,[20] and Alex Rosenberg[21] agree with Hayek and Popper that the difference between the social and natural science is to be accounted for in terms of complexity. But this is a view that seems questionable. After all, physical systems too can be immensely complex. The difference between the merely clarifactory social science and the predictively efficacious natural sciences is not a product of differential complexity and had best be located elsewhere. Perhaps the most effective account of the difference in view would seem to be one that proceeds in terms of volatility rather than complexity. For to all appearances the "laws" we encounter in the social sciences are not strict and omnitemporal but rather represent the merely transitory regularities of particular centuries of societies, and institutions that fail to achieve strict permanence and universality. Take history for example. The historical generalizations we use for explanation in this domain are well-confirmed statements concerning the actions of an organized group of agents under certain restrictive conditions (such group actions being intended to include those of systems composed conjointly of men and nonhuman instrumentalities under their physical control). Examples of such laws are "A census takes place in the United States in every decade year"; "Heretics were persecuted in seventeenth-century Spain"; and "In the sea battles of sailing vessels in the period 1653-1803, large formations were too cumbersome for effectual control as single units." Such historical generalizations are not unrestricted or universal in the manner in which the laws of the physical sciences are: they are not valid for all times and places. For instance, the statement about sailing-fleet tactics has (among others) an implicit or tacit condition relating to the state of naval ordnance in the eighteenth century. In elaborating such conditions, the historian delineates what is typical of the place and period rather than what is so with rigid universality.

And so, we face in the human sciences a situation different from that of the natural sciences. Here, the prominent role of phenomenological novelty due to innovation makes for a different situation with respect to the objects at issue. (Carbon atoms are ever the same whereas socio-technological units like mores are ever changing.) The comparative anarchy (i.e., lawlessness) of the social sciences in point of strict universality is thus best explained obliquely through their volatility— the fact that chance and change propels us into the region of quasi-laws. For the fact is that deliberate innovation and functional destabilization pervades this domain.[22] The complexity of social science lies in the final analysis not so much in the multiplicity of its internal parameters as in the changeability of their interrelationships.

Notes

1. Herbert Spencer, *First Principles*, 7th ed. (London: Methuen, 1889); see sect's. 14-17 of part II, "The Law of Evolution."
2. On the process in general see John H. Holland, *Hidden Order: How Adaptation Builds Complexity* (Reading, MA: Addison Wesley, 1995). Regarding the specifically evolutionary aspect of the process see Robert N. Brandon, *Adaptation and Environment* (Princeton: Princeton University Press, 1990.)
3. On the issues of this paragraph compare Stuart Kaufmann, *At Home in the Universe: To Search for the Laws of Self-Organization and Complexity* (New York and Oxford: Oxford University Press, 1995).
4. For further details see the author's *Induction* (Oxford: Basil Blackwell, 1980).
5. An interesting illustration of the extent to which lessons in the school of better experience have accustomed us to expect complexity is provided by the contrast between the pairs: rudimentary/nonanced; unsophisticated/sophisticated; plain/elaborate; simple/intricate. Note that in each case the second, complexity-reflective alternative has a distinctly more positive (or less negative) connotation than its opposite counterpart.
6. Hans Reichenbach, *Experience and Prediction* (Chicago: University of Chicago Press, 1938), p. 376. "Compare: Imagine that a physicist . . . wants to draw a curve which passes through [points on a graph that represent the data observed]. It is well known that the physicist chooses the simplest curve; this is not to be regarded as a matter of convenience. . . . [For different] curves correspond as to the measurements observed, but they differ as to future measurements; hence they signify different predictions based on the same observational material. The choice of the simplest curve, consequently, depends on an inductive assumption: we believe that the simplest curve gives the best predictions. . . . If in such cases the question of simplicity plays a certain role for our decision, it is because we make the assumptions that the simplest theory furnishes the best predictions." (*Ibid.*, pp. 375-76.)
7. *Science and Hypothesis* (New York: Dover Press, 1914), pp. 145-46.
8. Note that in explaining the behavior of people we always presume normalcy and rationality on their part—a presumption that is, to be sure, defeasible and only holds "until proven otherwise."
9. Kant was the first philosopher clearly to perceive and emphasize this crucial point: "But such a principle [of systematicity] does not prescribe any law for objects. . . , it is merely a subjective law for the orderly management of the possessions of our understanding, that by the comparison of its concepts it may reduce them to the smallest possible number; it does not justify us in demanding from the objects such uniformity as will minister to the convenience and exten-

sion of our understanding; and we may not, therefore, ascribe to the [methodological or *regulative*] maxim ['Systematize knowledge!'] any objective [or descriptively *constitutive*] validity" (CPuR, A306 = B362). Compare also C. S. Peirce's idea that the systematicity of nature is a regulative matter of scientific attitude rather than a constitutive matter of scientific fact. See Charles Sanders Peirce, *Collected Papers*, vol. 7 (Cambridge, MA: Harvard University Press, 1958), sect. 7.134.

10. On this process see sections 2 and 3 of chapter 5.

11. See B. W. Petley, *The Fundamental Physical Constants and the Frontiers of Measurement* (Bristol and Boston: Hilger, 1985).

12. On the structure of dialectical reasoning see the author's *Dialectics* (Albany: State University of New York Press, 1977), and for the analogous role of such reasoning in philosophy see *The Strife of Systems* (Pittsburgh, PA: University of Pittsburgh Press, 1985).

13. See John Dupré, *The Disorder of Things: Metaphysical Foundations of the Disunity of Science* (Cambridge, MA: Harvard University Press, 1993).

14. See Steven Weinberg, *Dreams of a Formal Theory* (New York: Pantheon, 1992). See also Edoardo Amaldi, "The Unity of Physics," *Physics Today*, vol. 261 (September, 1973), pp. 23-29. Compare also C. F. von Weizsäcker, "The Unity of Physics" in Ted Bastin (ed.) *Quantum Theory and Beyond* (Cambridge: Cambridge University Press, 1971).

15. For variations on this theme see the writer's *The Limits of Science* (Berkeley and Los Angeles: University of California Press, 1984).

16. Some of this chapter's themes are also explored in the author's *Scientific Progress* (Oxford: Basil Blackwell, 1978).

17. F. A. Hayek, "The Theory of Complex Phenomena" in his *Studies in Philosophy, Politics, and Economics* (Chicago: University of Chicago Press, 1967), pp. 22-42.

18. Karl R. Popper, "Prediction and Prophecy in the Social Science" in his *Conjectures and Refutations* (New York: Harper & Row, 1968).

19. For a good survey of the lay of the land here see Lee C. McIntyre, "Complexity and Social Scientific Laws," *Synthese*, 97 (1993) 209-27.

20. May Brodbeck, "On the Philosophy of the Social Sciences" in E. C. Harwood (ed.), *Reconstruction of Economics*, 3rd ed. (Great Barrington: American Institute for Economic Research, 1962), pp. 39-58.

21. Alexander Roseberg, *Philosophy of the Social Sciences* (Boulder, CO: Westview Press, 1988; 2nd ed., 1995).

22. Some futher ramifications of this state of affairs are discussed in Olaf Helmer and Nicholas Rescher, "The Epistemology of the Inexact Sciences," *Management Science*, vol. 6 (1959) 25-52.

4

Complex Knowledge: The Growth of Science and the Law of Logarithmic Returns

(1) Natural science has been growing exponentially throughout recent history in terms of its size and scope as a human enterprise. (2) However, scientific knowledge *does not correlate with the brute volume of scientific* information, *but only with its logarithm. (3) The rationale for this situation lies in the way in which the most significant information is always enveloped by lesser detail, obscured amidst a fog of insignificance. (4) In consequence, the progress of knowledge makes ever-escalating demands upon researchers, a circumstance that bears in a profound and ominous way upon the issue of the growth of scientific knowledge over time. (5) To be sure, the phenomenon of a logarithmic return on investment in natural science pivots on assessing the* quality *of the work at issue, since anything deserving of the name of* scientific knowledge *will be information of the highest quality level. The result of this state of affairs is that the construction of an ever more cumbersome and complex account of things is part of the unavoidable cost of scientific progress.*

1. The Expansion of Science

The increasing complexity of the scientific enterprise itself is reflected in the fact that research and development expenditures in the U.S. grew exponentially after World War II, increasing at a rate of some 10 percent per annum. By the mid 1960s, America was spending more on scientific research and development than the entire federal budget before Pearl Harbor. This growth in the costs of science has various significant ramifications and manifestations.

Take manpower, for example, where the recent growth of the scientific community is a particularly striking phenomenon. During most of the present century the number of American scientists has been increasing at 6 percent to yield an exponential growth-rate with a doubling time of roughly twelve years.[1] A startling consideration—one often but deservedly repeated—is that well over 80 percent of ever-existing scientists (in even the oldest specialties such as mathematics, physics, and medicine) are alive and active nowadays.[2]

Again, consider the growth of the scientific literature. It is by now a familiar fact that scientific information has been growing at the (reasonably constant) exponential rate over the past several centuries. Overall, the printed literature of science has been increasing at an average of some 5 percent annually throughout the last two centuries, to yield an exponential growth-rate with a doubling time of ca. fifteen years— an order-of-magnitude increase roughly every half century. The result is a veritable flood of scientific literature. The *Physical Review* is currently divided into six parts, each of which is larger than the whole journal was a decade or so ago. It is reliably estimated that, from the start, about 10 million scientific papers have been published and that currently some 30,000 journals publish some 600,000 new papers each year. In fact, it is readily documented that the number of books, of journals, of journal-papers has been increasing at an exponential rate over the recent period.[3] By 1960, some 300,000 different book titles were being published in the world, and the two decades from 1955 and 1975 saw the doubling of titles published in Europe from around 130,000 to over 270,000.[4] And science has had its full share of this literature explosion. The amount of scientific material in print is of a scope that puts it beyond the reach not only of individuals but also of institutions as well. No university or institute has a library vast enough to absorb or a faculty large enough to digest the relevant products of the world's printing presses.

Then too there is the massively increasing budget of science. The historic situation regarding the costs of American science was first delineated in the findings of Raymond Ewell in the 1950s.[5] His study of research and development expenditures in the U.S. showed that growth here has also been exponential; from 1776 to 1954 we spent close to $40 billion, and half of that was spent after 1948.[6] Projected at this rate, Ewell saw the total as amounting to what he viewed as an astronomical $6.5 billion by 1965—a figure that actually turned out to be far too conservative.

Moreover, the proliferation of scientific facilities has proceeded at an impressive pace over the past hundred years. (In the early 1870s there were only eleven physics laboratories in the British Isles; by the mid-1930s there were more than three hundred[7]; today there are several thousand.) And, of course, the scale of activities in these laboratories has also expanded vastly. It is perhaps unnecessary to dwell at length on the immense cost in resources of the research equipment of contemporary science.[8] Radiotelescopic observatories, low-temperature physics, research hospitals, and lunar geology all involve outlays of a scale that require the funding and support of national governments—sometimes even consortia thereof. In a prophetic vein, Alvin M. Weinberg (then director of the Oak Ridge National Laboratory) wrote, "When history looks at the 20th century, she will see science and technology as its theme; she will find in the monuments of Big Science—the huge rockets, the high-energy accelerators, the high-flux research reactors—symbols of our time just as surely as she finds in Notre Dame a symbol of the Middle Ages."[9] Of course, exponential growth cannot of course continue indefinitely. But the fact remains that that science has become an enormous industry that has a far-flung network of *training* centers (schools, colleges, universities), and of *production* centers (laboratories and research-institutes).

Science, in sum, has become a vast and expensive business. But what sort of relationship obtains between resource investment and returns here? Just how productive is the science enterprise?

2. The Law of Logarithmic Returns

There is no question but that the complexification *of* science produced by its growth as a productive enterprise also makes for a complexification *in* science as a cognitive resource. But this occurs at a far lesser rate. And it is instructive to consider the reason why.

En route to knowledge we must begin with information. How is one to measure the volume of information generated in a field of scientific or scholarly inquiry? Direct methods are hard to come by, but various oblique ways suggest themselves. The size of the literature of a field (as measured by the sheer bulk of publication in it) affords one possible measure, and there are various other possibilities as well. For one can make one's estimates here by way of inputs rather than outputs, measuring, for example, the aggregate time that investigators devote to their topics, or the volume of resource investment in research-supportive technology. So much, then, for the quantitative assessment of *information*. But what about *knowledge*?

While information is a matter of data, knowledge, by contrast, is something more select, more deeply issue-resolving—to wit, *significant and well-consolidated* information. Anyone who has ever struggled with the statistical analysis of masses of data knows viscerally the difference between basic information and the sort of insight at issue with actual knowledge. (Not every insignificant smidgeon of information constitutes knowledge, and the person whose body of information consists of utter trivia really *knows* virtually nothing.)

For the sake of a crude illustration of the information/knowledge distinction, suppose an object-descriptive color taxonomy—for the sake of example, an oversimple one based merely on Blue, Red, and Other. Then that single item of *knowledge* represented by "knowing the color" of an object—viz. that it is red—is bound up with many different items of (correct) *information* on the subject (that it is not Blue, is rather similar to some shades of Other, etc.). As such information proliferates, we confront a situation of redundancy and diminished productiveness. Any knowable fact is always surrounded by a vast penumbral cloud of relevant information. And as our information grows to be ever more extensive, those really *significant* facts become more difficult to discern. Knowledge certainly increases with information, but at a far less than proportionate rate.[10]

A single step in the advancement of knowledge is thus accompanied by a massive increase in the proliferation of information. Thus with n concepts, one can construct n^2 two-concept combinations, and with m facts, one can project m^2 fact-connecting juxtapositions, each representing some sort of characteristic relationship.[11] Extending the previous example, let us also contemplate *shapes* in addition to *colors*, again supposing only three of them: Rectangular, Circular, Other. When we thus *combine* color and shape there will be $9 = 3 \times 3$ possibilities in the resultant (cross-) classification. So with this enlarged, dual-aspect piece of knowledge (color + shape) we also launch into a vastly amplified—specifically *multiplied*—information spectrum over that increased classification-space. In moving cognitively from n to $n + 1$ cognitive parameters, knowledge is increased additively but the information field expands multiplicatively.

It is instructive to view the matter from a different vantage point. Knowledge commonly develops via distinctions (*A* vs. non-*A*) that are introduced with ever greater elaboration and sophistication to address the problems and difficulties that one encounters with less sophisticated approaches. A situation obtains that is analogous to the "Game of 20 Questions" with an exponentially exfoliating possibility-space unfolding stepwise $(2, 4, 8, 16, \ldots, 2^n, \ldots)$. With n descriptors one can specify for 2^n potential descriptions that specify exactly how, over all, a given object may be characterized. When we add a new descriptor we increase by one additional unit the amount of knowledge, but double the amount of available information. The *information* at hand grows with 2^n, but the knowledge acquired merely with n. With conceptual elaboration increases in informative detail always ratchet up exponentially. The cognitive yield of increasing information is subject to dramatically diminishing returns.

Consider another example, this time from the field of paleography. The yield of knowledge from information afforded by legibility-impaired manuscripts, papyri, and inscriptions in classical paleography provides an instructive instance. If one can decipher 70 percent of the letters in such a manuscript one can reconstruct a given phrase. If one can make out 70 percent of the phases one can pretty well figure out the sentences. If one can read 70 percent of its sentences one can understand the message of the whole text. So in favorable conditions some one-third of the letters suffice to carry the whole message. A vast load of information stands coordinate with a modest body of knowledge. From the standpoint of knowledge, information is highly redundant, albeit unavoidably so. A helpful perspective on this situation comes to view through the communication-theoretic conception of "noise," seeing that expanding bodies of information encompass so much cognition-impeding redundancy and unhelpful irrelevancy that it takes successive many-fold increases in information to effect successive fixed-size increases in actual knowledge.

Two ideas can profitably be brought together in this context:

1. Knowledge is distinguished from mere information as such by its significance. In fact: *Knowledge is simply particularly significant information*—information whose significance exceeds some threshold level (say

q). (In principle there is room for variation here according as one sets the quality level of entry qualification and the domain higher or lower.)

2. The significance of *additional* information is determined by its impact upon *pre-existing* information. Importance or significance in this sense is a matter of the relative (percentage-wise) increase that the new acquisitions effect upon the body of pre-existing information (I), which may—to reiterate—be estimated in the first instance by the sheer volume of the relevant body of information: the literature of the subject, as it were. Accordingly: *The significance of incrementally new information can be measured by the ratio of the increment of new information to the volume of information already in hand*: $\Delta I / I$.

Putting these two considerations together, we find that a new item of actual knowledge is one for which the ratio of information increments to preexisting information exceeds a fixed threshold-indicative quantity *q*:

$$\frac{\Delta I}{I} > q$$

Thus knowledge-constituting *significant* information arise when the proportional extent of the change effected by a new item in the preexisting situation (independently of what that preexisting situation is) exceeds a duly fixed threshold.

On the basis of such a construal of *knowledge*, it follows that the cumulative total amount of knowledge (*K*) encompassed in an overall body of information of size *I* is given by the *logarithm* of *I*. This is so because we have

$$K = \int \frac{dI}{I} = \log I + \text{const} = \log Ic$$

where *K* represents the volume of actual *knowledge* that can be extracted from a body of bare *information* *I*.[12] (Here the constant at issue is open to treatment as a unit-determinative parameter of the measuring scale, so that the equation at issue can be simplified without loss to $K = \log I$.[13] We accordingly arrive at the *law of logarithmic returns* governing the extraction of significant *knowledge* from bodies of mere *information*.

The ramifications of such a principle for cognitive progress are not difficult to discern. Nature imposes increasing resistance barriers to intellectual as to physical penetration. Consider the analogy of extracting air for creating a vacuum. The first 90 percent comes out rather easily. The next 9% is effectively as difficult to extract than all that went before. The next 0.9 is just as difficult. And so on. Each successive order-of-magnitude step involved a massive cost for lesser progress; each successive fixed-size investment of effort yields a substantially diminished return. Intellectual progress is exactly the same: when we extract *knowledge* (i.e., high-grade, nature-descriptively significant information from mere information of the routine, common "garden variety," the same sort of quantity/quality relationship obtained. Initially a sizable proportion of the available is high grade—but as we press further this proportion of what is cognitively significant gets ever smaller. To double knowledge we must quadruple information.

It should thus come as no surprise that knowledge coordinates with information in multiplicative layers. With texts we have the familiar stratification: article/chapter, book, library, library system. Or pictographically: sign, scene (= ordered collection of signs), cartoon (= ordered collection of scenes to make it a story). In such layering, we have successive levels of complexity corresponding to successive levels of informational combining combinations, proportional with n, n^2, n^3, etc. The logarithm of the levels—$\log n$, $2\log n$, $3\log n$, etc.—reflect the amount of "knowledge" that is available through the information we obtain about the state of affairs prevailing at each level. And this is something that increases only one unit step at a time, despite the exponential increase in information.

The general purport of such a law of logarithmic returns as regards expanding information is clear enough. Letting $K(I)$ represent the quantity of knowledge inherent in a body of information I, we begin with our fundamental relationship: $K(I) = \log I$. On the basis of this fundamental relationship, the knowledge of a two-sector domain increases additively notwithstanding a multiplicative explosion in the amount of information that is now upon the scene. For if the field (F) under consideration consists of two sub-fields (F_1 and F_2), then because of the cross-connections obtaining within the information-domains at issue the overall information complex will take on a multiplicative size:

$$I = \inf(F) = \inf(F_1) \times \inf(F_2) = I_1 \times I_2$$

With compilation, information is multiplied. But in view of the indicated logarithmic relationship, the knowledge associated with the body of compound information I will stand at:

$$K(I) = \log I = \log (I_1 \times I_2) = \log I_1 + \log I_2 = K(I_1) + K(I_2)$$

The knowledge obtained by joining two information-domains (subfields) into an overall aggregate will (as one would expect) consist simply in *adding* the two bodies of knowledge at issue. Whereas compilation increases *information* by multiplicative leaps and bounds, the increase in *knowledge* is merely additive.

3. The Rationale and Implication of the Law

The law of logarithmic returns constitutes an epistemological analogue of the old Weber-Fechner law of psychophysics, which asserts that inputs of geometrically increasing magnitude are required to yield *perceptual* outputs of arithmetically increasing intensity. This makes for a parallelism of perception and conception in this regard: on both sides we have it that informational inputs of geometrically increasing magnitude are needed to provide for cognitive outputs of arithmetically increasing magnitude. This is illustrated in display 4.1. There is an immense K/I imbalance: with ongoingly increasing information I, the corresponding increase in knowledge K, shrinks markedly. To increase knowledge by equal steps we must amplify information by successive orders of magnitude.

Perhaps the principal reason for such a K/I imbalance may be found in the efficiency of intelligence in securing a view of the modus operandi of a world whose law-structure is comparatively simple, since here one can learn a disproportionate amount of general fact from a modest amount of information. (Note that whenever an infinite series of 0's and 1's, as per 01010101 . . ., is generated—as this series indeed is—by a relatively *simple* law, then this circumstance can be gleaned from a comparatively short initial segment of this series.) We thus have a plausible reason for that K/I disparity: where order exists in the world, intelligence is rather efficient in finding it. (And it is with observing in this context that if the world were not orderly—were not amenable to the probes of intelligence—then intelligent beings would not and could not have emerged in it through evolutionary mechanisms.)

And the matter can be viewed in another perspective. Nature imposes increasing resistance barriers to intellectual as to physical penetration. Extracting knowledge from information thus requires ever

DISPLAY 4.1
The Structure of the Knowledge/Information Relation

I	Ic (with $c = .1$)	$\log Ic$ ($=K$)	$\Delta(K)$	K as % of I	ΔK as % of K
100	10	1	—	1.0	—
1,000	100	2	1	.2	50
10,000	1000	3	1	.03	33
100,000	10,000	4	1	.004	25

greater effort. For the greater a body of information, the larger the *patterns of order* that can potentially obtain and the greater the effort needed to bring particular orderings to light. With two-place combinations of the letters A and B (yielding the four pairs AA, AB, BA, and BB) we have only two possible patterns of order—namely "The same letter all the way through" (AA and BB), and "Alternating letters" (AB and BA). But as we add more letters, the possibilities proliferate massively. There is accordingly a law of diminishing returns in operation here: each successive fixed-size investment of effort yields a substantially diminished return. Intellectual progress is exactly the same: when we extract actual *knowledge* (i.e., high-grade, nature-descriptively significant information) from mere information of the routine, common "garden variety," the same sort of quantity/quality relationship obtained. Initially a sizable proportion of the available is high grade—but as we press further this proportion of what is cognitively significant gets ever smaller. And so, as science progress, the important discoveries that represent real increases in knowledge are surrounded by an ever increasing penumbra of mere items of information. (The mathematical literature of the day yields an annual crop of over 200,000 new theorems.[14])

This resultant situation is reflected in Max Planck's appraisal of the demands of scientific progress. He wrote that *"with every advance [in science] the difficulty of the task is increased; ever larger demands are made on the achievements of researchers,* and the need for a suitable division of labor becomes more pressing."[15] The law of logarithmic returns at once characterizes and explains this phenomenon or substantial findings being thicker on the informational ground in the earlier phase of a new discipline and growing ever attenuated in the natural course of progress. The upshot is that increasing complexity is the unavailable accompaniment of scientific progress as ever more elaborate processes are required to engender an equimeritious product.

4. The Growth of Knowledge

The law of logarithmic returns clearly has substantial implications for the *rate* of scientific progress.[16] In particular, it stipulates a swift and steady decline in the comparative cognitive yield of accession to our body of mere information. With the enhancement of scientific technology, the size and complexity of this body of data inevitably grows, expanding on quantity and diversifying in kind. Historical experience indicates that our knowledge is ongoingly enhanced through this broadening of our database. But of course this expansion of knowledge proceeds at a far slower rate than the increase of bare information.

It is illuminating to look at the implications of this state of affairs in an historical perspective. The salient point is that the growth of knowledge over time involves ever escalating demands. Progress is always possible—there are no absolute limits. But increments of the same cognitive magnitude have to be obtained at an ever increased price in point of information development and thus of resource commitment as well. The circumstance that knowledge stands proportionate to the logarithm of information ($K \propto \log I$) means the growth of knowledge over time stands to the increase of information in a proportion fixed by the *inverse* of the volume of already available information:

$$\frac{d}{dt} K \approx \frac{d}{dt} \log I \approx \frac{1}{I} \frac{d}{dt} I$$

The more knowledge we already have in hand, the slower (by a very rapid decline) will be the rate at which knowledge grows with newly acquired information. And the larger the body of information we have, the smaller will be the proportion of this information that represents real knowledge.

In developmental perspective, there is good reason to suppose that our body of bare *information* increases more or less in proportion with our resource investment in information-gathering. Accordingly, if this investment grows exponentially over time (as we have seen above to have historically been the case in the recent period), we shall in consequence have it that

$$I(t) \approx c^t \text{ and correspondingly also } \frac{d}{dt} I(t) \approx c^t$$

This means that

$$K(t) \approx \log I(t) \approx \log c^t = t$$

and consequently

$$\frac{d}{dt} K(t) = \text{constant}$$

It will follow on this basis that, since *exponential* growth in *I* is coordinated with a merely *linear* growth in *K*, the rate of progress of science in the information-exploding past has actually remained essentially constant.

And in fact it is not all that difficult to find empirical substantiation of our law of logarithmic returns ($K \approx \log I$). The phenomenology of the situation is that while scientific information has increased exponentially in the past (as shown by the exponential increase in journals, scientists, and outlays for the instrumentalities of research)—as was documented above—a good case can be made for maintaining that the progress of authentic scientific knowledge as measured in the sort of first-rate discoveries of the highest level of significance has to all appearances progressed at a more or less linear rate. For there is much evidence to substantiate this. It suffices to consider the size of encyclopedias and synoptic textbooks, or again, the number of awards given for "really big contributions" (Nobel Prizes, academy memberships, honorary degrees), or the expansion of the classificatory taxonomy of branches of science and problem areas of inquiry.[17] All of these measures of preeminently *cognitive* contribution conjoin to indicate that there has in fact been a comparative constancy in year-to-year progress, the exponential growth of the scientific enterprise notwithstanding.

And so, *viewing science as a cognitive discipline*—a growing body of knowledge whose task is the unfolding of a rational account of the modus operandi of nature—the progress of science stands correlative with its accession of really major discoveries: the seismically significant, cartography-revising insights into nature. And this perspective lays the foundation for our present analysis—that the historical situation has been one of a *constant* progress of science as a *cognitive discipline* notwithstanding its *exponential* growth as a *productive enterprise* (as measured in terms of resources, money, manpower, publications, etc.). The law of logarithmic returns says it all.[18]

5. The Centrality of Quality and Its Implications

The present deliberations also serve to indicate, however, why the question of the rate of scientific progress is delicate and rather tricky. For this whole issue turns rather delicately on fundamentally *evaluative* considerations. Thus consider once more the development of science in the recent historic past. As we saw above, at the crudest—but also most basic—level, where progress is measured simply by the growth of the scientific literature, there has for centuries been the astonishingly swift and sure progress of an exponential growth with a doubling time of roughly fifteen years. And at the more sophisticated, and demanding level of high-quality results of a suitably "important" character, there has also been exponential growth—though only at the pace of a far longer doubling time, perhaps thirty years, approximating the reduplication with each successive generation envisaged by Henry Adams at the turn of this century.[19] Finally, at the maximally exacting level of the really crucial insights—significant scientific knowledge that fundamentally enhances our understanding of nature—our analysis has it that in recent times science has been maintaining a merely constant pace of progress.

It is this last consideration that is crucial for present purposes, carrying us back to the point made at the very outset. For what we have been dealing with that essentially seismological standard of importance based on the question: "If a certain finding were abrogated or abandoned, how extensive would the ramifications and implications of this circumstance be? How great would be the shocks and tremors felt throughout the whole range of what we (presumably) know?" And what is at issue is exactly a kind of cognitive Richter Scale based on the idea of successive orders of magnitude of impact. The crucial determinative factor for increasing importance is the extent of seismic disturbance of the cognitive terrain. Would we have to abandon and/or rewrite the entire textbook, or a whole chapter, or a section, or a paragraph, or a sentence, or a mere footnote?

And so, while the question of the rate of scientific progress does indeed involve the somewhat delicate issue of the evaluative standard that is at issue, our stance here can be rough and ready—and justifiably so because the precise details do not affect the fundamental shape of the overall evaluation. *Viewing science as a cognitive discipline*—a body of knowledge whose task is the unfolding of a rational account of the modus operandi of nature—we have it that progress stands correlative with its accession of really major discoveries: the seismically significant, cartography-revising insights into nature. And this has historically been growing at a rate that sure and steady—but essentially linear. However, this perspective lays the foundation for our present analysis—that the historical situation has been one of a CONSTANT progress of science as a *cognitive discipline* notwithstanding its EXPONENTIAL growth as a *productive enterprise* (as measured in terms of resources, money, manpower, publications, etc.).

In the struggle for cognitive control over nature, we have been confronting an enterprise of ever escalating demands. And so, while one cannot hope to predict the *content* of future science, the *F/I*-relationship does actually put us into a position to make plausible estimates about its *volume*. To be sure, there is, on this basis, no inherent limit to the possibility of future progress in scientific knowledge. But the exploitation of this theoretical prospect gets ever more difficult, expensive, and demanding in terms of effort and ingenuity. New findings of equal significance require ever greater aggregate efforts. In the ongoing course of scientific progress, the earlier investigations in the various departments of inquiry are able to skim the cream, so to speak: they take the "easy pickings," and later achievements of comparable significance require ever deeper forays into complexity and call for ever increasing bodies of information. (And it is important to realize that this cost increase is not because latter-day workers are doing *better* science, but simply because it is harder to achieve *the same level* of science: one must dig deeper or search wider to achieve results of the same significance as before.)

A mixed picture emerges. On the one hand, the course of scientific progress is a history of the successive destabilization of theories. On the other hand, the increasing resource requirement for digging into ever deeper layers of complexity is such that successive triumphs in our cognitive struggles with nature are only to be gained at an increasingly greater price. The world's inherent complexity renders the task of its cognitive penetration increasingly demanding and difficult. The process at issue with the growth of scientific knowledge in our complex world is one of drastically diminishing returns. This situation means that grappling with ever vaster bodies of information in the construction of an ever more cumbersome and complex account of the natural world is the unavoidable requisite of scientific progress.

To be sure, we constantly seek to "simplify" science, striving for an ever smaller basis of ever more powerful explanatory principles. But in the course of this endeavor we invariably complicate the structure of science itself. We secure greater power (and, as it were, *functional* simplicity) at the price of greater complexity in *structural* regards.[20] By the time the physicists get that grand unified theory, the physics they will have on their hands will be complex to the point of almost defying comprehension. The mathematics gets ever more elaborate and powerful, the training transit to the frontier ever longer. And so, despite its quest for greater operational simplicity (economy of principles), science itself is becoming ever more complex (in its substantive content, its reasonings, its machinery, etc.). Simplicity of process is here more than offset by complexity of product. And the phenomenon of diminishing returns reflects the price that this ongoing complexification exacts.[21]

Notes

1. The older figures are given in S. S. Visher, "Starred Scientists, 1903-1943" in *American Men of Science* (Baltimore, MD, 1947). For many further details regarding the development of American science see the author's *Scientific Progress* (Oxford: Blackwell, 1978).
2. See, e.g., Derek J. Price, *Little Science, Big Science* (New York: Columbia University Press, 1963), p. 11.
3. Cf. Derek J. Price, *Science Since Babylon*, 2nd ed. (New Haven CN: Yale University Press, 1975); see in particular chap. 5, "Diseases of Science."
4. Data from *An International Survey of Book Production During the Last Decades* (Paris: UNESCO, 1985).
5. Raymond Ewell, "The Role of Research in Economic Growth," *Chemical and Engineering News*, vol. 33 (1955), pp. 2980-85.
6. It is worth noting for the sake of comparison that for more than a century now the *total* U.S. federal budget, its *nondefense subtotal*, and the aggregate budgets of all federal agencies concerned with the environmental sciences (Bureau of Mines, Weather Bureau, Army Map Service, etc.) have all grown at a uniform per annum rate of 9 percent. (See H. W. Menard, *Science: Growth and Change* [Cambridge, MA: Harvard University Press, 1971], p. 188.)
7. Data from William George, *The Scientist in Action* (New York: Arno Press, 1938).
8. Du Pont's outlays for research stood at $1 million per annum during World War I (1915-1918), $6 million in 1930, $38 million in 1950, and $96 million in 1960. (Data from Fritz Machlup, *The Production and Distribution of Knowledge in the United States* [Princeton, NJ 1962], pp. 158-59; and see pp. 159-60 for the relevant data on a larger scale.) In the U.S. at large, overall expenditures for scientific research and its technological development (R & D) stood at $ .11 x 10^9 in

1920, and had risen to $ .13 x 10^9 in 1930, $ .38 x 10^9 in 1940, $ 2.9 x 10^9 in 1950, $ 5.1 x 10^9 in 1953-54, $ 10.0 x 10^9 in 1957-58, $ 11.1 x 10^9 in 1958-59, and had risen to ca. 14.0 x 10^9 in 1960-61 (*ibid.*, pp. 155 and 187). Machlup thinks it a not unreasonable conjecture that no other industry or economic activity in the U.S. has grown as fast as R & D (*ibid.*, p. 155).

9. "Impact of Large-Scale Science on the United State," *Science*, vol. 134 (1961; 21 July issue), pp. 161-64 (see p. 161). Weinberg further writes: "The other main contender [apart from space-exploration] for the position of Number One Event in the Scientific Olympics is high-energy physics. It, too, is wonderfully expensive (the Stanford linear accelerator is expected to cost $ 100 x 10^6), and we may expect to spend $ 400 x 10^6 per year on this area of research by 1970." (*Ibid.*, p. 164).

10. The "knowledge" at issue here need not be necessarily *correct*: it is merely *putative* knowledge that represents a comprehensively contrived best estimate of what the truth of the matter actually is.

11. Note that a self-concatenated concept or fact is still a concept or fact, even as a self-mixed color is still a color.

12. In information theory, *entropy* is the measure of the information conveyed by a message, and is there measured by $k \log M$, where M is the number of structurally equivalent messages formulable with the available sorts of symbols. By analogy, the $\log I$ measure of the knowledge contained in a given body of information might be seen in the same light. Either way, the concept at issue measures informative actuality in relation to informative possibility. For there are two types of informative possibilities (1) structural/syntactical as dealt with in classical information theory, and (2) hermeneutic/semantical (i.e., genuinely meaning-oriented) as dealt with in the present discussion.

13. Some writers have suggested that the subcategory of significant information included in an overall body of crude data of size I should be measured by I^k (for some suitably adjusted value $0 < k < 1$)—for example by the "Rousseau's Law" standard of $\sqrt{I}$). (For details see Chapter VI of the author's *Scientific Progress* [Oxford: Blackwell, 1978].). Now since $\log I^k = k \log I$ which is proportional to $\log I$, the specification of *this* sort of quality level for information would again lead to a $K \approx \log I$ relationship.

14. See Stanislaw M. Ulam, *Adventures of a Mathematician* (New York: Scribner, 1976).

15. Max Planck, *Vorträge und Erinnerungen*, 5th ed. (Stuttgart: S. Hirzel, 1949), p. 376; italics added. Shrewd insights seldom go unanticipated, so it is not surprising that other theorists should be able to contest claims to Planck's priority here. C. S. Peirce is particularly noteworthy in this connection.

16. It might be asked: "Why should a mere accretion in scientific 'information'—in mere belief—be taken to constitute *progress*, seeing that those later beliefs are not necessarily *true* (even as the earlier one's were not)?" The answer is that they are in any case better *substantiated*—that they are "improvements" on the earlier one's by way of the elimination of shortcomings. For a detailed consideration is the relevant issues, see the author's *Scientific Realism* (Dordrecht: D. Reidel, 1987).

17. The data here are set out more fully in the author's *Scientific Progress* (Oxford: Blackwell, 1978).

18. To be sure, we are caught up here in the usual cyclic pattern of all hypothetico-deductive reasoning. In addition to explaining the various phenomena we have

been canvassing that projected K/I relationship is in turn substantiated by them. This is not a vicious circularity but simply a matter of the systemic coherence that lies at the basis of inductive reasonings.

19. See Henry Brooks Adams, *The Education of Henry Adams: An Autobiography* (Boston: Houghton Mifflin, 1918).

20. The situation with automobiles is analogous. Modern cars are simpler to operate (self-starting, self-shifting, power steering, etc.). But they are much more complex to manufacture, repair, maintain, etc.

21. For other discussions relevant to this chapter's themes see also the author's *Scientific Progress* (Oxford: Blackwell, 1978) and *Cognitive Economy* (Pittsburgh, PA: University of Pittsburgh Press, 1989).

5

Technological Escalation and the Exploration Model of Natural Science

(1) The cognitive competence of humans in a complex environment is well explained by our evolutionary niche in the world's scheme of things. (2) And the development of inquiry in natural science is help-fully understood on analogy with exploration—to be sure, not explora-tion in the geographical realm, but rather in nature's parametric space of such physical quantities as temperature, pressure, velocity, and field strength. (3) The technology-mediated parametric exploration at issue here involves an interaction between us humans and nature. And this exploration becomes increasingly difficult (and expensive) as we move ever farther away from the home base of the accustomed envi-ronment of our evolutionary heritage. The ongoing development of natural science accordingly requires technological escalation. An as-cent to successively higher levels of technological sophistication and power is unavoidably required for the production of the observational data needed by science. Scientific progress is a struggle with nature's unending complexity.

1. Accounting for Our Cognitive Competence in Managing Complexity

How is it that we humans are actually so competent in coping with matters of cognitive complexity? How is it that we possess the intel-lectual talent to create mathematics, medicine, science, engineering, architecture, literature, and other comparably splendid cognitive disci-plines? What explains the immense power of our intellectual capacities?

91

At a level of high generality the answer is relatively straightforward. Basically, we are so intelligent because this is our place in evolution's scheme of things. Different sorts of creatures have different ecological niches, different specialties that enable them to find their evolutionary way along the corridor of time. Some are highly prolific, some protected by hard shells, some swift of foot, some difficult to spot, some extremely timid. But Homo sapiens is different. For the evolutionary instrument of our species is *intelligence*—with everything that this involves in the way of abilities and versatilities. And we have all these splendid intellectual capacities because we require them in order to be ourselves: if we were not so cognitively competent, we would not be here as the sort of creatures we are.

Of course it is not all just a matter of fate's lottery happening to bring intelligence our way. Evolution's bio-engineering is the crucial factor. Bees and termites can achieve impressive prodigies of collective effort. But an insect developed under the aegis of evolution could not become as smart as man because the information-processing requirements of its lifestyle are too modest to push its physical resources to the development of intelligence. The development of our brain, of our bodies, and of our lifestyle have proceeded hand in hand.

Intelligence functions as an inherent concomitant of our physical endowment. Our bodies have many more independently movable parts (more "degrees of freedom") than do those of most other creatures.[1] This circumstance has significant implications. Suppose a system with n switches, each capable of assuming an on or off position. There are then 2^n states in which the system can find itself. With $n = 3$ there are only eight system-states, but with n doubling to six there are already sixty-four states. As a body grows more complex and its configuration takes on more degrees of freedom, the range of alternative possible states expands rapidly (exponentially). Merely keeping track of its actual position is already difficult. To plan ahead is more difficult yet. If there are m possible states which the system can now assume, then when it comes to selecting its next position there are also m choices, and for the next two there are $m \times m$ alternatives overall (ignoring unrealizable combinations). So with a two-step planning horizon the three-state system has sixty-four alternatives while that six-state system has 4,096. With a mere doubling of states, the planning problem has become complicated by a factor of sixty-four.

Considerations of this sort render it evident that a vertebrate creature that has a more highly articulated skeleton which equips it with many independently operable bones and bone-complexes, faces vastly greater difficulties in management and manipulation—in what military jargon calls "command and control." Versatile behavior involves more complex supervision. And so, physically more versatile animals have to be smarter simply because they are physically more versatile. The degrees of freedom inherent in variable movement over time are pivotal considerations here. The moment one walks upright and begins to develop the modes of motion that this new posture facilitates—by way of creeping, running, leaping, etc.—one has many more factors of physical movement to manage.

Environmental surveillance is crucial for our lifestyle. The complexity of our sophisticated surveillance mechanisms in the context of friend-or-foe identification is an illustration. We can observe at a considerable distance that people are looking at us, discriminating minute differences in eye orientation in this context. The development of our sophisticated senses with their refined discrimination of odors, colors, and sounds is another example. We have to know which feature of our environment to heed and which can safely be ignored. The handling of such a volume of information calls for selectivity and for sophisticated processing mechanisms—in short, for intelligence. Not only must our bodies be the right size to support our physical operations and activities, but our brains must be so as well.

We humans are driven to devising greater capabilities for information acquisition and processing by the greater exigencies of the lifestyle of our ecological niche. The complexities of information management and processing pose unrelenting evolutionary demands. To process a large volume of information, nature must fit us out with a large brain. A battleship needs more elaborate mechanisms for guidance and governance than a row boat. A department store needs a more elaborate managerial apparatus than a corner grocery. Operating a sophisticated body requires a sophisticated mind. And how one makes one's living matters: insect-eating and fruit-eating monkeys have heavier brains, for their size, than leaf-eating ones do.[2] The evolution of the human brain is the story of nature's struggles to provide the machinery of information management and operative control needed by creatures of increasing physical versatility. A feedback cycle comes into play—a complex body requires a larger brain for command and control, and a larger brain requires a larger body whose operational efficiency in turn places greater demands on that brain for the managerial functions required to provide for survival and the assurance of a posterity. As can be illustrated by comparing the brain weights of different mammalian species, the growing complexities and versatilities of animal bodies involve a physical lifestyle whose difficulties of information processing and management requires increasingly powerful brains.

Here then is the immediate (and rather trivial) answer to our question: We are as intelligent as we are because that is how we have had to evolve to achieve our niche in nature's scheme of things. We are so smart because evolution's bio-engineering needs to provide those smarts for us to achieve and maintain the lifestyle appropriate to our ecological niche.

But there remains the problem of why evolution would take this course? Surely we did not need to be *that* smart to outwit the saber toothed tiger or domesticate the sheep. Let us explore this developmental aspect of the matter a little.

The things we have to do to manage our lifestyle must not only be *possible* for us, they must in general be *easy* for us (so easy that most of them can be done unthinkingly and even unconsciously). If our problem-solving resources were frequently strained to the limit, often groaning under the weight of difficulty of the problems that they are called on by nature to solve in the interests of our lifestyle, then we just wouldn't have achieved the sort of place we actually occupy in the world's scheme of things.

For evolution to do its work, the survival problems that creatures confront must by and large be easily manageable by the mechanisms at their disposal. And this fundamental principle holds just as true for cognitive as for biological evolution. If cognitive problem-solving were too difficult for our mental resources, we wouldn't evolve as problem-solving creatures. If we had to go to as great lengths to work out $2 + 2$ as to extract the cube root of a number, or if it took us as long to discriminate three- from four-sided figures as it takes to discriminate between 296 and 297-sided ones, then these sorts of issues would simply remain outside our intuitive repertoire. The "average" problems of survival and thriving that are posed by our lifestyle must be of the right level of difficulty for us—that is, they must be relatively easy. And this calls for excess capacity. All of the "ordinary" problems of one's mode of life must be solvable quickly in real time—and with enough idle capacity left over to cope with the unusual.

A brain that is able to do the necessary things when and as needed to sustain the life of a complex and versatile creature will remain underutilized much of the time. To cope during times of peak demand, it will need to have a great deal of excess capacity to spare for other issues at slack times. And so, any brain powerful enough to accomplish those occasionally necessary tasks must have the excess capacity to pursue at most normal times various challenging projects that have nothing whatsoever to do with survival.

These deliberations resolve the objection that evolution cannot explain our intellectual capacities because we are a lot smarter than evolution demands—that, after all, nature does not quiz us on higher mathematics or theoretical physics. What is being maintained here is not the absurd contention that development of such sophisticated disciplines is somehow an evolutionary requisite. All that is being said is that the capacities and abilities that make such enterprises possible are evolutionarily advantageous—that evolution equips us with a reserve capacity that makes them possible as a side benefit. The point is that an intelligent creature whose capacities do not allow of development in these abstract directions just could not be able to pass evolution's examinations in other matters—that is, would not after all be able successfully to make intelligence its evolutionary specialty.

The brain/computer analogy once again proves helpful in this connection. As we have seen, very different things can be at stake with being "simple": the simplicity of "hardware" involved with comparatively less complex *computers* is one sort of thing, while the simplicity of "software" at issue with comparatively less complex *programs* is something quite different. And there are clearly tradeoffs here: solving problems of the same level of difficulty is generally easier to program on a more sophisticated (more complex) computing machines. Something of an inverse relationship obtains: complicating a machine can make its effective actual use easier and less demanding.

To be sure, evolution is not, in general, overgenerous. For example, evolution will not develop creatures whose running speed is vastly greater than what is needed to escape their predators, to catch their prey, or to realize some other such survival-facilitating objective. But intelligence and its works are a clear exception to this general rule, owing to their self-catalyzing nature. With *cognitive* artifacts as with many *physical* artifacts, the character of the issues prevents a holding back; when one can do a little with calculation or with information processing, one can in principle do a great deal. Once evolution cracks open the door to intelligence, it gets "the run of the house." When bio-design takes the route of intelligence to secure an evolutionary advantage for a creature, it embarks on a slippery slope. Having started along this road, there is no easy and early stop. For once a species embarks on using intelligence as its instrument for coping with nature, then the pressure of species-internal competition enters as a hothouse forcing process. Intelligence itself becomes a goad to further development simply because intelligence is, as it were, developmentally self-energizing.

The result of the preceding deliberations is straightforward. Intelligence is the evolutionary specialty of Homo sapiens. If we were markedly less smart than we in fact are, we would not have been able to survive—or rather, more accurately, we would not have been able to develop into the sort of creatures we have become. Intelligence constitutes the characteristic specialty that provides the comparative advantage which has enabled our species to make its evolutionary way into this world's scheme of things. We are so smart because this is necessary for *us* to be here at all.

In the course of deploying our intelligence to grapple with the complexities of the world about us, we arrived ultimately at the project of natural science. Gradually our natural curiosity got the better of us and we began to push the project of inquiry beyond the level of actual need. It is not that we require scientific smarts to exist in our evolutionary niche (thank goodness!) Instead, the fact is that what we require for occupying our evolutionary niche is a body of skills that also render the development of science possible.[3]

2. The Exploration Model of Scientific Inquiry

One of the most striking and important facts about scientific inquiry is that the ongoing resolution of significant new questions faces increasingly high demands for obtaining and processing data. In advancing science we scan nature for interesting phenomena and grope about for the explanatorily useful regularities they may exhibit. But as this process advances further, the quest for new phenomena imposes ever greater demands which can be met only with an increasingly more powerful technology of data exploration and management.

In theory, a prospect of unending scientific progress lies before us.

But its practical realization is something else again. Though the veins of cognitive gold run on, they become increasingly difficult—and expensive—to mine.

In developing natural science, we humans began by exploring the world in our own locality, not just our spatial neighborhood but—more far-reachingly—our *parametric* neighborhood in the space of physical variables such as temperature, pressure, and electric charge. Near the "home base" of the state of things in our accustomed natural environment, we can—thanks to the evolutionary attunement of our sensory and cognitive apparatus—operate with relative ease and freedom through using our unassisted senses to scan nature for data regarding its modes of operation. But in due course we accomplish everything that can be managed by these straightforward means. To do more, we have to extend our probes into nature more deeply, deploying increasingly technical sophistication to achieve more and more demanding levels of interactive capability. We have to move ever further away from our evolutionary home base in nature toward increasingly remote frontiers. From the egocentric standpoint of our local region of parametric space, we journey ever more distantly outward to explore nature's various parametric dimensions in the search for cognitively fertile phenomena. This perspective of exploration provides a conception of scientific research as a prospecting search for the new phenomena required for significant new scientific findings.

The appropriate picture is not, of course, one of geographical exploration but rather of the physical exploration—and subsequent theoretical systematization—of phenomena distributed over the parametric space of the physical quantities spreading out all about us. As we increase the range of telescopes, the energy of particle accelerators, the effectiveness of low-temperature instrumentation, the potency of pressurization equipment, the power of vacuum-creating contrivances, and the accuracy of measurement apparatus—that is, as our capacity to move about in the parametric space of the physical world is enhanced—new phenomena always come into view. A homely fishing analogy of Arthur Eddington's is useful here. He saw the experimentalists as akin to a fisherman who trawls nature with the net of his equipment for detection and observation. Now suppose, said Eddington, that a fisherman trawls the seas using a fishnet of two-inch mesh. Then fish of a smaller size will simply go uncaught, and those who analyze the catch will have an incomplete and distorted view of aquatic life. The situation in science is the same. Only by improving our observational means of trawling nature can such imperfections be mitigated.[4] After the major findings accessible via the data of a given level of technological sophistication have been achieved, further major findings become realizable only when one ascends to the next level of sophistication in data-relevant technology. Thus the key to the great progress of contemporary physics lies in the enormous strides which an ever more sophisticated scientific technology has made possible by enlarging the observational and experimental basis of our theoretical knowledge of natural processes.

3. Technological Escalation: An Arms Race Against Nature

Natural science is fundamentally empirical, with its advance critically dependent not on human ingenuity alone but also on the ongoing enhancement of our technologically facilitated experiential interactions with nature. Experiment and observation are the key here. The days are long past when useful scientific data can be had by unaided sensory observation of the ordinary course of nature. Artifice has become an indispensable route to the acquisition and processing of scientifically useful data. The sorts of data on which discovery in natural science nowadays depends can be obtained only by technological means. The discoveries of today cannot be made with yesterday's equipment and techniques. To conduct new experiments, to secure new observations, and to detect new phenomena, an ever more powerful investigative technology is needed. This technology of inquiry falls into relatively distinct levels or stages in sophistication—correlatively with successively "later generations" of instrumentation and manipulative machinery, which are generally separated from one another by substantial (roughly, order-of-magnitude) capacity improvements in regard to such information-providing parameters as measurement exactness, data-processing volume, detection sensitivity, high voltages, high or low temperatures, and the like.

Given that we can only learn about nature by interacting with her, Newton's third law of countervailing action and reaction becomes a fundamental principle of epistemology. Everything depends on just how and *how hard* we can push against nature in situations of observational and detectional interaction. As Bacon saw, nature will never tell us more than we can forcibly extract from her with the means of interaction at our disposal. And because this extraction can only be realized by ever deeper probings, this state of affairs has far-reaching implications for the perfectibility of science. The impetus to augment our science demands an unremitting and unending effort to enlarge the domain of effective experimental intervention.

Physicists often remark that the development of our understanding of nature moves through successive layers of *theoretical* sophistication.[5] But scientific progress is clearly no less dependent on continual improvements in strictly *technical* sophistication:

> Some of the most startling technological advances in our time are closely associated with basic research. As compared with 25 years ago, the highest vacuum readily achievable has improved more than a thousand-fold; materials can be manufactured that are 100 times purer; the submicroscopic world can be seen at 10 time higher magnification; the detection of trace impurities is hundred of times more sensitive; the identification of molecular species (as in various forms of chromatography) is immeasurably advanced. These examples are only a small sample. . . . Fundamental research in physics is crucially dependent on advanced technology, and is becoming more so.[6]

Without an ever improving technology, scientific progress would cease. Scientific progress depends crucially and unavoidably on our technical capability to penetrate into the increasingly distant—and increasingly difficult—reaches of the spectrum of physical parameters in order to explore and to explain the ever more remote phenomena encountered there. Pioneering scientific research will always operate at the technological frontier. For revealing here further "secrets" nature inexorably exacts a drastically increasing effort in the acquisition and processing of data. This accounts for the recourse to more and more sophisticated technology for research in natural science. Once the potential of a given state-of-the-art level has been exploited, not all our piety or wit can lure the technological frontier back to yield further significant returns at this stage. The need for enhanced data forces us to look further away and further from humanity's familiar natural "home base" in the parametric space of nature.

No doubt, nature is in itself uniform as regards the distribution of its diverse processes across the reaches of parameter space. It does not favor us by clustering them in our accustomed parametric vicinity: significant phenomena do not dry up outside our parochial neighborhood. And phenomenological novelty is seemingly inexhaustible: we can never feel confident that we have got to the bottom of it. Nature always has fresh reserves of phenomena at her disposal, hidden away in those ever more remote regions of paramative space. Successive stages in the technological resources of scientific inquiry accordingly lead us to ever different views about the nature of things and the character of their laws.

The requirement for technological progress to advance scientific knowledge has far-reaching implications for the nature of the enterprise. For the increasing technological demands that are requisite for scientific progress means that each step ahead gets more complex and more expensive as those new parametric regions grow increasingly remote. With the progress of science, nature becomes less and less yielding to the efforts of further inquiry. We are faced with the need to push nature harder and harder to achieve cognitively profitable interactions. The dialectic theory and experiment carries natural science ever deeper into the range of greater efforts and costs.

The pursuit of natural science as we know it embarks us on a literally endless endeavor to improve the range of effective experimental intervention, because only by operating under new and heretofore inaccessible conditions of observational or experimental systemization—attaining extreme temperature, pressure, particle velocity, field strength, and so on—can we realize situations that enable us to put knowledge-expanding hypotheses and theories to the test. The discoveries of today cannot be advanced with yesterday's instrumentation and techniques. As one acute observer has rightly remarked: "Most critical experiments [in physics] planned today, if they had to be constrained within the technology of even ten years ago, would be seriously compromised."[7]

That there is "pay dirt" deeper down in the mine avails us only if we can actually dig there. New forces, for example, may well be in the offering, if one able physicist is right:

> We are familiar, to varying degrees, with four types of force: gravity, electricity, the strong nuclear force that holds the atomic nucleus together and the weak force that brings about radioactive decay by the emission of electrons. . . . Yet it would indeed be astonishing if . . . other types of force did not exist. Such other forces could escape out notice because they were too weak to have much distinguishable effect or because they were of such short range that, no matter whether they were weak or not, the effects specifically associated with their range were contained within the objects of the finest scale that our instruments had so far permitted us to probe.[8]

But, of course, such weak forces would enter into our picture of nature only if our instrumentation were able to detect them. This need for a constant enhancement of scientifically relevant technology lies at the basis of the enormous increase in the human and material resources needed for modern experimental science.

Frontier research is true *pioneering*: what counts is not just doing it but doing it *for the first time*. Aside from the initial reproduction of claimed results needed to establish the reproducibility of reproducibility of results, repetition in *research* is in general pointless. As one acute observer has remarked, one can follow the diffusion of scientific technology "from the research desk down to the schoolroom":

> The emanation electroscope was a device invented at the turn of the century to measure the rate at which a gas such as thorium loses its radioactivity. For a number of years it seems to have been used only in the research laboratory. It came into use in instructing graduate students in the mid-1930's, and in college courses by 1949. For the last few years a cheap commercial model has existed and is beginning to be introduced into high school courses. In a sense, this is a victory for good practice; but it also summarizes the sad state of scientific education to note that in the research laboratory itself the emanation electroscope has long since been removed from the desk to the attic.[9]

We thus arrive at the phenomenon of *technological escalation*. The need for new data forces us to look further and further in parametric space. Thus while scientific progress is in principle always possible—there being no absolute or intrinsic limits to significant scientific discovery—the realization of this ongoing prospect demands a continual enhancement in the technological state of the art of data extraction or exploitation. In science, as in a technological arms race, one is simply never called on to keep doing what was done before. One is always forced further up the mountain, ascending to ever higher levels of technological performance—and of expense. As science endeavors to extend its "mastery over nature," it becomes enmeshed in a technology-intensive arms race against nature, with all of the practical and economic implications characteristic of such process.

The exploration of nature's parametric space confronts us with the reality of physical limits: particle velocities in accelerations are limited by the speed of light, temperatures in low-temperature research are limited by absolute zero, vacuums are limited by condition of emptiness, temperatures by the cosmic boiling point of the big bang. And such limits amount to resistance barriers. With every step we take towards them—every time we move from where we are to 90 percent closer yet—we find it exponentially more difficult to take yet further steps as the technological demands for further progress grow increasingly massive. Seen from the vantage point of a creature of our inexorably limited capabilities, nature's depths are effectively limitless.

The enormous power, sensitivity, and complexity deployed in present-day experimental science have not been sought for their own sake but rather because the research frontier has moved on into an area where this sophistication is the indispensable requisite of ongoing progress. The onus of increasing difficulty is unavoidable: the need for an ever deeper penetration into nature's inherent complexity means that in natural science, as in war, the battles of the present cannot be fought effectively with the armaments of the past.[10]

Notes

1. The human skeleton has some 220 bones, about the same number as a cat when tail bones are excluded. A small monkey has around 120. Of course, what matters for present purposes is *independently* moving parts. This demotes "thousand leggers" and—thanks to fingers, among other things—takes us out of the cat's league.
2. At any given time in evolutionary history, the then-current herbivores tended to have smaller brains than the contemporary carnivores. See Richard Dawkins, *The Blind Watchmaker* (New York: Norton, 1986), p. 190.
3. Some of the issues of this section are explored more extensively in the author's *A Useful Inheritance* (Savage, MD: Rowman & Littlefield, 1990).
4. See Arthur S. Eddington, *The Nature of the Physical World* (New York: The Macmillan Company; Cambridge, Eng.: The University Press, 1929).
5. "Looking back, one has the impression that the historical development of the physical description of the world consists of a succession of layers of knowledge of increasing generality and greater depth. Each layer has a well defined field of validity; one has to pass beyond the limits of each to get to the next one, which will be characterized by more general and more encompassing laws and by discoveries constituting a deeper penetration into the structure of the Universe than the layers recognized before." (Edoardo Amaldi, "The Unity of Physics," *Physics Today*, vol. 261, no. 9 [September 1973], p. 24.) See also E. P. Wigner, "The Unreasonable Effectiveness of Mathematics in the Natural Sciences, " *Communication on Pure and Applied Mathematics*, vol. 13 (1960), pp. 1-14; as well as his "The Limits of Science," *Proceedings of the American Philosophical Society*, vol. 93 (1949), pp. 521-26. Compare also the classic account in chapter 8 of Henry Margenau, *The Nature of Physical Reality* (New York: McGraw-Hill, 1950).
6. D. A. Bromley et al., *Physics in Perspective, Student Edition* (Washington, DC, 1973; National Research Council/National Academy of Science Publications), p. 23.
7. D. A. Bromley et al. *Physics in Perspective*, pp. 13, 16. See also Gerald Holton, "Models for Understanding the Growth and Excellence of Scientific Research," in

Stephen R. Graubard and Gerald Holton, eds., *Excellence and Leadership in the Democracy* (New York: Columbia University Press, 1962), p. 115.

8. Sir Denys H. Wilkinson, *The Quarks and Captain Ahab* or: *The Universe as Artifact* (Stanford, CA: Schiff Memorial Lecture, 1977), pp. 12-13.

9. Gerald Holton, "Models for Understanding the Growth and Excellence of Scientific Research," in Stephen R. Graubard and Gerald Holton (ed.), *Excellence and Leadership in a Democracy* (New York: Columbia University Press, 1962), p. 115.

10. Some of the issues of this section are also addressed in chapter 7 "Cost Escalation in Empirical Inquiry" of the author's *Cognitive Economy* (Pittsburgh: University of Pittsburgh Press, 1989). *Scientific Progress* (Oxford: Basil Blackwell, 1978) and *The Limits of Science* (Berkeley and Los Angeles: University of California Press, 1984) are also relevant as regards the broader issues.

6

The Theoretical Unrealizability
of Perfected Science

*(1) Perfected science would have to realize four theoretical desiderata:
(a) erotetic completeness (including explanatory completeness); (b)
pragmatic completeness; (c) predictive completeness; and (d) temporal finality (the ω-condition). (2) - (5) There is, as a matter of fundamental general principle, no practicable way for us to establish that
any one of these desiderata is realized. In this complex world of ours,
science must be seen as inherently incompletable, with an ever reced-
ing horizon separating where we are from where we would ideally like
to be. (6) Perfection is dispensable as a goal for natural science; we
need not presuppose its potential attainability to validate the enterprise. The motive force of scientific progress is not the* a fronte *pull of
an unattainable perfection but the* a tergo *push of recognized shortcomings. (7) Perfected science is not a realizable condition of things
but an idealization that provides a useful contrast-conception to highlight the limited character of what we do and can attain. (8) The
unachievability of perfected science constrains us to recognize that
natural science affords a no more than imperfect picture of reality in
its full complexity.*

1. Conditions for Perfected Science

How far can the scientific venture advance toward achieving a definitive understanding of this complex world of ours? Can science
attain a point of recognizable completion? Is the realization of perfected science a genuine possibility, even in theory, if we put all of the
"merely practical" obstacles aside as somehow incidental?

What would *perfected science* be like? What sort of standard would it have to meet? Clearly, it would have to complete in full the discharge of natural science's mandate or mission. Now, the goal-structure of scientific inquiry covers a good deal of ground. It is diversified and complex, spreading across both the cognitive/theoretical and active/practical sectors. It encompasses the traditional quartet of description, explanation, prediction, and control in line with the following array:

theoretical goals
$\begin{cases}
\textit{description}\text{: answering } \textit{what}? \text{ and,} \\
\quad \textit{how}? \text{ questions about nature} \\
\textit{explanation}\text{: answering } \textit{why}? \\
\quad \text{questions about nature}
\end{cases}$

practical goals
$\begin{cases}
\textit{prediction}\text{: successful alignment} \\
\quad \text{of our expectations with} \\
\quad \text{nature} \\
\textit{control}\text{: effective intervention in} \\
\quad \text{nature to alter the course of} \\
\quad \text{events in desired directions}
\end{cases}$

Accordingly, if we are to claim that it has attained a perfected condition, our science would have to satisfy (at least) the following conditions.

1. *Erotetic completeness*: It must answer, in principle at any rate, all those descriptive and explanatory questions that it itself countenances as legitimately raisable, and must explain everything it deems explicable.
2. *Predictive completeness*: It must provide the cognitive basis for accurately predicting those eventuations that are in principle predictable (that is, that it itself recognizes as such).
3. *Pragmatic completeness*: It must provide the requisite cognitive means for doing whatever is feasible for beings like ourselves to do in the circumstances in which we labor.
4. *Temporal finality* (the ω-condition): It must leave no room for thinking that further changes in the existing state of scientific knowledge can be achieved.

Each of these requisites deserves detailed consideration.

2. Theoretical Adequacy: Issues of Erotetic Completeness

Erotetic completeness is an unattainable mirage. We can never exhaust the possibility of questions. For we have no choice but to come to terms with the Kantian principle of question-propagation to the effect that in matters of factual investigation the answers to our questions always open up new questions in turn. And this means that inquiry—the dialectic of questions and answers—can never get to the ultimate bottom of things.

Any adequate theory of inquiry must recognize that the ongoing process of science is a process of *conceptual* innovation that always leaves certain theses wholly outside the cognitive range of the inquirers of any particular period. This means that there will always be facts (or plausible candidate-facts) about a thing that we do not *know* because we cannot ever *conceive* of them. For to grasp such a fact calls for taking a perspective of consideration that we simply do not have, since the state of knowledge (or purported knowledge) is not yet advanced to a point at which its entertainment is feasible. In bringing conceptual innovation about, cognitive progress makes it possible to consider new possibilities that were heretofore conceptually inaccessible.

The language of emergence can perhaps be deployed profitably to make the point. But what is at issue is not an emergence of *the features of thing* but an emergence in our *knowledge* about them. The blood circulated in the human body well before Harvey; uranium-containing substances were radioactive before Becquerel. The emergence at issue relates to our cognitive mechanisms of conceptualization, not to the *objects* of our consideration in and of themselves. Real-world objects are conceived of as antecedent to any cognitive interaction—as being there right along, or "pregiven," as Edmund Husserl puts it. Any cognitive changes or innovations are to be conceptualized as something that occurs on our side of the cognitive transaction, and not on the side of the objects with which we deal.[1]

The concept of a thing so functions in our conceptual scheme that things are thought of as having an identity, a nature, and a mode of comportment wholly indifferent to the cognitive state of the art regarding them, and presumably very different from our conceptions of the matter. But this is something we presume or postulate; it is certainly not something we have discovered—or ever could discover. We are not—and will never be—in a position to evade or abolish the contrast between "things as we think them to be" and "things as they actually and truly are." Their susceptibility to further elaborative detail—and to changes of mind regarding this further detail—is built into our very conception of a "real thing." To be a real thing is to be something regarding which we can always in principle acquire more information. The world's furnishings are cognitively opaque; we cannot see to the bottom of them. Knowledge can become more extensive without thereby becoming more complete. And this view of the situation is supported rather than impeded if we abandon a cumulativist/ preservationist view of knowledge or purported knowledge for the view that new discoveries need not supplement but can displace old ones.

And much the same story holds when our concern is not with things but with *types* of things. To say that something is copper (or is magnetic) is to say more than that is has the properties we associate with copper (or magnetic things), and indeed is to say more than that it meets our test-conditions for being copper (or being magnetic). It is to say that this thing *is* copper (or magnetic). And this is an issue regarding which we are prepared at least to contemplate the prospect that we've got it wrong.

There is thus good reason of general principle to think that erotetic completeness is unachievable. But another line of consideration is no less decisive for our present purposes.

Could we ever actually achieve the condition of being able to resolve, in principle, all of our (legitimately posable) question about the world? Could we ever find ourselves in this seemingly fortunate position?[2]

In theory, yes. A body of science certainly could be such as to provide answers to all those questions it allows to arise. But just how meaningful would this mode of completeness be?

It is sobering to realize that the erotetic completeness of a state of science does not necessarily betoken its comprehensiveness of sufficiency. It might reflect the paucity of the range of questions we are prepared to contemplate—a deficiency of imagination, so to speak. When the range of our knowledge is sufficiently restricted, then erotetic completeness will merely reflect this impoverishment rather than its intrinsic adequacy. Conceivably, if improbably, science might reach a purely fortuitous equilibrium between problems and solutions. It could eventually be "completed" in the narrow erotetic sense—providing an answer to every question one can ask in the then-existing (albeit still imperfect) state of knowledge—without thereby being completed in the larger sense of answering the questions that would arise if only one could probe nature just a bit more deeply. And so, our corpus of scientific knowledge could be erratically complete and yet fundamentally inadequate. Yet even if realized, this erotetic mode of completeness would not be particularly meaningful. (To be sure, this discussion proceeds at the level of supposition contrary to fact. The exfoliation of new questions from old in the course of scientific inquiry that is at issue in Kant's principle of question-propagation spells the infeasibility of ever attaining erotetic completeness.)

The preceding considerations illustrate a more general circumstance. Any claim to the realization of a *theoretically* complete science of physics would be one that affords "a complete, consistent, and unified theory of physical interaction that would describe all possible observations."[3] But to check that the state of physics on hand actually meets this condition, we would need to know exactly what physical interactions are indeed *possible*. And to warrant us in using the state of physics on hand as a basis for answering *this* question, we would *already* have to be assured that its view of the possibilities is correct—and thus already have preestablished its completeness. The idea of a consolidated erotetic completeness in science is shipwrecked on the infeasibility of finding a meaningful way to monitor its attainment.

After all, any judgment we can make about the laws of nature—any cognitive model we can contrive regarding how things work in the world—is a product of theoretical triangulation from the data at our disposal. And we should never have unalloyed confidence in the definitiveness of our data base or in the adequacy of our exploitation of it. Observation can never settle decisively just what the laws of nature are. In principle, different law-systems can always yield the same observations output: as philosophers of science are wont to insist, observations *undermine* laws. To be sure, this worries working scientists less than it does philosophers, because they deploy powerful regulative principles—simplicity, economy, uniformity, homogeneity, and so on—to constrain uniqueness. But neither these principles themselves nor the uses to which they are put are unproblematic. No matter how comprehensive our data of how great our confidence in the inductions we base upon them, the potential inadequacy or our claims cannot be averted. One can never feel secure in writing *finis* on the basis of purely theoretical considerations.

We can reliably estimate the amount of gold or oil yet to be discovered, because we know a priori the earth's extent and can thus establish a proportion between what we know and what we do not. But we cannot comparably estimate the amount of knowledge yet to be discovered, because we have and can have no way of relating what we know to what we do not. At best, we can consider the proportion of available questions we can in fact resolve; and this is an unsatisfactory procedure. The very idea of cognitive limits has a paradoxical air. It suggests that we claim knowledge about something outside knowledge. But (to hark back to Hegel), with respect to the realm of knowledge, we are not in a position to draw a line between what lies inside and what lies outside—seeing that, *ex hypothesi*, we have no cognitive access to that latter. One cannot make a survey of the relative extent of knowledge or ignorance about nature except by basing it on some picture of nature that is already in hand—that is, unless one is prepared to take at face value the deliverances of existing science. This process of judging the adequacy of our science on its own telling is the best we can do, but it remains an essentially circular and consequently inconclusive way of proceeding. The long and short of it is that there is no cognitively adequate basis for maintaining the completeness of science in a rationally satisfactory way.

To monitor the theoretical completeness of science, we accordingly need some theory-external control on the adequacy of our theorizing, some belief-independent reality principle to serve as a standard of adequacy. We are thus driven to abandon the road of pure theory and proceed along that of the practical goals of the enterprise. This gives special importance and urgency to the pragmatic sector.

3. Pragmatic Completeness

The arbitrament of praxis—not theoretical merit but practical capability—affords the best standard of adequacy for our scientific proceedings that is available. But could we ever be in a position to claim that science has been completed on the basis of the success of its practical applications? On this basis, the perfection of science would have to manifest itself in the perfecting of control—in achieving a perfected technology. But just how are we to proceed here? Could our natural science scheme manifest perfection on the side of control over nature? Could it ever underwrite a recognizably perfected technology?

The issue of "control over nature" is far more subtle than may appear on first view. For just how is this conception to be understood? Clearly, in terms of bending the course of events to our will, of attaining our ends within nature. But this involvement of "*our ends*" brings to light the prominence of our own contribution. For example, if we are inordinately modest in our demands (or very unimaginative), we may even achieve "complete control over nature" in the sense of being in a position to do *whatever we want* to do, but yet attain this happy condition in a way that betokens very little real capability.

One might, to be sure, involve the idea of omnipotence, and construe a "perfected" technology as one that would enable us to do literally *anything*. But this approach would at once run into the old difficulties already familiar to the medieval scholastics. Their theological deliberations faced them with the challenge: "If God is omnipotent, can he annihilate himself (contra his nature as a *necessary* being), or can he do evil deeds (contra his nature as a *perfect* being), or can he make triangles have four angles (contrary to *their* definitive nature)?" Sensibly enough, the scholastics inclined to solve these difficulties by maintaining that an omnipotent God need not be in a position to do literally *anything* but rather simply anything that it *is possible* for him to do. Similarly, we cannot explicate the idea of technological omnipotence in terms of a capacity to produce *any* result, wholly without qualification. We cannot ask for the production of a *perpetuum mobile*, for spaceships with "hyperdrive" enabling them to attain transluminar velocities, for devices that predict essentially stochastic processes such as the disintegrations of transuranic atoms, or for piston devices that enable us to set *independently* the values for the pressure, temperature, and volume of a body of gas. We cannot, in sum, ask of a "perfected" technology that it should enable us to do anything that we might take it into our heads to do, no matter how "unrealistic" this might be.

All that we can reasonably ask of it is that perfected technology should enable us to do anything *that it is possible for us to do*—and not just what we might *think* we can do but what we really and truly *can* do. A perfected technology would be one that enabled us to do anything that *can possibly* be done by creatures circumstanced as we are. But how can we deal with the pivotal conception of "can" that is at issue here? Clearly, only science—real, true, correct, *perfected* science—could tell us what indeed is realistically possible and what circumstances are indeed inescapable. Whenever our "knowledge" falls short of this, we may well "ask the impossible" by way of accomplishment (for example, spaceships in "hyperdrive"), and thus complain of incapacity to achieve control in ways that put unrealistic burdens on this conception.

Power is a matter of the "effecting of things possible"—of achieving control—and it is clearly cognitive state of the art in science which, in teaching us about the limits of the possible, is itself the agent that must shape our conception of this issue. *Every* law of nature serves to set the boundary between what is genuinely possible and what is not, between what can be done and what cannot, between which questions we can properly ask and which we cannot. We cannot satisfactorily monitor the adequacy and completeness of our science by its ability to effect "all things possible," because science alone can inform us about what is possible. As science grows and develops, it poses new issues of power and control, reformulating and reshaping those demands whose realization represents "control over nature." For science itself brings new possibilities to light. (At a suitable stage, the idea of "splitting the atom" will no longer seem a contradiction in terms.) To see if a given state of technology meets the condition of perfection, we must *already* have a body of perfected science in hand to tell us what is indeed possible. To validate the claim that our technology is perfected, we need to *preestablish* the completeness of our science. The idea works in such a way that claims to perfected control can rest only on perfected science.

In attempting to travel the practicalist route to cognitive completeness, we are thus trapped in a circle. Short of having supposedly perfected science in hand, we could not say what a perfected technology would be like, and thus we could not possibly monitor the perfection of science in terms of the technology that it underwrites.

Moreover, if ever (*per impossible*) a "pragmatic equilibrium" between what we can and what we wish to do in science were to be realized, we could not be warrantedly confident that this condition will remain unchanged. The possibility that "just around the corner" things will become unstuck can never be eliminated. Even if we "achieve control" to all intents and purposes, we cannot be sure of not losing our grip upon it—not because of a loss of power but because of cognitive changes that produce a broadening of the imagination and a widened apprehension as to what "having control" involves.

Accordingly, the project of achieving practical mastery over nature can never be perfected in a satisfactory way. The point is that control hinges on what we want, and what is conditioned by what we think possible, and *this* is something that hinges crucially on theory—on our beliefs about how things work in this world. And so control is something deeply theory-infected. We can never safely move from apparent to real adequacy in this regard. We cannot adequately assure that seeing perfection is more than just that. We thus have no alternative but to *presume* that our knowledge (that is, our purported knowledge) is inadequate at this and indeed at any other particular stage of the game of cognitive completeness.

One important point about control must, however, be noted with care. Our preceding negative strictures all relate to attainment of perfect control—of being in a position to do everything possible. No such problems affect the issue of amelioration—of doing some things better and *improving* our control over what it was. It makes perfectly good sense to use its technological applications as standards of scientific advancement. (Indeed, we have no real alternative to using pragmatic standards at this level, because reliance on theory alone is, in the end, going to be circular.) While control does not help us with *perfection*, it is crucial for monitoring *progress*. Standards of assessment and evaluation are such that we can implement the idea of improvements (progress), but not that of completion (realized perfection). We can determine when we have managed to *enlarge* our technological mastery, but we cannot meaningfully say what it would be to *perfect* it. (Our conception of the *doable* keeps changing with changes in the cognitive state of the art, a fact that does not, of course, alter our view of what *already has been done* in the practical sphere.)

4. Predictive Completeness

The difficulties encountered in using physical control as a standard of "perfection" in science all also hold with respect to *prediction*, which, after all, is simply a mode of *cognitive* control.

Suppose someone asks: "Are you really still going to persist in plaints regarding the incompleteness of scientific knowledge when science can predict *everything*?" The reply is simply that science will *never* be able to predict literally everything: the very idea of predicting *everything* is simply unworkable. For then, whenever we predict something, we would have to predict also the effects of making those predictions, and then the ramification of *those* predictions, and so on *ad indefinitum*. The very most that can be asked is that science put us into a position to predict, not *everything*, but rather *anything* that we might choose to be interested in and to inquire about. And here it must be recognized that our imaginative perception of the possibilities might be much too narrow. We can only make predictions about matters that lie, at least broadly speaking, within our cognitive horizons. Newton could not have predicted findings in quantum theory any more than he could have predicted the outcome of American presidential elections. One can only make predictions about what one is cognizant of, takes note of, deems worthy of consideration. In this regard, one can be myopic either by not noting or by losing sight of significant sectors of natural phenomena.

Another important point must be made regarding this matter of unpredictability. Great care must be taken to distinguish the ontological and the epistemological dimensions, to keep the entries of these two columns apart:

unexplainable	not (yet) explained
by chance	by some cause we do not know of
spontaneous	caused in a way we cannot identify
random	lawful in ways we cannot characterize
by whim	for reasons not apparent to us

It is tempting to slide from epistemic incapacity to ontological lawfulness. But we must resist this temptation and distinguish what is inherently uncognizable from what we just don't happen to cognize. The nature of scientific change makes it inevitably problematic to slide from present to future incapacity.

Sometimes, to be sure, talk in the ontological mode is indeed warranted. The world no doubt contains situations of randomness and chance, situations in which genuinely stochastic processes are at work in a ways that "engender unknowability." But these ontological claims must be rooted in knowledge rather than ignorance. They can only be claimed appropriately in those cases in which (as in quantum theory) *we can explain inexplicability*—that is, in which we can account for the inability to predict/explain/control within the framework of a positive account of why the item at issue is actually unpredictable/unexplainable/unsolvable.

Accordingly, these ontological based incapacities do *not* introduce matters that "lie beyond the limits of knowledge." On the contrary, positive information is the pivot point. the only viable limits to knowability are those rooted in knowledge—that is, in a model of nature which entails that certain sorts of things are unknowable. It is not a matter of an incapacity to answer appropriate questions ("We 'just don't know' why that stochastic process eventuated as it did"). Rather, in the prevailing state of knowledge, these question are improper; they just do not arise.

Science itself sets the limits to predictability—insisting that some phenomena (the stochastic processes encountered in quantum physics, for example) are inherently unpredictable. And this is always to some degree problematic. The most that science can reasonably be asked to do is to predict what it itself sees as in principle predictable—to answer every predictive question that it itself countenances as proper. And here we must once more recognize that any given state of science might have gotten matters quite wrong.

With regard to predictions, we are thus in the same position that obtains with regard to actually interventionist (rather than "merely cognitive") control. Here, too, we can unproblematically apply the idea of improvement—of progress. But it makes no sense to contemplate the *achievement* of perfection. For its realization is something we could never establish by any practicable means.[4]

5. Temporal Finality

Scientists from time to time indulge in eschatological musings and tell us that the scientific venture is approaching its end.[5] And it is, of course, entirely *conceivable* that natural science will come to a stop, and will do so not in consequence of a cessation of intelligent life but in C. S. Peirce's more interesting sense of completion of the project: of eventually reaching a condition after which even indefinitely ongoing inquiry will not—and indeed in the very nature of things *cannot*—produce any significant change, because inquiry has come to "the end of the road." The situation would be analogous to that envisaged in the apocryphal story in vogue during the middle 1800s regarding the commissioner of the United States Patents who resigned his post because there was nothing left to invent.[6]

Such a position is in theory possible. But here, too, we can never determine that it is actual.

There is no practicable way in which the claim that science has achieved temporal finality can be validated. The question "Is the current state of science, *S*, final?" is one for which we can never legitimate an affirmative answer. For the prospect of future changes of *S* can never be precluded. One cannot plausibly move beyond "We have (in *S*) no good reason to think that *S* will ever change" to obtain "We have (in *S*) good reason to think that *S* will never change." To take this posture towards *S* is to *presuppose its completeness*. It is not simply to take the natural and relatively unproblematic stance that that for which *S* vouches is to be taken as true but to go beyond this to insist that whatever is true finds a rationalization within *S*. This argument accordingly embeds *finality* in *completeness*, and in doing so jumps from the frying pan into the fire. For it shifts from what is difficult to what is yet more so. To hold that if something is so at all, then *S* affords a good reason for it is to take so blatantly ambitious (even megalomaniacal) a view of *S* that the issue of finality seems almost a harmless appendage.

Moreover, just as the appearance of erotetic and pragmatic equilibrium can be a product of narrowness and weakness, so can temporal finality. We may think that science is unchangeable simply because we have been unable to change it. But that's just not good enough. Were science ever to come to a seeming stop, we could never be sure that it had done so not because it is at "the end of the road" but because we are at the end of our tether. We can never ascertain that science has attained the ω-condition of final completion, since from our point of view the possibility of further change lying "just around the corner" can never be ruled out finally and decisively. No matter how final a position we *appear* to have reached, the prospect of its coming unstuck cannot be precluded. As we have seen, future science is inscrutable. We can never claim with assurance that the position we espouse is immune to change under the impact of further data—that the oscillations are dying out and we are approaching a final limit. By its very nature, science "in the limit" related to what happens in the long run, and this is something about which we *in principle* cannot gather information: any information we can actually gather inevitably pertains to the short run and not the long run. We can never achieve adequate assurance that *apparent* definitiveness is *real*. We can never consolidate the claim that science has settled into a frozen, changeless pattern. The situation in natural science is such that our knowledge of nature must ever be presumed to be incomplete.

The idea of achieving a state of recognizably completed science is totally unrealistic. Even as widely variant modes of behavior by three dimensional objects could produce exactly the same two-dimensional shadow projections, so very different law systems could in principle engender exactly the same phenomena. We cannot make any definitive inferences from phenomena to the nature of the real. The prospect of perfected science is bound to elude us.

One is thus brought back to the stance of the great Idealist philosophers (Plato, Spinoza, Hegel, Bradley, Royce) that human knowledge inevitably falls short of recognizably "perfected science" (the Ideas, the Absolute), and must accordingly be looked upon as incomplete.

We have no alternative but to proceed on the assumption that the era of innovation is not over—that in this complex world of ours *future* science can and will prove to be *different* science.

As these deliberations indicate, the conditions of perfected science in point of description, explanation, prediction, and control are all unrealizable. Our information will inevitably prove inconclusive. We have no reasonable alternative to seeing our present-day science as suboptimal, regardless of the question of what date the calendar shows.

Note that the present discussion does not propound the *ontological* thesis that natural science cannot be pragmatically complete, ω-definitive, and so on, but the *epistemological* thesis that science cannot ever be *known to be so*. The point is not that the requirements of definitive knowledge cannot in the nature of things be satisfied but that they cannot be *implemented* (that is, be *shown* to be satisfied). The upshot is that science must always be presumed to be incomplete, not that it necessarily always is so. No doubt this is also true. It cannot, however, be demonstrated on the basis of epistemological general principles but requires the substantive considerations regarding the metaphysics of inquiry that will be developed in the next chapter.

6. The Dispensability of Perfection

The cognitive situation of natural science invites description in theological terms. The ambiguity of the human condition is only too manifest here. We cannot expect ever to reach a position of definitive finality in this imperfect dispensation: we do have "knowledge" of sorts, but it is manifestly imperfect. Expelled from the Garden of Eden, we are deprived of access to "the God's-eye point of view."

Definitive and comprehensive adequacy is denied us: we have no basis for claiming to know "the truth, the whole truth, and nothing but the truth" in scientific matters. We yearn for absolutes, but have to settle for plausiblities; we desire what is definitively correct, but have to settle for conjectures and estimates.

In this imperfect epistemic dispensation, we have to reckon with the realities of the human condition. Age disagrees with age; different states of the art involve naturally discordant conceptions and incommensurate positions. The moral of the story of the Tower of Babel applies.

The absolutes for which we yearn represent an ideal that lies beyond the range of practicable realizability. We simply have to do the best we can with the means at our disposal. To aspire to absolutes— for definitive comprehensiveness—is simply unrealistic.

It is sometimes maintained that such a fallibilist and imperfectionist view of science is unacceptable. To think of science as *inevitably* incomplete and to think of "the definitive answers" in scientific matters as *perpetually* unattainable is, we are told, to write science off as a meaningful project.

But in science as in the moral life, we can operate perfectly well in the realization that perfection is unattainable. No doubt here and there some scientists nurse the secret hope of attaining some fixed and final definitive result that will stand, untouchable and changeless, through all subsequent ages. But unrealistic aspirations are surely by no means essential to the scientific enterprise as such. In science as in other domains of human endeavor, it is a matter of doing the best we can with the tools that come to hand.

For the fact that *perfection* is unattainable does nothing to countervail against the no less real fact that *improvement* is realizable—that progress is possible. The undeniable prospect of realizable progress— of overcoming genuine defects and deficiencies that we find in the work of our predecessors—affords ample impetus to scientific innovation. Scientific progress is not generated *a fronte* by the pull of an unattainable ideal; it is stimulated *a tergo* by the push of dissatisfaction with the deficiencies of achieved positions. The labors of science are not pulled forward by the mirage of (unattainable) perfection. We are pushed onward by the (perfectly realizable) wish to do better than our predecessors in the enterprise. The idea of *improving* our science can be implemented without difficulty, since we can clearly improve our performance as regards its goals of prediction, control, and the rest. But the idea of *perfecting* our science cannot be implemented.

With regard to technical perfectibility, we must recognize that (1) there is no reason to expect that its realization is possible, even in principle, and (2) it is not monitorable: even if we had achieved it, we would not be able to claim success with warranted confidence. In the final analysis, then, we cannot regard the *realization* of "completed science" as a meaningful prospect—we cannot really say what it is that we are asking for. (To be sure, what is meaningless here is not the idea of perfected science as such but the idea of *achieving* it.) These deliberations further substantiate the idea that in this complex world we must always presume our knowledge to be incomplete in the domain of natural science.

7. "Perfected Science" as an Idealization that Affords a Useful Contrast Conception

Reasons of general principle block us from ever achieving a position from which we can make good the claim that the several goals of science have actually been reached. Perfection is simply no a goal or *telos* of the scientific enterprise. It is not a realizable condition of things but at best a useful contrast conception that keeps actual science in its place and helps to sensitize us to its imperfections. The validation of this idealization lies not in its future *achievability* but in its ongoing *utility* as a regulative ideal that affords a contrast to what we do actually attain—so as to highlight its salient limitations.

Ideal science is not something we have in hand here and now. Nor is it something toward which we are moving along the asymptotic and approximative lines envisaged by Peirce.[7] Existing science does not and never will embody perfection. The cognitive ideals of completeness, unity, consistency, and definitive finality represent an aspiration rather than a coming reality, an idealized *telos* rather than a realizable condition of things. Perfected science lies outside history as a useful contrast-case that cannot be secured in this imperfect world.

The idea of "perfected science" is that *focus imaginarius* whose pursuit canalizes and structures out inquiry. It represents the ultimate *telos* of inquiry, the idealized destination of a journey in which we are *still* and indeed are *ever* engaged, a grail of sorts that we can pursue but not possess. The ideal of perfection thus serves a fundamentally regulative role to mark the fact that actuality falls short of our cognitive aspirations. It marks a contrast that *regulates* how we make and must view our claims, playing a role akin to that of the functionary who reminded the Roman emperor of his mortality in reminding us that our pretensions are always vulnerable. Contemplation of this idea reminds us that the human condition is suspended between the reality of imperfect achievement and the ideal of an unattainable perfection. In abandoning this conception—in rejecting the idea of an "ideal science" that alone can properly be claimed to afford a definitive grasp of reality—we would abandon an idea that crucially regulates our view regarding the nature and status of the knowledge to which we lay claim. We would then no longer be constrained to characterize our view of things as *merely* ostensible and purported. We would be tempted to regard our picture of nature as real, authentic, and final in a manner that we, at bottom, realize it does not deserve.

What is being maintained here is not the "completed/perfected science" is a senseless idea as such but that the idea of *attaining* it is senseless. It represents a theoretically realizable state whose actual realization we can never achieve. What is unrealizable is not perfection as such but the *epistemic condition* of recognizing its attainment. (Even if we arrive, we can never tell that we're there!)

Does this situation not destroy "the pursuit of perfection" as a meaningful endeavor? Here it is useful to heed the distinction between a *goal* and an *ideal*. A goal is something that we hope and expect to achieve. An ideal is merely a wistful inkling, a "wouldn't it be nice if"—something that figures in the mode of aspiration rather than expectation. A goal motivates us in striving for its attainment; an ideal stimulates and encourages. An ideal does not provide us with a destination that we have any expectation of reaching; it is something for whose actual attainment we do not even hope. It is in *this* sense that "perfected science" is an ideal.

Here, as elsewhere, we must reckon appropriately with the standard gap between aspiration and attainment. In the practical sphere—in craftsmanship, for example, or the cultivation of our health—we may *strive* for perfection, but cannot ever claim to *attain* it. And the situation in inquiry is exactly parallel with what we encounter in such other domains—ethics specifically included. The value of an ideal, even of one that is not realizable, lies not in the benefit of its attainment (obviously and *ex hypothesi*!) but in the benefits that accrue from its pursuit. The view that it is rational to pursue an aim only if we are in a position to achieve its attainment or approximation is mistaken; it can be perfectly valid (and entirely rational) if the indirect benefits of its pursuit and adoption are sufficient—if in striving after it, we realize relevant advantages to a substantial degree. An unattainable ideal can be enormously productive. And so, the legitimation of the ideas of "perfected science" lies in its facilitation of the ongoing evolution of inquiry. In this domain, we arrive at the perhaps odd-seeming posture of an invocation of practical utility for the validation of an ideal.[8]

With respect to the moral aspirations of man's will, Kant wrote:

> Perfection [of the moral will] is a thing of which no rational being is the world of sense is at any time capable. But since it is required [of us] as practically necessary, it can be found only in an endless progress to that complete fitness; on principles of pure practical reason, it is necessary to assume such a practical progress as the real object of our will. . . . Only endless progress from lower to higher stages of moral perfection is possible to a rational but finite being.[9]

Much the same story surely holds on the side of the cognitive perfecting of man's knowledge. here, comparable regulative demands are at work governing the practical venture of inquiry, urging us to the ever fuller realization of the potentialities of the human intellect. The discontent of reason is a noble discontent. The scientific project is a venture in self-transcendence; one of the strongest motivations of scientific work is the urge to go beyond present science—to "advance the frontiers." Man's commitment to an ideal of reason in his pursuit of an unattainable systematic completeness is the epistemic counterpart of our commitment to moral ideals. It reflects a striving toward the rational ultimates of completeness, totality, and systematic finality—a striving that is all the more noble because it is not finally attainable. And complexity has its compensations here. If the work of inquiring reason in the sphere of natural science were completable, this would be something utterly tragic for us.

8. Science and Reality

We are now in a position to place into clearer relief one of the really big questions of philosophy: How close a relationship can we reasonably claim to exist between the answers we give to our factual questions at the level of scientific generality and precision and the reality they purport to depict?

Scientific realism is the doctrine that *science describes the real world*— that the world actually is as science takes it to be, and that its furnishings are as science envisages them to be.[10] If we want to know about the existence and the nature of heavy water or quarks, of man-eating mollusks or a luminiferous aether, we are referred to the natural sciences for the answers. On this realistic construction of scientific theorizing, the theoretical terms of natural science refer to real physical entities and describe their attributes and comportments. For example, the "electron spin" of atomic physics refers to a behavioral characteristic of a real, albeit unobservable, object—and electron. According to this currently fashionable theory, the declarations of science are—or will eventually become—factually true generalizations about the actual behavior of objects that exist in the world. Is this "convergent realism" a tenable position?

It is quite clear that it is not. There is clearly insufficient warrant for and little plausibility to the claim that the world indeed is as our science claims it to be—that we've got matters altogether right, so that *our* science is *correct* science and offers the definitive "last word" on the issues. We really cannot reasonably suppose that science as it now stands affords the real truth as regards its creatures-of-theory.

One of the clearest lessons of the history of science is that where scientific knowledge is concerned, further discovery does not just *supplement* but generally *emends* our prior information. Accordingly, we have little alternative but to take the humbling view that the incompleteness of our purported knowledge about the world entails its potential incorrectness as well. It is now a matter not simply of *gaps* in the structure of our knowledge, or errors of omission. There is no realistic alternative but to suppose that we face a situation of real *flaws* as well, of errors of commission. This aspect of the matter endows incompleteness with an import far graver than meets the eye on first view.[11]

Realism equates the paraphernalia of natural science with the domain of what actually exists. But this equation would work only if science, as it stands, has actually "got it right." And this is something we are surely not inclined—and certainly not *entitled*—to claim. We must recognize that the deliverances of science are bound to a methodology of theoretical triangulations from the data which binds them inseparably to the "state of the art" of technological sophistication in data acquisition and handling.

The supposition that the theoretical commitments of our science actually describes the world is viable only if made *provisionally*, in the spirit of "doing the best we can now do, in the current state of the art" and giving our best estimate of the matter. The step of reification is always to be taken qualifiedly, subject to a mental reservation of presumptive revisability. We do and must recognize that we cannot blithely equate *our* theories with *the* truth. We do and must realize that the declarations of science are inherently fallible and that we can only "accept" them with a certain tentatively, subject to a clear realization that they may need to be corrected or even abandoned.

These considerations must inevitably constrain and condition our attitude toward the natural mechanisms envisaged in the science of the day. We certainly do not—or should not—want to reify (hypostasize) the "theoretical entities" of current science, to say flatly and unqualifiedly that the contrivances of *our* present-day science correctly depict the furniture of the real world. We do not—or at any rate, given the realities of the case, should not—want to adopt categorically the ontological implications of scientific theorizing in just exactly the state-of-the-art configurations presently in hand. Scientific fallibilism precludes the claim that what we purport to be scientific knowledge is in fact *real* knowledge, and accordingly blocks the path to a scientific realism that maintains that the furnishings of the real world are exactly as our science states them to be. Scientific theorizing is always inconclusive.

Convergent scientific realism of the Peircean type, which pivots on the assumption of an ultimately complete and correct scientific theory (let alone those stronger versions of realism that hinge on our ability to arrive at recognizably true scientific theories), is in deep difficulty. For we have little choice but to deem science's grasps of "the real truth of things" as both tentative and imperfect.

According to one expositor, the scientific realist "maintains that if a theory has scientific merit, then we are thereby justified in concluding that . . . the theoretical entities characterized by the theory really do exist."[12] But this sort of position encounters insuperable difficulties. Phlogiston, caloric, and the luminiferous aether all had scientific merit in their day, but this did not establish their existence. Why, then, should things be all that different with us? Why should *our* "scientific merit" now suddenly assure actual existence? What matters for real existence is clearly (and only) the issue of truth itself, and not the issue of what is *thought* to be true at some particular stage of scientific history. And here problems arise. For its changeability is a fact *about* science that is as inductively well established as any theory of science itself. Science is not a static system but a dynamic process.

We must accordingly maintain a clear distinction between *our conception of reality* and *reality as it really is*. Given the equation,

Our (conception of) reality = the condition of things as seen from the standpoint of "our *putative* truth" (= the truth as we see it from the vantage point of the science of the day)

we realize full well that there is little justification for holding that our present-day science indeed describes reality and depicts the world as it really is. In our heart of hearts, then, our attitude toward our science is one of *guarded* affirmation. We realize that there is a decisive difference between what science *accomplishes* and what it *endeavors* to accomplish.

The world *that we describe* is one thing, the world, *as we describe it* is another, and they would coincide only if our descriptions were totally correct—something that we are certainly not in a position to claim. The world-as-known is a thing of our contrivance, and artifact we devise on our own terms. Even if the "data" uniquely determined a corresponding picture of reality, and did not underdetermine the theoretical constructions we base upon them (as they always to), the fact remains that altered circumstances lead to altered bodies of "data." Our recognition of the fact that the world-picture of science is ever changing blocks our taking the view that it is ever *correct*.

Accordingly, we cannot say that the world *is* such that the paraphernalia of our science actually exist as such. Given the necessity of recognizing the claims of our science to be tentative and provisional, one cannot justifiably take the stance that it depicts reality. At best, one can say that it affords an *estimate* of it, an estimate that will presumably stand in need of eventual revision and whose creatures-of-theory may in the final analysis not be real at all. This feature of science must crucially constrain our attitude toward its deliverances. Depiction is in this regard a matter of intent rather than one of accomplishment. Correctness in the characterization of nature is achieved not by *our* science but only by *perfected* or *ideal* science—only by that (ineradicably hypothetical!) state of science in which the cognitive goals of the scientific enterprise are fully and definitively realized. There is no plausible alternative to the view that reality is depicted by *ideal* (or perfected or "complete") science, and not by the real science of the day. But, of course, it is this latter science that is the only one we've actually got—now or ever.

A viable scientific realism must therefore turn not on what *our* science takes the world to be like but on what *ideal or perfected* science takes the world to be like. The thesis that "science describes the real world" must be looked upon as a matter of intent rather than as an accomplished fact, of aspiration rather than achievement, of the ideal rather than the real state of things. Scientific realism is a viable position only with respect to that idealized science which, as we full well realize, we do not now have—regardless of the "now" at issue. We cannot justifiably be scientific realists. Or rather, ironically, we can be so only in an idealistic manner—namely, with respect to an "ideal science" that we can never actually claim to possess.

The posture of scientific realism—at any rate, or a duly qualified sort—is nevertheless built into the very goal-structure of science. The characteristic task of science, the definitive mission of the enterprise, is to respond to our basic interest in getting the best answers we can to our questions about the world. On the traditional view of the matter, its question-resolving concern is the raison d'être of the project—to celebrate any final victories. It is thus useful to draw a clear distinction between a *realism of intent* and a *realism of achievement*. We are certainly not in a position to claim that science as we have it achieves a characterization of reality. Still, science remains unabashedly realistic in *intent* or *aspiration*. Its *aim* is unquestionably to answer our questions about the world *correctly* and to describe the world "as it actually is." The orientation of science is factual and objective: it is concerned with establishing the *true* facts about the *real* world. The theories of physics purport to describe the actual operation of real entities; with those Nobel prizes awarded for discovering the electron, the neutron, the pi meson, and anti-protron, the quark, and so on, we intended to recognize an enlargement of our understanding of nature, not to reward the contriving of plausible fictions or the devising of clever ways of relating observations.

The language of science is descriptively committal. At the semantical level of the content of its assertions, science makes firm claims as to how things stand in the world. A realism of intent or aspiration is built into science because of the genesis of its questions. The factually descriptive status of science is ultimately grounded in just this erotetic continuity of its issues with those of "prescientific" everyday life. We begin at the prescientific level of the paradigmatic realities of our prosaic everyday-life experience—the things, occurrences, and processes of our everyday world. The very reason for being of our scientific paraphernalia is to resolve our questions about this real world of our everyday-life experience. Given that the teleology of the scientific enterprise is rooted in the "real world" that provides the stage of our being and action, we are committed *within its framework*, to take the realistic view of its mechanisms. Natural science does not address itself to some world-abstracted realm of its own. Its concern is with this familiar "real world" of ours in which we live and breathe and have our being—however differently science may characterize it. While science may fall short in performance, nevertheless in aspiration and endeavor it is unequivocally committed to the project of modeling "the real world," for in this way alone could it realize its constituting mandate of answering our questions as to how things work in the world.

Our position, then, is one not of skepticism but of realism—in two senses: (1) it is realistic about our capabilities of recognizing that here, as elsewhere, we are dealing with the efforts of an imperfect creature to do the best it can in the circumstances; and (2) it recognizes the mind-transcendent reality of a "real world" that our own best efforts in the cognitive sphere can only manage to domesticate rather imperfectly. We do, and always must, recognize that no matter how far we manage to extend the frontiers of natural science, there is more to be done. Within a setting of vast complexity, reality outruns our cognitive reach; there is more to this complex world of ours than lies—now or ever—within our ken. Reality is just too many-faceted for its cognitive domestication by us to be more than very partial.[13]

Notes

1. One possible misunderstanding must be blocked at this point. To learn about nature, we must interact with it. And so, to determine some feature of an object, we may have to make some impact upon it that would perturb its otherwise obtaining condition. (The indeterminacy principle of quantum theory affords a well-known reminder of this.) It should be clear that this matter of physical interaction for data-acquisition is not contested in the ontological indifference thesis here at issue.

2. Note that this is independent of the question "Would we ever want to do so? Do we ever want to answer all those predictive questions about ourselves and our

environment, or are we more comfortable in the condition in which "ignorance is bliss"?

3. S. W. Hawking, "Is the End in Sight for Theoretical Physics?" *Physics Bulletin*, vol. 32 (1981), pp. 15-17.

4. On further aspects of cognitive pediction see the author's *Predicting the Future* (Albany: State University of New York Press, 1997).

5. This sentiment was abroad among physicists of the *fin de siècle* era of 1890-1900. (See Lawrence Badash, "The Completeness of Nineteenth-Century Science," *Isis*, vol. 63 [1972], pp. 48-58.) and such sentiments are coming back into fashion today. See S. W. Hawking, "Is the End in Sight for Theoretical Physics?" (op. cit.)

6. See Eber Jeffrey, "Nothing Left to Invent," *Journal of the Patent Office Society*, vol. 22 (July 1940), pp. 479-81.

7. See the author's *Peirce's Philosophy of Science* (Notre Dame, IN: University of Notre Dame Press, 1978).

8. Note, however, that to say that some ideal can be legitimated by practical considerations is not to say that all ideals must be legitimated in this way.

9. Immanuel Kant, *Critique of Practical Reason*, p. 122 [Akad.]

10. For some recent discussions of scientific realism, see Wilfred Sellars, *Science Perception and Reality* (London: Humanities Press, 1963); E. McKinnon, ed., *The Problem of Scientific Realism* (New York: Appleton-Century-Crofts, 1972); Rom Harré, *Principles of Scientific Thinking* (Chicago: University of Chicago Press, 1970); and Frederick Suppe, ed., *The Structure of Scientific Theories*, 2nd, ed. (Urbana: University of Illinois Press, 1977).

11. Some of the issues of this discussion are developed at greater length in the author's *Methodological Pragmatism* (Oxford: Oxford University Press, 1977), *Scientific Progress* (Oxford: Oxford University Press, 1979), and *Cognitive Systematization* (Oxford: Oxford University Press, 1979).

12. Keith Lehrer, "Review of *Science, Perception, and Reality* by Wilfred Sellars," *The Journal of Philosophy*, vol. 63 (1966), pp. 269.

13. Some of the themes of this chapter are also treated in the author's *Empirical Inquiry* (Totowa, NJ: Rowman & Littlefield, 1982) and *Scientific Realism* (Dordrecht: D. Reidel, 1987).

7

Extraterrestrial Science

(1) The science of another, astronomically remote, alien civilization is likely to be very different from ours. (2) A critique of the uniformitarian thesis that since there is only one world which all intelligent beings share, there is bound to be only one uniform science. Even though there might well be enormously many intelligent civilizations in space, the probability that any have our scientific posture is negligibly small. (3) Cognition is an evolutionary product that is bound to attune its practitioners to the local peculiarities of their particular ecological niche in the world-order. (6) We must assume that their intellectual journey of reasoned inquiry will take them in an altogether different direction. The world's inherent complexity means that science is limited by the very fact of being our *science.*

1. The Potential Diversity of "Science"

We come here to a yet very different aspect of the world's cognitive complexity. For when we address the issues of complexity for cognition, the question also arises: for whose cognition? Here the natural tendency is to answer *for us humans*. But of course one need not be so parochial about it. There is, after all, also the prospect of very different sorts of intelligent beings in the world. And there is every possibility that nature will present very different sorts of vistas to different sorts of perceivers and that other sorts of intelligent beings equipped with very different sorts of perceptual and cognitive resources will conceptualize the world in ways very different from ourselves. It not only can but must be supposed that among the features of the world's complexity there is also this, that physical nature will present itself differently to whatever different kinds of intelligent creatures it may bring to realization.

To what extent would the *functional equivalent* of natural science built up by the inquiring intelligences of an astronomically remote civilization be bound to resemble our science? In reflecting on this question and its ramifications, one soon comes to realize that there is an enormous potential for diversity.

To begin with, the *machinery of formulation* used in expressing their science might be altogether different. Specifically, their mathematics might be very unlike ours. Their dealings with quantity might be entirely anumerical—purely comparative, for example, rather than quantitative. Especially if their environment is not amply endowed with solid objects or stable structures congenial to measurement—if, for example, they were jellyfish-like creatures swimming about in a soupy sea—their "geometry" could be something rather strange, largely topological, say, and geared to flexible structures rather than fixes sizes or shapes. Digital thinking might be undeveloped, while certain sorts of analogue reasoning might be highly refined. Or, again, an alien civilization might, like the ancient Greeks, have "Euclidean" geometry without analysis. In any case, given that the mathematical mechanisms at their disposal could be very different from ours, it is clear that their description of nature in mathematical terms could also be very different. (Not necessarily truer or falser, but just different.)

Secondly, the *orientation* of the science of an alien civilization might be very different. All their efforts might conceivably be devoted to the social sciences—to developing highly sophisticated analogues of psychology and sociology, for example. In particular, if the intelligent aliens were a diffuse assemblage of units comprising wholes in ways that allow of overlap,[1] then the role of social concepts might become so paramount for them that nature would throughout be viewed in fundamentally social categories, with those aggregates we think of as physical structures contemplated by them in social terms.

Then, too, their natural science might deploy *procedural mechanisms* very different from ours. Communicating by some sort of "telepathy" based upon variable odors or otherwise "exotic" signals, they might devise a complex theory of emphatic thought-wave transmittal through an ideaferous aether. Again, the aliens might scan nature very differently. Electromagnetic phenomena might lie altogether outside the ken of alien life-forms; if their environment does not afford them lodestone and electrical storms, the occasion to develop electromagnetic theory might never arise. The course of scientific development tends to flow in the channel of practical interests. A society of porpoises might lack crystallography but develop a very sophisticated hydrodynamics; one comprised of mole-like creatures might never dream of developing optics or astronomy. One's language and thought processes are bound to be closely geared to the world as one experiences it. As is illustrated by the difficulties we ourselves experience in bringing the language of everyday experience to bear on subatomic phenomena, our concepts are ill-attuned to facets of nature different in scale or structure from our own. We can hardly expect a "science" that reflects such parochial preoccupations to be a universal fixture.

The interests of creatures shaped under the remorseless pressure of evolutionary adaptations to very different—and endlessly variable—environmental conditions might well be oriented in directions very different from anything that is familiar to us.

Laws are detectable regularities in nature. But detection will of course vary drastically with the mode of observations—that is, with the sort of resources that different creatures have at their disposal to do their detecting. Everything depends on how nature pushes back on our senses and their instrumental extensions. Even if we detect everything we can, we will not have got hold of everything available to others. And the converse is equally true. The laws that we (or anybody else) manage to formulate will depend crucially on one's place within nature—on how one is connected into its wiring diagram, so to speak.

A comparison of the "science" of different civilizations here on earth suggests that it is not an outlandish hypothesis to suppose that the very *topics* of alien science might differ dramatically from those of ours. In our own case, for example, the fact that we live on the surface of the earth (unlike whales, the fact that we have eyes (unlike worms) and thus can *see* the heavens, the fact that we are so situated that the seasonal positions of heavenly bodies are intricately connected with agriculture—all these facts are clearly connected with the development of astronomy. The fact that those distant creatures would experience nature in ways very different from ourselves means that they can be expected to raise very different sorts of questions. Indeed, the mode of emplacement within nature of alien inquirers might be so different as to focus their attention on entirely different aspects of constituents of the cosmos. If the world is sufficiently complex and multifaceted, they might concentrate upon aspects of their environment that mean nothing to us, with the result that their natural science is oriented in directions very different from ours.[2]

Moreover, the *conceptualization* of an alien science might be very different, for we must reckon with the theoretical possibility that a remote civilization might operate with a drastically different system of concepts in its cognitive dealings with nature. Different cultures and different intellectual traditions, to say nothing of different sorts of creatures, are bound to describe and explain their experience—their world as they conceive it—in terms of concepts and categories of understanding substantially different from ours. They would diverge radically with respect to what the Germans call their *Denkmittel*—the conceptual; instruments they employ in thought about the facts (or purported facts) of the world. They could, accordingly, be said to operate with different conceptual schemes, with different conceptual tools used to "make sense" of experience—to characterize, describe, and explain the items that figure in the world as they view it. The taxonomic and explanatory mechanisms by means of which their cognitive business is transacted might differ so radically from ours that intellectual contact with them would be difficult or impossible.

Epistemologists have often said things to the effect that people whose experience of the world is substantially different from our own are bound to conceive of it in very different terms. Sociologists, anthropologists, and linguists talk in much the same terms, and philosophers of science have recently also come to say the same sorts of things. According to Thomas Kuhn, for example, scientists who work within different scientific traditions—and thus operate with different descriptive and explanatory "paradigms"—actually "live in different worlds."[3]

It is (or should be) clear that there is no simple, unique, ideally adequate concept-framework for "describing the world." The botanist, horticulturists, landscape gardener, farmer, and painter will operate from diverse cognitive "points of view" to describe one selfsame vegetable garden. It is merely mythology to think that the "phenomena of nature" can lend themselves to only one correct style of descriptive and explanatory conceptualizations. There is surely no "ideal scientific language" that has a privileged status for the characterization of reality. Different sorts of creatures are bound to make use of different conceptual schemes for the representation of their experience. To insist on the ultimate uniqueness of science is to succumb to "the myth of the God's-eye view." Different cognitive perspectives are possible, no one of them more adequate or more correct than any other independently of the aims and purposes of their users.

Supporting considerations for this position have been advanced from very different points of view. One example is a *Gedankenexperiment* suggested by Georg Simmel in the last century, which envisaged an entirely different sort of cognitive being: intelligent and actively inquiring creatures (animals, say, or beings from outer space) whose experiential modes are quite different from our own.[4] Their senses respond rather differently to physical influences: they are relatively insensitive, say, to heat and light, but substantially sensitized to various electromagnetic phenomena. Such intelligent creatures, Simmel held, could plausibly be supposed to have operated within a largely different framework of empirical concepts and categories; the events and objects of the world of their experience might have been very different from those of our own: their phenomenological predicates, for example, might have altogether variant descriptive domains. In a similar vein, Williams James wrote:

> Were we lobsters, or bees, it might be that our organization would have led to our using quite different modes from these [actual ones] of apprehending our experiences. It *might* be too (we cannot dogmatically deny this) that such categories unimaginable by us to-day, would have proved on the whole as serviceable for handling our experiences mentally as those we actually use.[5]

The science of a different civilization would inevitably be closely tied to the particular pattern of their interaction with nature as funneled through the particular course of their evolutionary adjustment to their specific environment. The "forms of sensibility" of radically different beings (to invoke Kant's useful idea) are likely to be radically diverse from ours. The direct chemical analysis of environmental materials might prove highly useful, and bioanalytic techniques akin to our senses of taste and smell could be very highly developed, providing them with environmentally oriented "experiences" of a very different sort.

The constitution of alien inquirers—physical, biological, and social—thus emerges as crucial for science. It would be bound to condition the agenda of questions and the instrumentalities for their resolution—to fix what is seen as interesting, important, relevant, and significant. Because it determines what is seen as an appropriate question and what is judged as an admissible solution, the cognitive posture of the inquirers must be expected to play a crucial role in shaping the course of scientific inquiry itself.

To clarify this idea of a conceptually different science, it helps to cast the issue in temporal rather than spatial terms. The descriptive characterization of *alien* science is a project rather akin in its difficulty to that of describing our own *future* science. It is a key fact of life that progress in science is a process of *ideational* innovation that always places certain developments outside the intellectual horizons of earlier workers. The very concepts we think in terms of become available only in the course of scientific discovery itself. Like the science of the remote future, the science of remote aliens must be presumed to be such that we really could not achieve intellectual access to it on the basis of our own position in the cognitive scheme of things. Just as the technology of a more advanced civilization would be bound to strike us as magic, so its science would be bound to strike us as incomprehensible gibberish—until we had learned it "from the ground up." They might (just barely) be able to *teach* it to us, but they could not *explain* it to us by transposing it into our terms.

The most characteristic and significant difference between one conceptual scheme and another arises when the one scheme is committed to something the other does not envisage at all—something that lies outside the conceptual range of the other. A typical case is that of the stance of Cicero's thought-world with regard to questions of quantum electrodynamics. The Romans of classical antiquity did not hold *different* views on these issues; they held no view at all about them. This whole set of relevant considerations remained outside their conceptual repertoire. The diversified history of *our* terrestrial science gives one some minuscule inkling of the vast range of possibilities along these lines.

The "science" of different civilizations may well, like Galenic and Pasteurian medicine, simply *change the subject* in key respects so as to no longer "talk about the same things," but deal with materials (e.g., humors and bacteria, respectively) of which the other takes no cognizance at all. The difference in regard to "conceptual scheme" between modern and Galenic medicine is not that the modern physician has a different theory of the operation of the four humors from his Galenic counterpart but that modern medicine has *abandoned* the four humors, and not that the Galenic physician says different things about bacteria and viruses but that he says *nothing* about them.

As long as the fundamental categories for the characterization of thought—the modes of spatiality and temporality, of structural description, functional connection, and explanatory rationalization—are not seen as necessary features of intelligence as such, but as evolved cognitive adaptations to particular contingently constituted modes of emplacement in and interaction with nature, there will be no reason to expect uniformity. Sociologists of knowledge tell us that even for us humans here on earth, our Western science is but one of many competing ways of conceptualizing the world's processes. And when one turns outward toward space at large, the prospects of diversity become virtually endless. It is a highly problematic contention even that beings constituted as we are and located in an environment such as ours must inevitably describe and explain natural phenomena in our terms. And with differently constituted beings, the basis of differentiation is amplified enormously. Our minds are the information-processing mechanisms of an organism interacting with a particular environment via certain particular senses (natural endowments, hardware) and certain culturally evolved methods (cultural endowments, software). With different sorts of beings, these resources would differ profoundly—and so would the cognitive products that would flow from their employment.

The more one reflects on the matter, the more firmly one is led to the realization that our particular human conception of the issues of science is something parochial, because we are physically, perceptually, and cognitively limited and conditioned by our specific situation within nature. Given intelligent beings with a physical and cognitive nature profoundly different from ours, one simply cannot assert with confidence what the natural science of such creatures would be like.

2. The One World, One Science Argument

One writer on extraterrestrial intelligence poses the question, "What can we talk about with our remote friends?" and answers with the remark, "We have a lot in common. We have mathematics in common, and physics, and astronomy."[6] Another maintains that "we may fail to enjoy their music, understand their poetry, or approve their ideals; but we can talk about matters of practical and scientific concern.":[7] But is it all that simple? With respect to his hypothetical Planetarians, the ingenious Christiaan Huygens wrote, three centuries ago:

> Well, but allowing these Planetarians some sort of reason, must it needs be the same with ours? Why truly I think 'tis, and must be so; whether we consider it as applied to Justice and Morality, or exercised in the Principles and Foundations of Science. . . . For the aim and design of the Creator is every where the preservation and safety of his Creatures. Now when such a reason as we are masters of, is necessary for the preservation of Life, and promoting of Society (a thing that they be not without, as we shall show) would it not be strange that the Planetarians should have such a perverse sort of Reason given them, as would necessarily destroy and confound what it was design'd to maintain and defend? But allowing Morality and Passions with those Gentlemen to be somewhat different from ours, . . . yet still there would be no doubt, but that in the search after Truth, in judging of the consequences of things, in reasoning, particularly in that form which belongs to Magnitude or Quantity about which their Geometry (if they have such a thing) is emplo'd, there would be no doubt I say, but that their Reason here must be exactly the same, and go the same way to work with ours, and that what's true in one part will hold true over the whole Universe; so that all the difference must lie in the degree of Knowledge, which will be proportional to the Genius and Capacity of the inhabitants.[8]

With the exception of a timely shift from a theological to a natural-selectionist rationale, this analysis is close to the sort of thing one hears advanced today.

It is tempting to reason: "Since there is only one nature, only one science of nature is possible." Yet, on closer scrutiny, this reasoning becomes highly problematic. Above all, it fails to reckon with the fact that while there indeed is only one world, nevertheless very different *thought-worlds* can be at issue in the elaborations of a "science."

It is surely naive to think that because one single object is in question, its description must issue in one uniform result. This view ignores the crucial impact of the describer's intellectual orientation. Minds with different concerns and interests and with different experiential backgrounds can deal with the selfsame items in ways that yield wholly disjoint and disparate result because different features of the thing are being addressed. The *things* are the same, but their significance is altogether different.

Perhaps it seems plausible to argue thus: "Common problems constrain common solutions. Intelligent alien civilizations have in common with us the problem of cognitive accommodation to a shared world. Natural science as we know it is *our* solution to this problem.

Therefore, it is likely to be *theirs* as well." But this tempting argument founders on its second premise. The problem-situation confronted by extraterrestrials is *not* common with ours. Their situation must be presumed substantially different exactly because they live in a significantly different environment and come equipped with significantly different resources—physical and intellectual alike. The common problems, common solutions line does not work: to presuppose a common problem is already to beg the question.

Science is always the result of *inquiry* into nature, and this is inevitably a matter of a *transaction* or *interaction* in which nature is but one party and the inquiry beings another. We must expect alien beings to question nature in ways very different from our own. On the basis of an *interactionist* model, there is no reason to think that the sciences of different civilizations will exhibit anything more than the roughest sorts of family resemblance.

Our alien colleagues scan nature for regularities, using (at any rate, to begin with) the sensors provided to them by their evolutionary heritage. They note, record, and transmit those regularities that they find to be useful or interesting, and then develop their inquiries by theoretical triangulation from this basis. Now, this is clearly going to make for a course of development that closely gears their science to their particular situation—their biological endowment ("their sensors"), their cultural heritage ("what is pragmatically useful"). Where these key parameters differ, we must expect that the course of scientific development will differ as well.

Admittedly, there is only one universe, and its laws and materials are, far as we can tell, the same everywhere. We share this common universe with all life-forms. However radically we differ in other respects (in particular, those relating to environment, to natural endowments, and to style or civilization), we have a common background of cosmic evolution and a common heritage of natural laws. And so, if intelligent aliens investigate nature at all, they will investigate the same nature we ourselves do. All this can be agreed. But the fact remains that the corpus of scientific information—ours or anyone's—is an ideational construction. And the sameness of the object of contemplation does nothing to guarantee the sameness of ideas about it. It is all too familiar a fact that even where only human observers are at issue, very different constructions are often placed upon "the same" occurrences. As is clearly shown by the rival interpretations of different psychological schools—to say nothing of the court testimony of rival "experts" —there need be little uniformity in the conceptions held about one selfsame object from different "perspectives of consideration." The fact that all intelligent beings inhabit the same world does not countervail the no less momentous fact that we inhabit very different ecological niches within it, engendering very different sorts of modus operandi.

The universality and intersubjectivity of our science, its repeatability and investigator-independence, still leave matters at the level of *human* science. As C. S. Peirce was wont to insist, the aim of scientific inquiry is to allay *our* doubts—to resolve the sorts of questions we ourselves deem worth posing. Different sorts of beings might well ask very different sorts of questions.

No one who has observed how very differently the declarations of a single text (the Bible, say, or the dialogues of Plato) have been interpreted and understood over the centuries—even by people of a common culture heritage—can be hopeful that that study of a common object by different civilizations must be lead to a uniform result. Yet, such textual analogies are oversimple and misleading, because the scientific study of nature is not a matter of decoding a preexisting text. There just is not one fixed basic text—the changeless "book of nature writ large"—which different civilizations can decipher in different degrees. Like other books, it is to some extent a mirror: what looks out depends on who looks in.

The development of a "science"—a specific codification of the laws of nature—always requires as input some inquirer-supplied element of determination. The result of such an interaction depends crucially on the contribution from both sides—from nature and from the intelligences that interact with it. A kind of "chemistry" is at work in which nature provides only one input and the inquirers themselves provide another— one that can massively and dramatically affect the outcome in such a way that we cannot disentangle the respective contributions of nature and the inquirer. Things cannot of themselves dictate the significance that an active intelligence can attach to them. Human organisms are essentially similar, but there is not much similarity between the medicine of the ancient Hindus and that of the ancient Greeks.

After all, throughout the earlier stages of man's intellectual history, different human civilizations developed their "natural sciences" in substantially different ways. The shift to an extraterrestrial setting is bound to amplify this diversity. The "science" of an alien civilization may be far more remote from ours than the "language" of our cousin the dolphin is remote from our language. We must face, however reluctantly, the fact that on a cosmic scale the "hard" physical sciences have something of the same cultural relativity that one encounters with the "softer" social sciences on a terrestrial basis.

There is no categorical assurance that intelligent creatures will *think* alike in a common world, any more than that they will *act* alike—that is, there is no reason why *cognitive* adaption should be any more uniform than *behavioral* adaption. Thought, after all, is simply a kind of action; and as the action of a creature reflects its biological heritage, so does its mode of thought.

These considerations point to a clear lesson. Different civilizations composed of different sorts of creatures must be expected to create diverse "sciences." Though inhabiting the same physical universe with us, and subject to the same sorts of fundamental regularities, they must be expected to create as cognitive artifacts different depictions of nature, reflecting their different modes of emplacement within it.

Each inquiring civilization must be expected to produce its own, perhaps ever changing, cognitive products—all more or less adequate in their own ways but with little if any actual overlap in conceptual content.

Natural science—broadly construed as inquiry into the ways of nature—is something that is in principle endlessly plastic. Its development will trace out a historical course closely geared to the specific capacities, interests, environment, and opportunities of the creatures that develop it. We are deeply mistaken if we think of it as a process that must follow a route generally parallel to ours and issue in a roughly comparable product. It would be grossly unimaginative to think that either the journey or the destination must be the same—or even substantially similar.

Factors such as capacities, requirements, interests, and course of development are bound to affect the shape and substance of the science and technology of any particular space-time region. Unless we narrow our intellectual horizons in a parochially anthropomorphic way, we must be prepared to recognize the great likelihood that the "science" and "technology" of a remote civilization would be something *very* different from science and technology as we know it. Our human sort of natural science may well be sui generis, adjusted to and coordinated with a being of our physical constitution, inserted into the orbit of the world's processes and history in our sort of way. It seems that in science, as in other areas of human endeavor, we are prisoners of the thought-world that our biological and social and intellectual heritage affords us.

Even a superficial scrutiny of the terrestrial situation suffices to show that the development of natural science is certainly not inevitable for cognitive beings but is closely linked to their internal constitution and their cultural orientation. And given the *immense* diversity to be expected among the various modes of "science" and "technology," the number of extraterrestrial civilizations possessing a science and technology that are duly consonant and contiguous with ours— and, in particular, oriented toward the mathematical laws of the electromagnetic spectrum—must be judged to be very small.

It must accordingly be recognized that sciences can vary (1) In their formal mechanisms of *formulation*—their "mathematics"; (2) in their *conceptualization* that is, in the kinds of explanatory and descriptive concepts they bring to bear; and (3) in their *orientation* toward the manifold pressures of nature, reflecting the varying "interest"-directions of their developers. While "science" as such is clearly not anthropocentric, science *as we have it*—the only "science" that we ourselves know—is a specifically human artifact that must be expected to reflect to a significant degree the particular characteristics of its makers. Consequently, the prospect that an alien "science"-possessing civilizations has a *science* that we would acknowledge (if sufficiently informed) as representing the same general inquiry as that in which we ourselves are engaged seems extremely implausible. The possibility that *their* science and technology are "sufficiently similar" in orientation and character to be substantively proximate to *ours* must be viewed as extremely remote.

3. First Principles

Diverse organisms have diverse requirements; diverse requirements engender diverse technologies; diverse technologies make for diverse styles of science. If a civilization of intelligent aliens develops a science at all, it seems reasonable to expect that they will develop it in another direction altogether and produce something that we, if we could come to understand it at all, would regard as simply disjoint in

content—though presumably not in intent—from science as we ourselves cultivate it.

There just is no unique itinerary of scientific/technological development that different civilizations travel in common with mere differences in speed or in staying power (not withstanding the penchant of
astrophysicists for the neat plotting of numerical "degrees of development" against time in the evolution of planetary civilizations).[9] In
cognitive and even in "scientific" evolution, we are not dealing with a
single railway line but with a complex network leading to mutually
remote destinations. Even as cosmic evolution involves a spatial red
shift that carries different star systems ever farther from each other, so
cognitive evolution may well involve an intellectual red shift that
carries different civilizations into thought-worlds ever more remote
from each other.

The literature created by extraterrestrial-intelligence enthusiasts is
pervaded by the haunting worry: "Where is everybody?" "Why haven't
we heard from them?" Are they simply too distant—or perhaps too
cautious[10] or too detached?[11] Our present discussion offers yet another line of response: they are simply too busy doing their own thing.
Radio communication is ours, theirs is something very, *very* different.
If alien civilizations inhabit alien thought-worlds, then this lack of
intellectual communion might well explain the lack of physical communication.

The rationale or our analysis emerges from the data of table 7.1.
What matters here is not the numerical detail but the general structure.
For these figures interestingly embody the familiar situation that as
one moves through successive stages of increasing complexity, one
encounters a greater scope for diversity: further layers of system complexity provide for an ever widening spectrum of possible states and
conditions. (The more fundamental the system, the narrower its correlative range of alternatives; the more complex, the wider.) If each
unit ("letter," "cell," "atom") can be configured in ten ways, then each
ordered group of ten such units ("words," "organs," "molecules") can
be configured in 10^{10} ways, and each complex of ten such groups
("sentences," "organisms," "objects") in $(10^{10})^{10} = 10^{100}$ ways. Thus
even if only a small fraction of what is realizable in theory is realizable in nature, any increase in organizational complexity will nevertheless be accompanied by an enormous amplification of possibilities.

To be sure, the specific particulars of the various computations that

TABLE 7.1
Conditions for the Development of Science

Planets of sufficient size for potential habitation	10^{22}
Fraction thereof with the right astrophysics for a temperature location	10^{-1}
Fraction thereof with the right chemistry for life-support	10^{-1}
Fraction thereof with the right biochemistry for the actual emergence of life	10^{-2}
Fraction there of with the right biology and psychology for the evolution of intelligence	10^{-4}
Fraction there of with the right sociology for developing a culture with a duly constructed "technology" and "science"	10^{-7}
Fraction thereof with the right epistemology for developing science as we know it	10^{-7}
Product of all these fractions	10^{-22}

comprise the quantitative thread of the discussion cannot be given much credence. But their general tendency nevertheless conveys an important lesson. For people frequently seem inclined to reason as follows:

> There are, after all, an immense number of planetary objects running about in the heavens. And proper humility requires us to recognize that there is nothing all that special about the Earth. If it can evolve life and intelligence and civilization and science, then so can other planets. And given that there are so many other runners in the race, we must assume that—even though we cannot see them in the cosmic darkness—some of them have got ahead of us in the race.

As one recent writer formulates this familiar argument: "Since man's existence on the earth occupies but an instant in cosmic time, surely intelligent life has progressed far beyond our level on some of these 100,000,000 (habitable) planets [in our galaxy]."[12] Such reasoning overlooks the critical probabilistic dimension. Admittedly, cosmic locales are very numerous. But when probabilities get to be very small, they will offset this fact. (No matter how massive N is, there is always that diminutive $1/N$ able to countervail it.) Even though there are an immense number of solar systems, and thus a staggering number of sizable planets (some 10^{22} by current estimates), nevertheless, a very substantial number of conditions must be met for "science" (as we understand it) to arise. The astrophysical, physical, chemical, biological, psychological, sociological, and epistemological parameters must all be in proper adjustment. There must be habitability, and life, and intelligence, and culture, and technology, and a technologically geared mode of inquiry and an appropriate subject-matter orientation of this intellectual product, and so on. By this reckoning, the number of civilization that possess a technologized science as we comprehend it is clearly not going to be very substantial: it might, in fact, be strikingly close to 1.

The developmental path from intelligence to science is strewn with substantial obstacles. Matters must be propitious not just as regards the physics, chemistry, biochemistry, evolutionary biology, and cognitive psychology of the situation; the sociological requisites for the evolution of science as a culture artifact must also be met. Economic conditions, social organization, and cultural orientation must all be properly adjusted before the move from intelligence to science can be accomplished. For scientific inquiry to evolve and flourish, there must, in the first place, be cultural institutions whose development requires specific economic conditions and favorable social organizations. And terrestrial experience suggests that such conditions for the social evolution of a developed culture are by no means always present where intelligence is. At this point, we would do well to recall that of the hundreds of human civilizations evolved here on earth, only one, the Mediterranean/European, managed to inaugurate natural science as we understand it. The successful transition from intelligence to science is certainly not a sure thing.

A great many turnings must go all right en route for science of a quality comparable to ours to develop. Each step along the way is one of finite (and often small) probability. And to reach the final destination, all these probabilities must be multiplied together, yielding a quantity that will be very small indeed. Even if there were only twelve turning points along this developmental route, each involving a chance of successful eventuation that is, on average, no worse than one in one hundred, the chance of an overall success would be diminutively small, corresponding to an aggregate success-probability of merely 10^{-24}.

George G. Simpson has rightly stressed the many chance twists and turns that lie along the evolutionary road, insisting that

the fossil record shows very clearly that there is no central line leading steadily, in a goal-directed way, from a protozoan to man. Instead there has been continual and extremely intricate branching, and whatever course we follow through the branches there are repeated changes both in the rate and in the direction of evolution. Man is the end of one ultimate twig. . . . Even slight changes in earlier parts of the history would have profound cumulative effects on all descendent organisms through the succeeding millions of generations. . . . The existing species would surely have been different if the start had been different, and if any stage of the histories of organisms and their environments had been different. Thus the existence of our present species depends on a very precise sequence of causative events through some two billion years or more. Man cannot be an exception to this rule. If the causal chain had been different, *homo sapiens* would not exist.[13]

The workings of evolution—be it of life or intelligence or culture or technology or science—are always the product of a great number of individually unlikely events. Any evolutionary process involves putting to nature a sequence of questions whose successive resolution produces a series reminiscent of the game "Twenty Questions," sweeping over a possibility-spectrum of awesomely large proportions. The result eventually reached lies along a route that traces out one particular contingent path within a possibility-space that encompasses an ever divergent fanning out of alternatives as each step opens up yet further eventuations. an evolutionary process is a very iffy proposition—a complex labyrinth in which a great many twists and turns in the road must be taken aright for matters to end up as they do.

If things had not turned out suitably at each stage, we would not be here to tell the tale. The many contingencies on the long route of cosmic, galactic, solar-system, biochemical, biological, social, cultural, and cognitive evolution have all turned out right; the innumerable obstacles have all been surmounted. In retrospect, it all looks easy and inevitable. The innumerable (unrealized) possibilities of variation along the way are easily kept out of sight and out of mind. The Whig interpretation of history beckons comfortably. It is so easy, so tempting, to say that a planet on which there is life will of course evolve a species with the technical capacity for interstellar communications.[14] It is tempting, but it is also nonsense. There are simply too many critical turnings along the road of cosmic and biological evolution. The fact is that many junctures along the way are such that, had things gone only a little differently, we would not be here at all.[15]

The ancient Greek atomists' theory of possibility affords an interesting lesson in this connection. Adopting a Euclideanly infinitistic view of space, they held to a theory of innumerable worlds:

There are innumerable worlds, which differ in size. In some worlds there is no sun and moon, in others they are larger than in our world, and others more numerous. The intervals between the worlds are unequal; in some parts there are more worlds, in others fewer; some are increasing, some at their height, some decreasing; in some parts they are arising, in others failing. They are destroyed by collision one with another. There are some worlds devoid of living creatures or plants or any moisture.[16]

On this basis, the atomists taught that every (suitably general) possibility is realized in fact someplace or other. Confronting the question of "Why do dogs not have horns; why exactly is the theoretical possibility that dogs be horned not actually realized?" the atomist replied that it indeed is realized, but only elsewhere—*in another region of space.* Somewhere within infinite space, there is another world just like ours in every respect save one: that its dogs have horns. That dogs lack horns is simply a parochial idiosyncrasy of the particular local world in which we interlocutors happen to find ourselves. Reality accommodates all possibilities of world alternative to this through spatial distribution: as the atomists saw it, *all* alternative possibilities are in fact actualized in the various subworlds embraced within one spatially infinite superworld.

This theory of virtually open-ended possibilities was shut off by the closed cosmos of the Aristotelian world-picture, which dominated European cosmological thought for almost two millennia. The breakup of the Aristotelian model in the Renaissance and its replacement by the "Newtonian" model is one of the great turning points of the intellectual tradition of the West—elegantly portrayed in Alexandre Koyré's splendidly entitled book, *From the Closed World to the Infinite Universe.*[17] One may recall Giordano Bruno's near-demonic delight with the explosion of the closed Aristotelian world into one opening into an infinite universe spread throughout endless spaces. Others were not delighted but appalled: John Donne spoke of "all coherence lost," and Pascal was frightened by "the eternal silence of infinite spaces," of which he spoke so movingly in the *Pensées.* But no one doubted that the onset of the "Newtonian" world-picture represented a cataclysmic event in the development of Western thought.

Strangely enough, the potential refinitization of the universe effected by Einstein's general relativity produced scarcely a ripple in philosophical or theological circles, despite the immense stir caused by other aspects of the Einsteinian revolution. (Einsteinian space-time is, after all, even more radically finitistic than the Aristotelian world-picture, which left open, at any rate, the prospect of an infinite future with respect to time.)

To be sure, it might perhaps seem that the finitude in question is not terribly significant because the distances and times involved in modern cosmology are so enormous. But this view is rather naive. The difference between the finite and the infinite is as big as differences can get to be. And it represents a difference that is—in this present context—of the most far-reaching significance. For it means that we have no alternative to supposing that a highly improbable set of eventuations is not going to be realized in very many places, and that something sufficiently improbable may well not be realized at all. The decisive *philosophical* importance of cosmic finitude lies in the fact that in a finite universe only a finite range of alternatives can be realized. A finite universe must "make up its mind" about its contents in a far more radical way than an infinite one. And this is particularly manifest in the context of low-probability possibilities. In a finite world, unlike an infinite one, we cannot avoid supposing that a prospect that is sufficiently unlikely is simply not going to be realized at all, that in piling improbability on improbability we eventually outrun the reach of the actual. It is therefore quite conceivable that our science represents a solution of the problem of cognitive accommodation that is terrestrially locale-specific.

4. Potential Plurality of Science

Our science is bound to be limited in crucial respects by the vary fact of its being *our* science. A tiny creature living its brief life span within a maple leaf could never recognize that such leaves are deciduous—themselves part of a cyclic process. The processes of this world of ours (even unto its utter disappearance) could make no cognitive impact upon a being in whose body our entire universe is but a single atom. No doubt the laws of our world are (part of) the laws of its world as well, but this circumstance is wholly without practical effect. Where causal processes do not move across the boundaries between worlds—where the levels of relevantly operative law are so remote that nothing happening at the one level makes any substantial impact on the other—there can be little if any overlap in "science." Science is limited to the confines of discernibility: as Kant maintained, the limits of our experience set limits to our science.

A deep question arises: Is the mission of intelligence in the cosmos uniform or diversified? Two fundamentally opposed philosophical views are possible with respect to cognitive evolution in its cosmic perspective. The one is a *monism* that sees the universal mission of intelligence in terms of a certain shared destination, the attainment of a common cosmic "position of reason as such." The other is a *pluralism* that sees each intelligent cosmic civilization as forging its own characteristic cognitive destiny, and takes it as the mission of intelligence as such to span a wide spectrum of alternatives and to realize a vastly diversified variety of possibilities, with each thought-form achieving its own peculiar destiny in separation from all the rest. The conflict between these doctrines must in the final analysis be settled by triangulation from the empirical data. This said, it must be recognized that the whole tendency of these present deliberations is toward the pluralistic side. It seems altogether plausible to see cognition as an evolutionary product that is bound to attune its practitioners to the characteristic peculiarities of their particular niche in the world-order.

There is, no doubt, a certain charm to the idea of companionship. It would be comforting to reflect that however estranged from them we are in other ways, those alien minds share *science* with us at any rate and are our fellow travelers on a common journey of inquiry. Our yearning for companionship and contact runs deep. It might be pleasant to think of ourselves not only as colleagues but as junior collaborators whom other, wiser minds might be able to help along the way. Even as many in sixteenth-century Europe looked to those strange pure men of the Indies (East or West) who might serve as moral exemplars for sinful European man, so we are tempted to look to alien inquirers who surpass us in scientific wisdom and might assist us in overcoming our cognitive deficiencies. The idea is appealing, but it is also, alas, very unrealistic.

In the late 1600s, Christiaan Huygens wrote:

> For 'tis a very ridiculous opinion that the common people have got among them, that it is impossible a rational Soul should dwell in any other shape than ours. . . . This can proceed from nothing but the Weakness, Ignorance, and rejoice of Men; as well as the humane Figure being the handsomest and most excellent of all others, when indeed it's nothing but a being accustomed to that figure that makes me think so, and a conceit . . . that no shape or colour can be so good as our own.[18]

People's tendency to place all rational minds into a physical structure akin to their own is paralleled by a tendency to emplace all rational knowledge into a cognitive structure akin to their own. Roland Pucetti even thinks that the fundamental legal and social concepts of extraterrestrial societies must be designed on our lines.[19]

Life on other worlds might be very different from the life we know. It could well be based on a multivalent element other than carbon and be geared to a medium other than water—perhaps even one that is solid or gaseous rather than liquid. In his splendid book entitled *The Immense Journey*, Loren Eiseley wrote:

> Life, even cellular life, may exist out yonder in the dark. But high or low in nature, it will not wear the shape of man. That shape is the evolutionary product of a strange, long wandering through the attics of the forest roof, and so great are the chances of failure, that nothing precisely and identically human is likely ever to come that way again.[20]

What holds for the material configuration of the human shape would seem no less applicable to the cognitive configuration of human thought. It is plausible to think that alien creatures will solve the problems of *intellectual* adjustment to their environment in ways as radically different from ours as those by which they solve the problems of physical adjustment. The physics of an alien civilization need resemble ours no more than does their physical therapy. We must be every bit as leery of *cognitive* anthropomorphism as of *structural* anthropomorphism. (Fred Hoyle's science fiction story entitled *The Black Cloud* is thought provoking in this regard.[21] The cloud tells a scientist what it knows about the world. The result is schizophrenia and untimely death for the scientist: the cloud's information is divergent and compelling.)

With respect to biological evolution it seems perfectly sensible to reason as follows:

> What can we say about the forms of life evolving on these other worlds? . . . [I]t is clear that subsequent evolution by natural selection would lead to an immense variety of organisms; compared to them, all organisms on Earth, from molds to men, are vary close relations.[22]

The same situation will surely obtain with respect to cognitive evolution. The "sciences" produced by different civilizations here on earth—the ancient Chinese, Indians, and Greeks for example—unquestionably exhibit an infinitely greater similarity than obtains between our present-day science and anything devised by astronomically remote alien civilizations. Specifically, the idea of a comparison in terms of "advance" or "backwardness" is highly implausible. The prospect that some astronomically remote civilization is "scientifically more advanced" than ourselves—that somebody else is doing "our sort of science" *better* than we ourselves—requires in the first instance that they be doing our sort of science at all. And this deeply anthropomorphic supposition is extremely dubious. (It should be stressed, however, that this consideration that "our sort of natural science" may well be unique is not so much a celebration of our intelligence as a recognition of our peculiarity.) The chance that an alien civilization might develop *our* sort of science as it stands in the year 2000 is remote, to put is mildly.

Accordingly, deliberations along these present lines have a profound and far-reaching bearing on the theme of the limits of science. The ultimate reason why we cannot expect alien intelligences to be at work doing our sort of science is that the possible sorts of science are almost endlessly diverse. Sciences—understood as such in the functional-equivalency terms laid down for the present discussion—are bound to vary with the cognitive instruments that are available through the physical constitution and mental mind-set of their developers and with the cognitive focus of interest of their cultural perspective and conceptual framework. In view of the world's inherent complexity, we must think of our sort of science as simply one alternative among others: our whole cognitive project is simply the intellectual product of one particular sort of cognitive life-form.

Immanuel Kant's insight holds: there is good reason to think that natural science as we know it is not something universally valid for all rational intelligences as such but a man-made creation correlative with out specifically human intelligence. The potential plurality of modes of judgment means that there is no single definitive way of knowing. It entails a radical cognitive Copernicanism which recognizes that our position is no more central in the cognitive than in the spatial order of things. The world's complexity means that we have little alternative to supposing that our science is limited precisely by its being *our* science.

Notes

1. Compare the discussion in Gösta Ehrensvärd, *Man on Another World* (Chicago: University of Chicago Press, 1965), pp. 146-48.
2. His anthropological investigations pointed Benjamin Lee Whorf in much this same direction. He wrote: "The real question is: What do different languages do, not with artificially isolated objects, but with the flowing face of nature in its motion, color, and changing form; with clouds, beaches, and yonder flight of birds? For as goes our segmentation of the face of nature, so goes our physics of the cosmos" ("Language and Logic," in *Language, Thought, and Reality*, ed. by J.

B. Carroll [Cambridge, MA: MIT Press,. 1956], pp. 240-41). Compare also the interesting discussion in Thomas Nagel, "What is it Like to be a Bat?" in *Mortal Questions* (Cambridge, Mass: Harvard University Press, 1976).

3. Thomas Kuhn, *The Structure of Scientific Revolutions* (Chicago: University of Chicago Press, 1962).

4. Georg Simmel, "Uber eine Beziehung der Selektionslehre zur Erkenntnistheorie," *Archiv für systematische Philosophie und Soziologie*, vol. 1 (1895), pp. 34-45 (see pp. 40-41).

5. William James, *Pragmatism* (New York: Longmans Green, 1907).

6. See E. Purcell in *Interstellar Communication: A Collection of Reprints and Original Contributions*, ed. by A.G.W. Cameron (New York and Amsterdam: W. A. Benjamin, 1963).

7. Poul Anderson, *Is There Life on Other Worlds?* (New York: Crowell-Collier, 1963), p. 130.

8. Christiaan Huygens, *Cosmotheoros: The Celestial Worlds Discovered—New Conjectures Concerning the Planetary Worlds, Their Inhabitants and Productions* (London, 1698), pp. 41-43.

9. John A. Ball, "Extraterrestrial Intelligence: Where Is Everybody?" *American Scientist*, vol. 68 (1980), pp. 565-663 (see p. 658).

10. Robert Nozick, "R.S.V.P.—A Story," *Commentary*, vol. 53 (1972), pp. 66-68.

11. John A. Ball, "The Zoo Hypothesis," *Icarus*, vol. 19 (1973), pp. 347-49.

12. See M. Calvin in A. G. W. Cameron, ed. *Interstellar Communication: A Collection of Reprints and Original Contributions* (New York and Amsterdam: W. A. Benjamin, 1963), p. 75.

13. George Gaylord Simpson, "The Nonprevalence of Humanoids," *Science*, 143 (1964): 769-775 = chapter 12 of *This View of Life: The World of an Evolutionist* (New York: Harcourt Brace & Co., 1964), see pp. 773.

14. A. G. W. Cameron, ed., *Interstellar Communication* (op. cit.).

15. Robert T. Rood and James S. Trefil, *Are We Alone? The Possibility of Extraterrestrial Civilization* (New York: Scribner's Reference, 1981).

16. Diels-Kranz 68 A 40 [for Leucippus and Democritus]; tr. G. S. Kirk and J. E. Raven, *The Presocratic Philosophers* (Cambridge: Cambridge University Press, 1957), p. 411.

17. Alexandre Koyré, *From the Closed World to the Infinite Universe* (New York: Peter Smith Publishers, 1957).

18. Christiaan Huygens, *Cosmotheoros: The Celestial Worlds Discovered—New Conjectures Concerning the Planetary Worlds, Their Inhabitants and Productions* (London, 1698), pp. 76-77.

19. Roland Pucetti, *Persons: A Study of Possible Moral Agents in the Universe* (New York: Macmillan, 1969), cf. Ernan McMullin in *Icarus*, 14 (1971): 291-94.

20. Loren Eiseley, *The Immense Journey* (New York: Vintage Books, 1937).

21. Fred Hoyle, *The Black Cloud* (New York: New American Library, 1965).

22. I. S. Shklovskii and Carl Sagan, *Intelligent Life in the Universe* (San Francisco, CA: Holden-Day, 1966), p. 350.

8

Are There Any Limits to the Problem-Solving Capacity of Computers?

(1) Could computers conquer all obstacles to problem solving? (2) To begin with, it is first necessary to clarify what is at issue with "solving" a problem. And on this basis it can be argued that this is something that computers can never manage altogether on their own. (3) But in any case, they clearly cannot overcome those limits that are a matter of theoretical general principle. However, such theoretical, in-principle limits do not qualify as real limitations. (4) There do, however, exist various sorts of practical or operational limits to what computers can achieve in problem solving. These include inadequate information, (5) limits to the representation of detail, (6) limits to compressing operations into real-time availability, (7) and limitations in matters of self-insight. (8) All in all, there are substantial practical limits to computer problem solving. (9) A sort of cognitive thermodynamics is at work: there is not and cannot be any cognitive engine that is perfectly efficient for descriptive, explanatory, or predictive purposes. (10) And these incapacities also hold for us humans—even though we may enjoy some advantages over computers in other respects. In a complex world every problem-solving resource faces some ultimately insuperable obstacles.

1. Could Computers Overcome Our Limitations?

Considering the difficulties and limitations that beset our human efforts at problem solving in a complex world, it becomes tempting to contemplate the possibility that computers might enable us to eliminate our cognitive disabilities and overcome all those epistemic frailties of ours. And so we may wonder: Are computers cognitively omnipotent? If a problem is to qualify as soluble at all, will computers always be able to solve it for us?

Of course, computers cannot bear human offspring, enter into contractual agreements, or offer meaningful consolation. But such processes address *practical* problems relating to the management of the affairs of human life and thus do not count in the present cognitive context. Then, too, we must put evaluative problems of human affectivity and sensibility aside. The issue presently at hand regards the capacity of computers to resolve *theoretical* problems of the strictly cognitive sort regarding matters of empirical or formal fact. The sort of problems that will concern us here are accordingly those that characterize natural science, in particular problems relating to the description, explanation, and prediction of the things, events, and processes that constitute the realm of physical reality. And to all visible appearances computers are ideal instruments for handling the matters of cognitive complexity that arise in such contexts.

The history of computation in recent times is one of a movement from triumph to triumph. Time and again, those who have affirmed the limitedness of computers have been forced into ignominious retreat as increasingly powerful machines implementing increasingly ingenious programs have been able to achieve the supposedly unachievable. But the question on the present agenda is not "Can computers *help* with problem-solving?"—an issue that demands a resounding affirmative that needs little further discussion. There is no doubt whatever that computers can do a lot. But there is an awesomely wide gap between a lot and *everything*.

2. Problem Solving by Computers

First some important preliminaries. To begin with, we must, in this present context, recognize that much more is at issue with a "computer" than a mere electronic calculating machine understood in terms of its operational hardware. For one thing, software also counts. And, for another, so does data acquisition. As we here construe computers, they are electronic information-managing devices equipped with data banks and augmented with sensors as autonomous data access. Such "computers" can not only *process* information they can *obtain* it as well. They can not only work with *givens* but also with *takens*. Moreover, the computers at issue here are, so we shall suppose, capable of discovering and learning, able significantly to extend and elaborate their own initially programmed modus operandi. Computers in this presently operative sense are not mere calculating machines, but general problem solvers along the lines of the fanciful contraptions envisioned by the aficionados of artificial intelligence. These enhanced computers are question-answering devices of a very ambitious order.

On this expanded view of the matter, we must also correspondingly enlarge our vision both of what computers can do and of what can reasonably be asked of them. For it is the potential of computers as an instrumentality for generalized problem solving (GPS) that concerns us here, and not merely their more limited role in the calculations of algorithmic decision theory (ADC). The computers at issue will thus be prepared to deal with substantive as will as merely formal (logico-mathematical) issues. And this means that the questions we can ask are correspondingly diverse. For here, as elsewhere, added power brings added responsibility. The questions it is appropriate to ask thus can relate not just to matters of calculation but to the things and processes of the world.

Moreover, a preliminary discussion of the nature of "problem solving" is also required because one has to become clear from the outset about what it is to *solve* a cognitive problem. Obviously enough, this is a matter of answering questions. Now "to answer" a question can be construed in three ways: to offer a *possible* answer, to offer a *correct* answer, and finally to offer a *credible* answer. It is the third of these senses that will be at issue here. Thus consider a problem solver that proceeds in one of the following ways: it replies "yes" to every yes/no question; or it figures out the range of possible answers and then randomizes to select one; or it proceeds by "pure guesswork." Even though these so-called "problem solvers" may give the correct response some or much of the time, they are systematically unable to resolve our questions in the presently operative credibility-oriented sense of the term. For the obviously sensible stance calls for holding that *a cognitive problem is resolved only when an appropriate answer is convincingly provided*—that is to say, when we have a solution that we can responsibly accept and acknowledge as such. Resolving a problem is not just a matter of having an answer, and not even of having an answer that happens to be correct. The actual resolution of a problem must be credible or convincing—with the answer provided in such a way that its cogency is recognizable. A response whose appropriateness as such cannot secure rational confidence is no answer at all.[1] In answering a mathematical question we want not just a thesis but a *theorem*—a thesis that comes equipped with a proof to establish its correctness. Analogously, in general problem solving we want not just a dictum but an *answer* —a response equipped with a contextual rationale to establish its credibility.

With this crucial preliminary out of the way, we are ready to begin.

3. Theoretical Limits are not Meaningful Limitations

The question before us is: "Are there *any* significant cognitive problems that computers cannot solve?" Now it must be acknowledged from the outset that certain problems are inherently unsolvable in the logical nature of things. One cannot square the circle. One cannot co-measure the incommensurable. One cannot decide the demonstrably undecidable nor prove the demonstrably unprovable. Such tasks represent absolute limitations whose accomplishment is theoretically impossible—unachievable for reasons of general principle rooted in the nature of the realities at issue.[2] And it is clear that inherently unsolvable problems cannot be solved by computers either.[3]

Other sorts of problems will not be unsolvable as such but will, nevertheless, be demonstrably prove to be computationally intractable. For with respect to *purely theoretical* problems it is clear from Turingesque results in algorithmic decision theory (ADT) that there will indeed be computer insolubilia—mathematical questions to which an algorithmic respondent will give the wrong answer or be unable to give any answer at all, no matter how much time is allowed.[4] But this is a mathematical fact which obtains of necessity so that this whole issue can be also set aside for present purposes. For in our present context of generalized problem solving (GPS) the necessitarian facts of Gödel-Church-Turing incompleteness become irrelevant. Here any search for *meaningful* problem-solving limitations will have to confine its attention to problems that are in principle solvable: *demonstrably* unsolvable problems are beside the point of present concern because an inability to do what is in principle impossible hardly qualifies as a limitation. The sort of limit that a rigid demonstration of impossibility establishes in our present context is one that bears not so much on question answering as on question askability, seeing that it makes no sense to ask for the demonstrably impossible.

For present purposes, then, it is limits of *capability* not limits of *feasibility* that matter. In asking about the problem-solving limits of computers we are looking to problems that *computers* cannot resolve but that other problem solvers conceivably can. The limits that will concern us here are accordingly not rooted in conceptual or logico-mathematical infeasibilities of general principle but rather in performatory limitations imposed upon computers by the world's modus operandi. And in view of this, the lay of the land in generalized problem solving (GPS) is very different from that obtaining in algorithmic decision theory (ADT) because the concept of what constitutes a problem and that of what constitutes a solution operative in the former domain are less regimented and more open-ended than is the case with the latter.

The landscape that opens up before us with respect to such performative problems deserves fuller exploration.

4. Practical Limits: Inadequate Information

Often the information needed for credible problem-resolution is simply unavailable. Thus no problem-solver can at this point in time provide credible answers to questions like "What did Julius Caesar have for breakfast on that fatal Ides of March?" or "Who will be the first auto accident victim of the next millennium?" In all problem-solving situations, the performance of computers is decisively limited by the quality of the information at their disposal. "Garbage in, garbage out," as the saying has it. But matters are in fact worse than this. Garbage can come out even where no garbage goes in. One clear example of the practical limits of computer problem-solving arises in the context of prediction. Consider the following two prediction problems:

Case 1

Data: X is confronted with the choice of reading a novel by Dickens or one by Trollope. And further: X is fond of Dickens.
Problem: To predict which novel X will read.

Case 2

Data: *Z* has just exactly $10.00. And further: *Z* promised to repay his neighbor $7.00 today. Moreover, *Z* is a thoroughly honest individual.

Problem: To predict what *Z* will do with his money.

On first sight, there seems to be little difficulty in arriving at a prediction in these cases. But now suppose that we acquire some further data to enlarge our background information: pieces of information supplementary to—but nowise conflicting with or corrective of—the given premisses:

Case 1:   *X* is extremely, nay *inordinately* fond of Trollope.

Case 2:   *Z* also promised to repay his other neighbor the $7.00 he borrowed on the same occasion.

Note that in each case our initial information is nowise abrogated but merely enlarged by the additions in question. But nevertheless in each case we are impelled, in the light of that supplementation, to *change* the response we were initially prepared and rationally well advised to make. Thus when I know nothing further of next year's Fourth of July parade in Centerville, I shall predict that its music will be provided by a marching band; but if I am additionally informed that the Loyal Sons of Old Hibernia have been asked to provide the music, then bagpipes will now come to the fore.

It should, accordingly, be recognized that the process of providing rationally appropriate answers to certain questions can be led astray not just by the *incorrectness* of information but by it *incompleteness* as well. The body of information that is actually at hand is not just important for problem resolution it is *crucial*. And we can never be unalloyedly confident of problem-resolutions based on incomplete information, seeing that further information can always come along to upset the apple cart. As available information expands, established problem-resolutions can always become destabilized. One crucial practical limitation of computers in matters of problem solving is thus constituted by the inevitable incompleteness (to say nothing of potential incorrectness) of the information at their disposal. And here the fact that computers can only ever ingest finite—and thus incomplete—bodies of information means that their problem-resolving performance is always at risk. (And this sort of risk exists quite apart from others, such as the fact that computerized problem-resolutions are always the product of many steps, each of which involves a nonzero probability of error.) If we are on a quest for certainty, computers will not help us to get there.

5. Practical Limits: Limits of Prediction— Real-Time Processing Problems

Then there is also the temporal aspect. To solve problems about the real world, a computer must of course be equipped with information about it. But securing and processing information is a time-consuming process and the time at issue can never be reduced to an instantaneous zero. Time-constrained problems that are enormously complex—ones whose solution calls for securing and processing a vast amount of data—are bound to be intractable for any computer. At some point it always becomes impossible to squeeze the needed operations into available time. There will always be some questions—namely those about the near-term future—to which a computer cannot deliver answers "on time." If the solution of a given problem requires data whose determination by observation or measurement involves days, the computer cannot solve the problem in minutes, and so if the problem is a predictive one it could find itself in the awkward position that it should have started yesterday on a problem only presented to it today. Thus even under the (fact-contravening) supposition that the computer can answer *all* of our questions, it cannot, if we are demanding enough, produce those answers whenever we might require them.

6. Practical Limits: Limitations of Representation in Matters of Detail Management

This situation is emblematic of a larger issue. Any computer that we humans can design and produce here on earth is going to be finite: its sensors will be finite, its memory (however large) will be finite, and its processing time (however fast) will be finite.[5] Moreover, the modus operandi of computers (in matters of software as well as hardware) is also based on processes that are digital, discrete, and finite. In particular, all computers operate in a context of finite instructions and finite inputs. Any representational model that functions by means of computers is of finite complexity in this sense. It is always a finitely characterizable system: Its descriptive constitution is characterized in finitely many information-specifying steps and its operations are always ultimately presented by finitely many instructions. And this array of finitudes means that a computer's modelling of the real will never capture the inherent ramifications of a natural universe that effectively is, to all appearances, infinitely complex in its detail and its machinations. The result is that the inherent make-up of reality exceeds the complexity of detail that computers are able to capture.

Now the modelling by means of finite and discrete representational resources of what is, in effect, an unendingly complex system is always imperfect. For nature itself has a complexity that is effectively endless so that no finistic model that purports to represent nature can ever replicate the detail of reality's make-up in a fully comprehensive way. Artifice cannot replicate the complexity of the real; reality is richer in its descriptive constitution and more efficient in its transformatory processes then human artifice can ever manage to realize. Descriptive finitude never fully encompasses the full complexity of ontologically infinite detail even as no architect's blueprint-plus-specifications can possibly specify *every* feature of the structure that is ultimately erected. The complications of a continuous universe cannot be captured completely by the resources of a discrete language. Consider an analogy. A page of print has (say) fifty lines of fifteen words each. If the average sentence has ten words, the page can make seventy-five statements. Now divide the page into small rectangles, by ruling (say) ten lines across and ten down. That gives you a hundred rectangles each of which has its own texture, its own blemishes, its own collection of inch-marks. Those seventy-five statements cannot begin to exhaust this range of facts. All endeavors to represent reality—computer models emphatically included—involve some element of oversimplification, and in general a great deal of it. Computers deal in the digitalized modelling of an analogue world to which computer modelling can never do full justice.

The fact of the matter is that reality is too complex for adequate cognitive manipulation. Cognitive friction always enters into matters of information management—our cognitive processing is never totally efficient, something is always lost in the process; cognitive entropy is always upon the scene. But as far as knowledge is concerned, nature does nothing in vain, and so it encompasses no altogether irrelevant detail. Oversimplification always makes for losses, for deficiencies in cognition. For representational omissions are never totally irrelevant, so that no oversimplified descriptive model can get the full range of predictive and explanatory matters exactly right. Put figuratively, it could be said that the only "computer" that can keep pace with reality's twists and turns over time is the universe itself. It would be unreasonable to expect any computer model less complex than this totality itself to provide a fully adequate representation of it, in particular because that computer model has to be incorporated *within* the universe.

7. Inherent Limits of Prediction—Self-Insight Problems

Another important sort of practical limitation to computer problem-solving arises not from the inherent intractability of questions but from their unsuitability for particular respondents. Specifically, one of the issues regarding which a computer can never function perfectly is its own predictive performance. One critical respect in which the self-insight of computers is limited arises in connection with what is known as "the Halting Problem" in algorithmic decision theory (ADC). Even if a problem is computer solvable—in the sense that a suitable computer will demonstrably be able to find a solution by keeping at it long enough—it will in general be impossible to foretell how long a process of calculation will actually be needed. There is not—and demonstrably cannot be—a *general* procedure for foretelling with respect to a particular computer and a particular problem: "Here is how long it will take to find the solution—and if the problem is not solved within this span then it is not solvable at all." No computer can provide general insight into how long it—or any other computer—will take to solve problems. The question "How long is long enough?" demonstrably admits of no general solution here.

And computers are—of necessity!—bound to fail even in much simpler self-predictive matters. Thus consider asking a predictor the question:

P_1: *When next you answer a question, will the answer be negative?*

This is a question which—for reasons of general principle—no predictor can ever answer satisfactorily.[6] For consider the available possibilities:

Answer given	Actually correct answer	Agreement?
YES	NO	NO
NO	YES	NO
CAN'T SAY	NO	NO

On this question, there just is no way in which a predictive computer's response could possibly agree with the actual fact of the matter. Nevertheless, the seemingly plausible response "I can't say" automatically constitutes a self-falsifying answer. For in giving this answer the predictor would then automatically make "No" into the response called for by the proprieties of the situation.

Here, then, we have a question that will inevitably confound any conscientious predictor and drive it into baffled perplexity. But of course this is a perfectly meaningful question to which *another* predictor could give a putatively correct answer—namely, by saying: "No— that predictor cannot answer this question at all; the question will condemn it (Predictor No. 1) to baffled silence." But of course the answer "I am responding with baffled silence" is one which that initial predictor cannot cogently offer. And as to that baffled silence itself, this is something which, as such, would clearly constitute a defeat for Predictor No. 1. Still, that question which impelled Predictor No. 1 into perplexity and unavoidable failure presents no problem of principle for Predictor No. 2. And this clearly shows that there is nothing improper about that question as such.

And there are, of course, other questions that a *given* respondent (be it human or otherwise) could not answer correctly even though another might have no difficulty with it. For example: "What would be an example of an idea that you never entertain?"

This line of thought opens up another relevant issue. Let us contemplate a supposedly perfected hypothetical predictive machine Pythia. Difficulties are clearly going to arise as long as Pythia's performance is itself part of the domain regarding which it is being asked to make predictions. For then there will, on grounds of theoretical general principle, be some issues with respect to which Pythia cannot function appropriately. Consider an example. The questions that one asks Pythia can be divided into two groups, the *anticipated* (which Pythia has at some prior point predicted it would be asked), and the *unanticipated* (which Pythia has never predicted before the occasion itself that it would be asked). Now suppose we now ask Pythia "What will be the next unanticipated predictive question that you will be asked?" It is clear that Pythia will be unable, in principle, to give a correct answer. While *we* ourselves—or some *other* predictor—might perfectly well predict correctly here, Pythia itself certainly cannot. Such an inherently meaningful question that a given respondent cannot possibly answer as a matter of theoretical general principle might be characterized not as being inappropriate in and of itself, but rather as being *unsuitable* for the particular respondent. (Presumably, it would only make sound logical sense to consider as somehow limitation-constituting only those questions which are "suitable" for a given respondent at issue and which nevertheless prove to be intractable for it.) The fact remains that a "perfected predictor" that correctly answers every meaningful and answerable predictive question—those regarding its own operations included—is an unrealizable impossibility. [4]

Such simple examples establish a significant result. No computer can possibly be a universal problem-solver (UPS): none can possibly provide a certifiably correct answer to every meaningful question that can be put to it. The long and short of it is that every predictor is bound to manifest versatility-incapacities with respect to it own predictive operations. No computer can manage to get a perfect grip on itself. Alan Turing's dream of a universal computer that can solve all computer-solvable problems is an illusion. For any *given* computer there will always be some cognitive problems that it cannot satisfactorily resolve. [5]

8. Practical Limits: Limits of Modeling— Cognitive Thermodynamics

These deliberations about computer limitations convey a larger and deeper lesson.

Thermodynamics teaches the impossibility of ever contriving a perfectly efficient engine because the inner "friction" of any realizable machine always precludes perfect efficiency in its operations. In its communicative bearing, it teaches that no transmitters of information are perfectly efficient—there is always "noise" that precludes perfection in the delivery of messages. And much the same sort of situation prevails in matters of computerized problem-solving. Our computer models of nature, as science enables us to realize them, in effect constitute transmitters of messages from nature to human minds, conveying the story of nature's operations to the cognitive domain. And here, as elsewhere, the transmission of information is never perfect. Something inevitably gets lost in the process. There is not and cannot be any cognitive engine that is perfectly efficient for descriptive, explanatory, or predictive purposes.

At this point, our earlier deliberations loom up once more. We can only achieve the cognitive domestication of nature by *oversimplifying*—alike with respect to its descriptive make-up and its processual mode of operation. There is just no way in which we can squeeze all of nature's details into our descriptive models nor all its processes into our functionally operational models. Any world-model is a theory-contrivance that we devise with the imperfect means at our disposal, and there is every reason to think that it will never be able to capture the full detail of a complex reality. For all such models are destined to involve some elements of oversimplification, and oversimplification matters. As far as knowledge is concerned, nature does nothing in vain, and so it encompasses no altogether irrelevant detail. Oversimplification always makes for losses, for deficiencies in cognition. For representational omissions are never totally irrelevant, so that no oversimplified descriptive model can get the full range of predictive and explanatory matters exactly right. Limits of adequacy are inherent in the inevitable imperfection (oversimplification) of our cognitive models. And therefore no model-based cognitive process is entirely risk free. (And the more we oversimplify, the riskier.) Modelling in information processing and the realm of information processing cognitive entropy will always take its toll. And so, adequacy limitations will always dog our steps in the domain of computerized problem solving.

9. The Human Element

The present discussion has not trespassed on the terrain of books along the lines of Hubert L. Dreyfus' *What Computers Still Can't Do*.[6] For the project that is at issue there is to critique "artificial intelligence" and the task at hand to identify various functions of human intelligence and behavior that computers cannot manage satisfactorily. Accordingly, such works are given to comparing computer information processing with human performance in an endeavor to show that there are things that humans can do that computers cannot accomplish. It is—or ought to be—clear that this sort of thing has not been the issue here. For our present discussion has proceeded with a view solely to problems that computers cannot manage to resolve. Whether *humans* can or cannot resolve them is a question that has to this point not even been raised here.

And so a big question yet remains untouched: Is there any sector of this problem-solving domain where the human mind enjoys a competitive advantage over computers? Or does it transpire that wherever computers are limited, humans are always limited in similar ways?

It will not do to shirk this issue entirely. So for what it is worth, here is the answer I am inclined to give.

The modus operandi of computers is governed by explicitly formulable rules. But conceivably people can manage information-handling processes that explicit rules cannot encapsulate (any more, say, than one can become a good writer by following rules). After all, skill is not just a matter of following rules: even as there may be achievements realizable by physical skills (e.g., playing tennis) that cannot be encapsulated in rules alone, so there may well be cognitive problem-solving skills that cannot be fully captured in this way. It may therefore seem plausible that, as various theorists contend, the human mind can resolve issues that evade any prospect of computational resolution. [7]

Still, this sort of thing is a very iffy proposition—and especially so when the idea of "computers" is understood in the very expansive, open-ended way at issue here. The fact remains that the various computer incapacities in point of description, explanation, and prediction that have been instanced here also represent things that people cannot do either. And whether this situation is altogether pervasive is somewhat besides our main point. For the main message of these present deliberations is not that all of the things that computers cannot accomplish in the way of problem solving are things people cannot accomplish either (which may or may not be true), but rather the no less sobering and unquestionably true point that much of what we would ideally like to do, computers cannot do either. They can indeed diminish but cannot eliminate our limitations in solving the cognitive problems we confront in dealing with a vastly complex world, a realm where every problem-solving resource faces some ultimately insuperable obstacles.

Notes

1. Note that the convincingness at issue here is something quite different from reliability in the usual sense of freedom from calculating errors.
3. On unsolvable problems, mathematical completeness, and computability see Martin Davis, *Computability and Unsolvability* (New York: McGraw-Hill, 1958; expanded reprint edition, New York: Dover, 1982). See also N. B. Pour-El and J. I. Richards, *Computability in Analysis and Physics* (Berlin: Springer Verlag, 1989) or on a more popular level Douglas Hofstadter, *Gödel, Escher, Bach: An Eternal Golden Braid* (New York: Basic Books, 1979).
4. Some problems are not inherently unsolvable but cannot in principle be settled by computers. An instance is "What is an example of word that no computer will ever use?" Such problems are inherently computer-inappropriate and for this reason a failure to handle them satisfactorily cannot be seen as a meaningful limitation of computers.
5. On Gödel's theorem see S. G. Shanker (ed.) *Gödel's Theorems in Focus* (London: Croom Helm, 1988), a collection of essays that provide instructive, personal, philosophical, and mathematical perspectives on Gödel's work.
6. For a comprehensive survey of the physical limitations of computers see Theodore Leiber, "Chaos, Berechnungskomplexität und Physik: Neue Grenzen wissenschaftlicher Erkenntnis," Reference???
7. As stated this question bears the coloration of anthropomorphism in its use of "you." But this is so only for reasons of stylistic vivacity. That "you" is, of course, only shorthand for "computer number such-and-such."
8. On the inherent limitation of predictions see the author's *Predicting the Future* (Albany: State University of New York Press, 1997).
9. To be sure, this does not countervail against Turing's principal thesis that there can be a machine that is universal in the sense that it can carry out any computation that any other machine of the same generic sort can possibly manage. On Turning Machines see R. Hesken (ed.), *The Universal Turning Machine* (Oxford: Oxford University Press, 1988).
10. Cambridge MA: MIT Press, 1992.
11. This line of thought is developed in considerable detail in Roger Penrose, *The Emperor's New Mind* (New York: Oxford University Press, 1989).

9

Coping with Cognitive Limitations:
Problems of Rationality in a Complex World

(1) In cognitive and practical contexts alike, even the most rational of problem solutions can misfire with situations of incomplete information. Throughout our rational deliberations, the conclusions we reach must be a function of the premises. In consequence, any changes in or additions to the available information can affect our issue-resolutions. The prevailing state of our information accordingly will—and should— decisively affect the determination of what is the best thing to do or to think. And with information acquisition, future changes are presently unforeseeable since present knowledge cannot speak for future knowledge. (2) We have no alternative but to act on the basis of what our conscientious cognitive efforts can here and now provide, recognizing that our available information in highly complex matters is all too often less than adequate—and almost never complete. Accordingly, in the informatively difficult and problematic setting of a complex world, reason faces the predicament of acknowledging that it must call on us to do that which, for aught we really know, may in the end prove totally inappropriate.

1. Stage-Setting for the Problem:
Issue Resolution Hinges on Available Information

Science is an inherently dynamical venture; the theories and theses of one scientific era will—and because of technological progress *must*— differ from those of another. And the wishes and preferences of scientists notwithstanding, the world-picture that they deliver into our hands grows increasingly complex over time. The history of science is a story of the ever renewed realization that things were not so simple as they previously seemed. What does this increasing complexity of our understanding of the world's ways portend? The answer to this question has some rather ominous consequences—both for matters of belief and for matters of practice as well.

Rational action encounters serious challenges in a complex world. For in such a world the information at the disposal of limited beings is bound to be incomplete, and in situations of imperfect information their very rationality can lead rational agents into difficulty. This becomes apparent with even the most simple of problem-solving situations. For consider such cases as the following:

Case 1: Informational gap-filling

DATA: A manuscript note contains the (partly illegible) passage: "He sent her a l-tter . . . "

QUESTION: How is that gap in that incomplete word "l-tter" to be filled in?

Case 2: Probabilistic reasoning

DATA: 1. X is a mechanical engineer.
            2. 90 per cent of mechanical engineers are male.

QUESTION: How probable is it that X is male?

Case 3: Inductive inference

DATA: A sequence starts 1, 10, 100.

QUESTION: What are we to expect at the 10th place?

Case 4: Prudential decision

DATA: 1. It is starting to rain.
            2. Yonder large tree affords the only shelter in the large, flat meadow that we are crossing.

QUESTION: Where should we go?

Case 5: Expert intervention

DATA: 1. X suffers from asthma.
            2. Antihistamines are the most effective available medicament for (most cases of) asthma.

PROBLEM: What course of action should we recommend to X?

In each case, we face a perfectly possible and clearly delineated situation of choice. And in each instance the "rationally appropriate resolution" seems rather obvious and straightforward. But now consider what happens when some additional, supplementary information is added. Let us assume that in these five cases we acquire some further, merely additional information:

Case 1: The passage continues: "to transport her wounded brother."

Case 2: We are also informed that X gave birth to a bouncing baby boy last week.

Case 3: We are further told that the sequence continues 1, 10, 100, 1, 10, 100, for the *next* six entries.

Case 4: We are given the supplemental datum that there is also much lightning and thunder.

Case 5: We are also informed that X is highly allergic to antihistamines.

Clearly, one and the same phenomenon recurs throughout. Informatively more amply grounded choices may or may not be better, but they will frequently be different.

In any and every domain, the rational resolution of problems is highly context-sensitive to the information in hand in such a way that what is a patently sensible and appropriate resolution in a given data-situation can cease to be so in the light of additional information—information that does not abrogate or correct our prior data, but simply augments it. Often as not, additional ramifications complicate matters by destabilizing seemingly obvious resolutions. For exactly what qualifies as the most rational resolution of a particular problem of belief, action, or evaluation is bound to depend upon the precise content of our data about the circumstances. And this dependency so functions that a "mere addition" to our information can radically transform the situation as regards optimality. For, as those preceding examples indicate, a mere *amplification* of the known circumstances may well indicate the appropriateness of doing something totally incompatible with that initial optimum. The fact is that the rationally appropriate resolution of a problem on the basis of one body of evidence or experience can always become undone when that body of evidence or experience is not actually *revised* but merely *enlarged*.

It is precisely here that complexity makes for difficulties. For when we operate in complex situations, we are constantly involved in learning new facts about them—facts which can all too easily upset the apple cart of our previous ideas. We thus confront the situation generated by the confluence of two considerations: that the rationality of a problem-resolution is "information-sensitive," and that amidst the complexities of the real world our information is always incomplete and open to supplementation.

It is clear that the rationally appropriate approach in any situation of problem solving—be it cognitive or practical—is to strive for the best resolution achievable in the light of the available data. Rationality enjoins us to adopt the optimal option: having surveyed the range of alternatives, the appropriate thing to do is to resolve the choice between them in what is, all considered, the overall most favorable way. To be sure, what is "favorable" will differ in some ways from context to context. But the fact remains that rationality is a matter of *optimization relative to constraints*—of doing the best one can in the prevailing circumstances. Yet in complex settings, circumstances are bound to change in the light of fuller understanding. And it is a trite fact—which nevertheless has enormously far-reaching implications—that the deployment of intelligence or *incomplete* information may well yield inadequate solutions.

In cognitive and practical contexts alike, even the most rational of problem-solutions can misfire in situations of incomplete information. For in all rational deliberation the conclusion is and must be a function of the premises. The prevailing state of our information will—and should—decisively affect the determination of what is the best thing to do or to think. And in consequence any changes in or additions to the available information can—and should—affect our issue-resolutions.

The history of the empirical sciences affords a familiar illustration. Beliefs in the luminiferous aether, the conservation of matter, and the like, were all sensible and rational in their day. Achieving a substantial enlargement of the data base on which we erect the structures of our theorizing has generally produced those changes of mind characterized as "scientific revolutions." As significantly enhanced experimental information comes to hand in a complex world, people are led to resolve their problems of optimal question-resolution in radically different ways.

2. Ideal vs. Practical Rationality: The Predicament of Reason

Rationality demands that we should think and act on the basis of the best available confirmation. But in this domain of information acquisition, future changes are presently unforseeable. Present knowledge does not—cannot—speak for future knowledge.[1]

We have no rationally superior alternative but to act on the basis of what our conscientious cognitive efforts can here and now provide, recognizing that our available information in highly complex matters is generally less than adequate—let alone complete. The predicament of reason residing in the irresolvable tension between the demands of rationality and its practical possibilities comes to view in the following aporetic situation:

1. As agents who pretend to rationality, we ought to act as fully rational agents do, namely to do what is in fact the rationally optimal thing.
2. In actual practice, we can do no more and no better than to opt for what *appears* to be the best option in the circumstances.
3. It cannot reasonably and rationally be asked of us to do more than the very best that is possible in the circumstances.
4. What *appears* to be the best option in various circumstances may not actually *be* the best option.

Since these theses create a conflict, a compromise must be effected and at least one of them must be sacrificed. Now since 2 and 4 represent unavoidable "facts of life," 1 and 3 are the plausible candidates here. Yet neither the rationality-abandonment of 1-rejection nor the unrealistic perfectionism of 3-rejection are attractive options. And the resulting situation is a thoroughly uncomfortable one—whence the characterization of a predicament. For in the informatively problematic setting of a complex world, reason faces the need for acknowledging that it must call on us to do that which, for aught we know, may in the end prove totally inappropriate.

Rational action in this world has to proceed in the face of the sobering recognition that while we doubtless should do the best we can in the circumstances, this may nevertheless eventuate as quite the wrong thing. It is the course of reason to *aim* at the absolute best, but nevertheless to *settle for* the best that is realistically available in the existing circumstances. (After all, it would be unreasonable, nay *irrational*, to ask for more.) But the predicament lies in our clear recognition of the inherent tension between these two commitments—the fact that while the ideal ends of rationality are achieved only under the ideal conditions of global totality, nevertheless the actual practice of rationality must inevitably be conducted at the level of local and imperfect conditions. We can never rest complacently confident that in following reason's directions we may not in fact be frustrating the very purposes for whose sake we are calling upon the guidance of reason. We have to recognize the "fact of life" that it is rationally advisable to do the best we can, while nevertheless realizing all the while that it may prove to be inappropriate. Reason calls on us to act on the basis of the best information that our conscientious efforts can here and now provide—notwithstanding the recognition that they may not in the end prove to be sufficient.

"But the problem is created by mere ignorance." True enough! But true in a way that provides no comfort. Imperfect information is an inevitable fact of life. A "rationality" that could not be implemented in these circumstances would be totally pointless. Were rationality to hinge on complete information, it would thereby manifest its irrelevance for our concerns. There is nothing "mere" about ignorance regarding how matters actually stand in this complex world of ours.

If we had "complete information," and in particular if we knew how our future efforts would eventuate—how matters will actually turn out when we decide one way or another—then rational decision making and planning would of course become something very different from what they are. But all we can ever actually manage to do is to be rational in the circumstances *as best we can determine them to be*. If rationality were only possible in the light of *complete* information it would perforce become totally irrelevant for us. It lies in the inevitable nature of things that we must exercise our rationality amidst conditions of imperfect information. A mode of "rationality" capable of implementation only in ideal circumstances is pointless; in this world, the real world, there is no work for it to do. We have to be realistic in our understanding of rationality—recognizing that we must practice this virtue in real rather than ideal circumstances. In fact, to ask more of rationality would not itself be rational. A conception of rationality that asks no more of us than doing the best we possibly can is the only one that makes sense—anything else would be ipso facto irrelevant. Clearly, if rationality is to be something that one can actually implement, then it has to be possible for its demands to be met in sub-ideal conditions—specifically including conditions of incomplete information as we (inevitably) confront them.

We standardly operate on the presumption that the available information is adequate to permit the appropriate resolution of the problems we face. (After all, we have no option but to do the best we can with the means in hand.) But all too frequently this presumption turns out ultimately falsified. Yet twentieth-century medicine is naturally not deficient for failing to apply twenty-first-century remedies. Rationality, like politics, is an art of the possible—a matter of doing the best that is achieved in the overall circumstances in which the agent functions—cognitive circumstances included. Our best available judgments—not only as to the actualities of things but also as regards their plausibilities and probabilities—will always be conditional judgments formed in the context and against the background of the then-available information as best we can determine it. And in this sphere future changes are presently unforeseeable.

It will not do to react to this state of affairs by saying: "Delay decision until your experience is perfected and your information altogether complete." To postpone a decision until then is tantamount to preventing its ever being made. A rationality we cannot deploy here and now, amidst the realities of an imperfect world, is altogether useless.

Still, the situation that we face is an ironic one. Categorical (unconditional) rational appropriateness always hinges on the *total* circumstances, involving the entirety of relevant information, be it present *and absent*. But obviously this second factor of "absent information" poses difficulties. In this world, our circumstances are inevitably subideal, our information unavoidably incomplete. The inconvenient fact is that here, as elsewhere, we simply cannot determine that nothing outside our cognitive reach has a certain character or tendency—that this is more than we can ever actually manage. This sort of situation obtains throughout all areas of rational deliberation: cognitive, prudential, evaluative—right across the board. Even our optimally evidentiated beliefs are not necessarily true; even our optimally well-advised actions are not necessarily successful; even our optimally crafted appraisals are not necessarily correct. The reality of limitation meets us in every direction.

We are comparatively simple creatures living in a comparatively complex world. And for this reason we occupy a position in which a good deal of skepticism is warranted. Not that we do not know any-thing—or indeed a great many things—but in a complex world our knowledge is bound to be of a changing, dynamic, progressive character, so that our presently available knowledge is imperfect—at any and every present. Evolution has equipped us with an intellect adequate to fare satisfactorily (though certainly not *perfectly*) with the environment as we find it—sufficiently to cope effectively in the statistical average with the situations relating to our well being as regards survival and reproduction. All the same, our knowledge is bound to be frequently inadequate to the situation that actually confronts us. And the problems of praxis that result are formidable, since we know full well on general principles that the actions we deem appropriate on the basis of even the most careful exploration of incomplete information can readily turn out to be entirely ineffective and inappropriate.

Rationality is undoubtedly the best resource that we have, but there is no failproof assurance that in the conditions of incomplete information that obtain in a complex world its guidance will prove good enough. And yet while rationality is an imperfect resource, there is nowhere else where we can—rationally—go. Virtually by definition, the rationally appropriate resolution will, in the circumstances, afford our best choice in point of rational appropriateness.

There thus stands before us the profound lesson of the biblical story of the Fall of Man, that in this complex world of ours there are simply no guarantees—not even for a life conducted on principles of reason. It is this sobering situation—doubtless unwelcome, but inevitable—that betokens the predicament of reason: the circumstance that rationality—our very best available guide—requires us to do "what seems best" in the full and clear recognition that, in a world whose complexities often prove to be too much for us, this may well fail to be, in actuality, anything like the best thing to do.[2]

Notes

1. On this theme see the author's *Predicting the Future* (Albany, NY: State University of New York Press, 1997).
2. Some of the themes of this section are further elaborated in the author's *Rationality* (Oxford: Oxford University Press, 1988).

10

Technology, Complexity, and Social Decision

(1) While technological innovation makes particular *tasks easier to perform, its overall effect is to make life as a whole more complicated. (2) For technical progress not only solves existing problems but creates new problems of its own. (3) Coping with the complexity that comes in the wake of technological progress always involves destabilizing leaps into the unknown. (4) Such novelty militates towards decision quandaries and gridlock in social decision making. (5) The natural developmental dynamic of our technology (be it physical or intellectual) carries us out of our depths. Increasingly, it impels us into an area where the magnitude of the problem that confronts us threatens to outrun the power of our capacities for problem resolution.*

1. Technological Progress Makes Life More Complicated

We members of Homo sapiens are amphibious creatures: we inhabit two realms, the realm of nature and the realm of human artifice. The former domain is one where we *find* matters in place; the latter is a *construct* that we ourselves produce under the guidance of intelligence. But on both sides alike we encounter an unfathomable complexity. Nature has levels of depth exceeding the reach of our cognitive powers, and human artifice also carries us ever further down the road of complexification.

Biological evolution under the aegis of natural selection makes for ever more specialized speciation, differentially selecting for organisms that branch off into particular varieties able to respond more effectively to the challenges of changing environmental conditions. This process makes for increasingly complex organisms—just as Herbert Spencer's law of evolution would have it. And technological evolution exhibits exactly the same tendency. In virtually every sphere of our human concerns we constantly encounter new obstacles. And new problems call for doing what we were unable to do before; they require new solutions which themselves call for new methods, new processes, new instrumentalities. Such escalating demands drive us to devising even more complex systems to put increasing performative sophistication at our disposal. We here encounter the fundamental law of technical progress: *Human artifice is caught up in a complexity tropism.* And the rationale of this situation is easy to understand on principles of economy of effort, seeing that rational creatures are naturally inclined to try simpler solutions first, maintaining them until such time as it becomes advantageous to replace them by something more complicated. In consequence, all of our creative efforts—in material, social, and intellectual contexts alike—manifest a historical tendency of moving from the simpler to the more complex.

People incline to think that technological progress makes life easier. It is faster and more convenient to cross oceans by plane than by sailing ship, to phone messages rather than mail letters, to type with word processors than write with quills. But while all his is true enough, there is the other side of the coin as well. New-gained technical capacity accordingly brings additional problems of management in its wake. Along the roadway of technological progress, ever more tracks branch off before us into different sectors of the realm of possibility. More choices mean more decisions which require more information. Think, for example, of travel and communication, where modern resources mean that we become linked in an increasingly large and complex system of operations. (No modern airline—or airplane—can operate without computers.) With this increase, however, the problems of choice and decision become increasingly elaborate, with ever more choices to be made—and more switches to be thrown. Notoriously, one virtually has to be a rocket scientist to program one's VCR. A modern car has many thousands of parts, but a jet aircraft can have over four million and a space rocket over six million. Only technical experts can carry out repairs or modifications: the era of string and sealing wax is over. And as regards system operation, the same story holds with ever more elaborate control processes being required. And what holds for function holds for malfunction as well. In the 1950s when an airplane plummeted from the sky, a pair of experts had comparatively little trouble figuring out what went wrong. But as the explosion of TWA's flight 800 demonstrated in 1996, determining the cause of the malfunction of a complex system can set a team of scores into prolonged bafflement.

The fact is that technological progress makes life vastly more complicated by widening the range of choice and opportunity. It increases the operational complexity of process all about us. The driver of a horse and buggy can afford to doze off, but the driver of a car can afford it far less, and the pilot of a supersonic fighter plane not at all. With more sophisticated camera equipment, film makers need to make many more detailed decisions about location, perspective, lighting, timing, etc. in making their pictures. And if we replace these human decision makers with automatic control devices, each must be vastly more complex and sophisticated than its more rudimentary compeers. With the growth of technology, the artifacts we devise threaten to become too complicated for effective human management. Modern superjets are so complex that pilots no longer possess the cognitive skills to fly them and could not manage to do so without the aid of computers. The problem of complexity management becomes shifted from operating the system itself to managing the functioning of its cybernetic governance. The drug industry is subject to far more extensive regulations today than the entire economy was fifty years ago. In combat, the pilot of a jet fighter makes a more decisions in five minutes than a sailing-era ship's naval captain did in a day.[1]

We pay for the advantages of sophisticated technology by confronting issues of operational choice and decision that are of ever increasing complexity. As technology advances, the problems of cognitive discrimination—just like those of visual discrimination—expand exponentially in line with the proliferation of possibilities.[2] And so, while technological progress—be it material or social—may indeed simplify and facilitate the performance of particular tasks, its aggregate effect is to make large-scale processes more complicated and difficult.

Complexity is the inseparable accompaniment of modernity. We encounter it throughout our science, throughout our technology, and throughout our social and cultural environment as well. Perhaps the clearest manifestation of this is the range of choice that confronts us on all sides in everyday life—with sources of information, means of entertainment and leisure activities, occupations, and even lifestyles. An ongoing proliferation in the multiplicity of cultural forms and the diversity of opportunities is a striking and salient feature of our age, and it is an unavoidable feature of what we are pleased to designate as "progress" that it confronts as with an ever more complex and diversified manifold of possibilities. And the obverse scale of such opportunity creation is the matter of *opportunity cost* inherent in the fact that every opportunity that we seize also represents a multiplicity of other opportunities forgone.

Progress itself pushes us deeper and deeper into difficulties. For every solution opens up new problems. Such a hydra effect is closely related to the principle of question propagation in matters of factual inquiry. The phenomenon of the ever-continuing "birth" of new questions was first emphasized by Immanuel Kant, who maintained that, "The solution of any factual (scientific) question gives rise to yet further unsolved questions."[3] This opening up of new and deeper questions in the course of our inquiries into matters of empirical fact is something that is empirically as well established as any encountered within our study of nature herself. The history of science forcefully substantiates this principle of question-proliferation in empirical inquiry. And it deserves emphasis that this phenomenon of escalating diversity and complexity holds just as much for *practical* as for *cognitive* problems.

But what of a "return to the past"—a nostalgia-satisfying reversion to the conditions of an earlier, simpler age? The short answer is that this is simply impracticable outside the limited range of museum-piece environments in isolated backwaters. For we would not have resorted to those complications in the first place if we had not been forced to them by the needs of the situation. After all, even in Adam Smith's day, so he informs us in *The Wealth of Nations*[4] some thousand people over all had a hand in making a woolen coat. In general, the price of a return is unaffordable. To be sure this is a matter of how things stand in the large and in the whole. It is possible to preserve islands of simplicity in human affairs. But this is possible only in exceptional and highly localized conditions. Overall, the later position in the realm of artifice is bound to be one where complexity is unavoidable and uneliminable.

In his amusingly written but brilliantly perceptive book, C. N. Parkinson took note of what might be called the managerial bloat of modern organizations.[5] In all sorts of enterprises as activity diminished, management flourished. Throughout the twentieth century, the British navy had ever more admirals as ever fewer ships were in commission. Everywhere while operations downsized, management upsized.

But of course the explanation of this phenomenon is straightforwardly a matter of complexity. To address more complex tasks more sophisticated operations are necessary. But more sophisticated operations require more elaborate processes and more elaborate processes require more sophisticated control and thus more elaborate management. And so even where the *scale* of operation is diminished as the technically more sophisticated processes grew more sophisticated and powerful, so nevertheless the problems of planning and control grow ever more elaborate. It is not boondoggling or diminished capacity that produces managerial bloat but the inexorable demands of dealing with greater complexity. And so the gigantism of the managerial machinery of the contemporary army or industrial enterprise or university is thus no accident. Designed for affording greater control over more complex systems, the administrative machine of such organizations is forced to meet even greater challenges in point of performative capability. As the functional capacity of such institutions expands under the pressure of technological progress, the scope of management operations expands also—and even more rapidly. With the modern technology of communication and information management, bureaucracy is thus bound to increase irrespective of the particular operational tasks for whose management the bureaucracy is instituted. And sometimes the functional complexities of a system make its effective control virtually unrealizable.

2. Problem Complexity Outpaces Solution Complexity

Throughout the progress of science, technology, and human artifice generally, complexity is self-potentiating because it engenders complications on the side of problems that can only be addressed adequately through further complication on the side of process and procedure. The increase in technical sophistication confronts us with a dynamic feedback interaction between problems and solutions that ultimately transforms each successive solution into a generator of new problems. And these feedback effects operate in such a way that to all intents and purposes the growth rate of the problem domain continually outpaces that of our capacity to produce solutions. Both the problems and the solutions grow more complex in the wake of technological progress, but the crux of the matter lies in the comparatively greater pace of the increase in problem complexity.

Of course, technology is not just part of the problem, it affords part of the solution as well. For while technological progress always poses new difficulties in the management of information and the control of operating procedures, it can of course also help with resolving issues of this sort. Where accurate and correct results matter, complex systems of quality control will always be needed. For the prevention of errors is clearly a strategy superior to correcting them. If a process involves the contributions of n subsidiary components each of which can malfunction in m ways, then when something goes wrong error diagnosis becomes the search for a needle in a haystack, seeing that there will be m x n possible ways in which things *could* have gone wrong. Safety engineering in all its forms—redundancy provision, fault detection sensors—together with the "cybernetic" automation of control mechanisms, and above all the use of computers in information management and decision implementation, all afford powerful resources for problem resolution in technological contexts. Process controls too can be handled in substantial measure by technological means. Interestingly enough, the electronics in a contemporary automobile cost some two thousand dollars more than the steel used to produce the same car.

However, there yet remains the crucial question of comparative pace. With technological progress, which grows the faster, the manifold of problems to be resolved or the reach and power of our instrumentalities of problem resolution? Now here it might seem that complex technology gives the advantage to problem resolution. After all, do not the cognitive resources that computers afford us offset the problems raised by increasing of complexity? Alas, not really.

First of all, it has to be recognized that computers help principally with information *processing* and do not equally address the problems information *acquisition*. And in the course of technological progress these become even more extensive and even more significant. Here the classic dictum holds good: as far as the efficacy of computational information manipulation is concerned, garbage in, garbage out. Moreover, the fact remains that computers do just exactly what they are programmed to do. The level of complexity management they are able to achieve is determined through—and thus limited by—the levels of ingenuity and conceptual adequacy of their programming. No central bank places unalloyed confidence in its economic models. And there is also the problem of unforeseen and unforeseeable interactions within the interact fabric of the operating processes. Such "bugs" can result in malfunctions in computer operation even as they can produce accidents in other sorts of systems. And the more elaborate and complex our programs get—particularly in areas where novelty and innovation are the order of the day—the larger the prospect and chances for such mishaps.[6] In every area, maiden voyages are notoriously fertile in bringing unanticipated difficulties to light.

The fact is that as technical systems become more complex, their operation becomes even more so. And over time managerial complexity generally outpaces processual efficacy. A more elaborate repertoire always imposes new and increasingly unmanageable difficulties in matters of operation and procedure, since as already noted in the preceding chapter, process concatenations always grow at a rate faster than the processes themselves.

Granted, computer automated problem solving is one of the wonders of the age. Computers fly planes, land rocket modules on the moon, win chess competitions, develop mathematical proofs. All the same, we have to come face to face here with what might be called a *hydra effect* after the mythological monster who managed to grow several heads to take the place for each one that was cut off. The fact is that there is a feedback symbiosis between problems and solutions which operates in such a way that the growth of the former systematically outpaces that of the latter. Accordingly, those sophisticated information and control technologies do not so much resolve problems of complexity as enlarge this domain by engendering complexity problems of their own. Despite the enormous advantages that they furnish to intellectual efforts at complexity management, computers nevertheless do not and cannot eliminate but only displace and magnify the difficulties that we encounter throughout the realm of increasing complexity. An information processing device that has a failure ratio on the order of 10^{-9} cannot be relied on without introducing various checks and balances if asked to carry out an inferential process with 10^8 steps.

In some ways, humans are better at managing complexity than are computers as we know them. For computers are programmed—their responses to situations are automatized. Humans, on the other hand, are flexible, spontaneous, able to innovate or to "wing it." So when complex systems malfunction or mis-function, as they are bound on occasion to do, humans can come to terms such a breakdown by fair means or foul, while the computer's response would be one of "crashing." A deficient, aberrant situation that can conceivably be handled by people would likely as not faze a computer. And the person who malfunctions into error or misunderstanding in the management of complexity may well be able to recover where a computer would plunge on into an ever deeper morass.

The long and short of it is that complexity management via computers will not remove the obstacles to managerial effectiveness exactly because complexity raises problems faster than it provides means for their solution. Computers—the very instruments that enhance our capacity for complexity management—widen the scope of the field of action and thereby augment the complexity we face. The technical resources that enlarge our powers in the area of problem resolution not only do not manage to *reduce* the overall size of the problem field that confronts us, but actually manage to *enlarge* it. The fact is that technological progress engenders what might be characterized as the "rolling snowball effect" because complexity breeds more complexity through engendering problem-situations from which only additional technical capacity can manage to extract us. As already noted in chapter 1, in the natural, unfettered course of things complexity tends to grow exponentially. Exponential growth is the automatic result when something grows in such a way that its size increases in proportion with the size that it has already attained. And so if the *management* of complexity (be it cognitive or operational) is to keep up, then it too must increase exponentially. Our technological capacity in this regard must grow by exponential leaps and bounds, passing through successively ever greater stages of capacity. The historical course of things has certainly seen this sort of technological escalation in complexity management, passing through successive phases of management by individuals, by groups, by mechanical devices, by single electronic computers, by groups or systems of electronic computers, and possibly by yet more powerful but as yet undreamt of resources. Eventually, no doubt, there will be an end of the line here, for it seems to be a law of nature that all exponential growth must ultimately come to an end.

And so in the final reckoning we must expect that our ability to manage ever greater complexity will eventually become saturated.

3. The Intimidating Impetus of the Unknown: Risk and Destabilization

The growing complexity that emerges in the wake of technical progress all too often engenders unexpected difficulties. And with every practical step that we take towards coping with these difficulties, unforeseeable consequences generally arise. All along the line, the law of unintended effects comes into operation. As technical sophistication increases, we penetrate ever further into a domain where we cannot see clearly along the road that lies ahead. We continually confront problem situations within which we not only cannot determine *optimal* solutions, but where even the identification of *desirable* solutions becomes problematic and imponderable.

This phenomenon has ominous implications. *Physical chaos*, it will be recalled, occurs when a system functions in so volatile a way that a minute difference in its initial condition—one that is so small as to lie beneath the threshold of observation and perhaps even of observability—can make for a vast difference for the outcome state. *Cognitive chaos* is exactly the same sort of thing transposed to the region of information processing. It occurs whenever a minute variation in input information can produce great difference in its inferential consequences—that is, whenever an inferential outcome is enormously sensitive to small variations on informational input (for example where even a "shadow of doubt" can spell the difference between manifest guilt and innocence). The prospect of subjecting such inferential processes to adequate cognitive control by way of systematic principled understanding are somewhere between small and nonexistent. And it is just here that complexity makes itself felt. For the prospect of insufficient or misleading information grows along with system complexity and, other things equal, sophisticated systems need to have more elaborate processes. Prediction too becomes less practicable, save at the level of statistical indefiniteness. The activities of a primitive tribe are easier to predict than those of the U.S. Congress; very heavy atoms are less stable than very light ones; strategy is easier to manage with tic-tac-toe than with chess. The general structure of the situation is reflected in the circumstance that while simple systems are more versatile and flexible but less effective and efficient; complex systems are more specialized but less adaptable. Screws are more complex than nails, but thereby more limited. They do a better job at holding things together, but are less versatile (all sorts of things can be nailed together while screws require a congenially porous material). Complex systems pay for their greater efficiency and effectiveness through being more specialized, more closely attuned to the circumstantial specifics of the case. They are, accordingly, easier to destabilize—more vulnerable to the interventions of chaos.

The number of cells in a human body is of the order of 10^{15} or 10^{16}. The number of neurons in the nervous system is of the order of 10^{10}. The compositional complexity of the organism is immense. But this structure has to be built up on principles that are much simpler. The DNA-coded instructions providing the blueprint for such a complex product must itself involve a far lesser degree of complexity and has to be built into a more compact structure. Ideally complex systems should be managed on simple principles. But this is possible only up to a point.

As the operations of a goal-directed system of any sort become more complex, the importance of safety engineering comes to the fore increasingly the need for devising contrivances that protect against potential for failure that is an inevitable accompaniment of increasing complexity. To be sure, part of that growing complexity may be invested in safety assurance—in building malfunction controls into the system operations and proliferating back-ups and redundancies. But problems are inevitable in this domain as well. The prospect of things going wrong will always slip "through the cracks," and complex systems for this very reason grow increasingly error-prone and susceptible to malfunction. And the seriousness of such mishaps is not only amplified by the complexity of the environment but also rendered less manageable by it.[7]

We devise those more complex systems because we need them. But their very existence creates new difficulties. For we soon come to depend on them and this dependence renders us increasingly vulnerable to frustration. Complex systems are inherently less amenable to successful comprehension, management, and control. It is evident that where double the number of steps must go right in a goal-pursuing context, we double the prospects of something's going wrong, other things being equal. Complexity generally enlarges the prospect of system failure—and where not in frequency, there in magnitude of effect. A washing machine can malfunction far more readily than a wash board—and with more extensive consequences. There is no clearer indication of the vulnerability that complexity engenders than the extent to which a single act of sabotage by a terrorist, or of dishonesty by a greedy or disgruntled employee, can inflict destructive damage on a large enterprise or an extensive organization.

This state of things engenders inevitable threats and dangers. Specifically, with the ongoing sophistication of human artifice we find that:

- with *cognitive* systems we face the threat of disintegration, disorganization, and cognitive dissonance.
- with *technical* systems we face the threat of breakdown and malfunction.
- with *social* systems we face the threat of gridlock and stalemate or—at the opposite extreme—of social chaos and anarchy.

Throughout the domain of human creativity—alike in matters of cognitive, technological, and social engineering—we encounter an increasing complexity that carries with it the inherent risks of system malfunction. Risk is a natural companion to complexity. It involves the (multiplicatively interactive) combination of two factors: the probability of failure and the magnitude of the consequences should failure occur. Increasing complexity generally enlarges risk. It does so not necessarily by increasing the probability of failure but by increasing the negative consequences should failure occur. (Precisely when failure probability is diminished we tend to increase our stake on success.) Increasing complexity thus tends to be associated with increasing risk.[7]

Our individual activity—say getting from home to work—is undoubtedly simplified by the technology of the automobile in contrast with that of the horse. But the entire system of automotive transport is something vastly more complex, penetrating pervasively into every aspect of our social and economic life. Local simplicity rides on the back of globally systemic complexity. The present-day motor vehicle code of U.S. states is more complex than the whole of their transport legislation in the 1890s. And no American who has lived through the months of the Arab oil embargo in the early 1970s can fail to realize the magnitude and power of the vulnerabilities to which such systemic complexification renders us subject.

The basic point that is at issue here is relatively straightforward. It is that in general and as a rule complex systems are by reason of their very complexity more expensive and more difficult to construct, operate, and maintain. And they are also more risky to use—not necessarily by way of an increased likelihood of malfunction but rather through the increased seriousness of the consequences that ensue when a malfunction occurs. In sum, the increased complexity of our systems does not come cost-free; to achieve its undoubted advantages we have to pay a substantial price, not in terms of money alone, but also in terms of risk.

4. Concretization Quandaries and Decision Gridlock

At the earlier, less sophisticated stages of technological progress, it was easier for people to understand the implications of change. For when changes occur in highly complex systems, the consequences are often unpredictable. It becomes somewhere between difficult and impossible to say in advance just what the result of modifications and innovations will be. We all too frequently cannot see our way clearly through the accompanying ramifications to grasp the implications of innovation for their management. For effective decision making requires the timely processing of full information. And both of these factors—readily acquiring and speedily processing information—tend to be more difficult and cumbersome in contexts of complexity. And the more complex the ramifications of a choice situation are, the more likely it is that any particular way of resolving it will be worrisome to some of the individuals or groups who have a stake in its outcome. Few of us have the engineering sophistication to be rocket scientists. But, effectively none of us today have the technical sophistication to be social engineers. And there is a real possibility that even all of us taken collectively do not have what it takes.

In particular, the measures that are required to cope with matters of social and economic policy become increasingly difficult and constantly more expensive to implement and to operate. The complexities that have to be taken account of outrun the grasp of ordinary understanding. (Think, for example, of Hillary Clinton's health care program, not to speak of the Federal Tax Code.) The management of

America's systems in the area of medical or social or economic processes and programs has grown so difficult throughout the successive decades of the present century that the political system is nowadays close to throwing up its hands in frustration.

And so the very power of technical progress brings new disabilities and incapacities in its wake. The operational dynamics of complexity expansion means that as we increase our problem-resolving capacity we will inevitably—preferences to the contrary notwithstanding—also increasingly loose our grip on the overall effectiveness of problem control. All too often, no one can form an accurate picture of how proposed changes of process and procedure in the management of complexity will work themselves out for those involved. And even where we ourselves think that we can see the way clear, there may well be precious few others who agree with us. This state of affairs manifests itself in the striking and by now familiar phenomenon that might be called the *cacophony of experts*. The difficulties of rational problem solution in complex situations engenders a variety of plausible but competingly alternative possibilities. And in the absence of a single clean-cut resolution a dissonance of theories arise. Pundits come upon the scene with their competing wares—each with a case that seems plausible and persuasive but is nevertheless insufficiently clear-cut and decisive to put its rivals out of business.

The destabilizing effect of technological change thus paves the way for social discord and procedural impotence. Here sheer stagnation is the natural result of risk-aversive "better the devil we know" thinking. All too often, life in our imperfect world proceeds in such a way that to all appearances certain abstractly desirable aims simply cannot be concretely realized by acceptable means. Let us inspect the ramifications of this process a bit more closely.

In an environment of increasing technological complexity we must develop ever more sophisticated control processes to address new problems. Such changes affect different people, different groups, different constituencies differently. And just here the eventual effects of the measures we take to address the challenges become lost in a fog of impredictability. For every winner there are some losers and various others who—not being able to see the way clear—come to feel threatened. When people confront more complex problems they find it difficult and sometimes impossible, to think their way through to satisfactory solutions. Everyone feels put to risk by some aspect of the ill understood consequence flow of potential innovation. And in the face of this perplexity, people become fearful lest any step away from the status quo—unhappy though the existing state of things may be—will plunge them into disaster. This sort of situation is an open invitation to gridlock.

What might be called a *concretization quandary* arises when it is—abstractly considered—a good idea to do A, while the only way to do so concretely is by doing A_1 or A_2 or A_3 (etc.), where nevertheless doing each of these alternative A_i is a bad idea. In such situations there is no concrete way of realizing a generically desirable objective, since this can be accomplished only in one or another of various particular ways, each of which is—individually—something negative.

Think, for example, of the story of the princess whose father is a kingly ogre who will release her from his paternal thralldom only on the condition of her marrying the princeling of some neighboring kingdom. But it turns out that all of the available princelings are quite ineligible: one is too ugly, another too stupid, a third too loutish, and the like. For the princess, marriage is a good idea in the abstract. Yet each of the actually available concrete alternatives for achieving this otherwise desirable objective is unsuitable and unacceptable. Or again, consider the plight of the younger son of an impoverished aristocrat. He finds himself so situated that taking up an appropriate career is somewhere between eminently desirable and absolutely necessary. But each of the specifically available alternatives is infeasible: he is too cowardly for the army, too hydrophobic for the navy, too skeptical for the church, and so on.

The schematic structure of such concretization quandary situations is clear. The circumstance that now arises is that while realizing a goal is desirable in the abstract, it nevertheless remains false that any and every concrete practicalization of this generic desideratum is in itself something undesirable. Those who face such a quandary situation are emplaced in the unhappy position where an outcome looks good—in the abstract, but only as long as one ignores the problematic details of its concrete actualizations. There is simply no acceptable way to get there from here.

Desiderata as such are, after all, nothing more than mere abstract wishes—mere indefinite wants: "Would that such-and-such a condition of things were realized." But effective means to this realization require concreteness: some certain *particular* way for that abstract desideratum to be concretely realized. An abstraction may be acceptable to and even desirable for us while nevertheless we shrink from each and every one of the concrete states that would bring it to realization in the actually prevailing circumstances. For it is evident that in adopting an end *we do not* and need not necessarily endorse any one of the particular means actually available for its realization. (Recall W. W. Jacobs' classic short story, "The Monkey's Paw.") In inauspicious circumstances it can, unfortunately, happen that the cultivation of what is, in and of itself, a perfectly proper desideratum may—in the prevailing circumstances—saddle us with collateral negativities. With such a concretization quandary, there just is no acceptable concretization for that deserved end. Here the apparently best course may well be to leave well enough alone. The princess might be better off staying home single with Daddy Ogre.

It is easy to see how concretization quandaries impact upon the workings of democracy in the context of the voting process. For situations frequently arise when policymaking reaches a stage where even though a social program or public work is generally acknowledged as something that is abstractly (or generically) desirable and desired, yet nevertheless each and every one of the concrete ways of realizing it is deemed unacceptable. Downsizing the market in illegal drugs, keeping teenage girls out of maternity wards or reducing the exploding public expenditures for medical services, are only a few examples of this. Here, on the question of achieving a result R-somehow vs. maintaining not-R, a decided majority is in favor of R. But equally, each and every one of the particular concrete ways of realizing R is opposed by a comparable majority. This sort of situation is something often encountered in the political arena, where we frequently read in the press stories of the following tendency:

> When asked what Congress should do about the federal deficit, two-thirds of the voters preferred cuts in major spending programs, but this support for spending cuts dissipated whenever it came to specific programs, with two-thirds of the voters opposed to each of the specific ways of achieving these cuts.

Despite an accepted "sense of the Congress" resolution, no implementing decision can manage to gain Congressional approval. In such a situation, society confronts a concretization quandary: there simply is no majoritatively acceptable way of reaching a majoritatively accepted goal. It is as when everyone agrees that there shall be a better round from *A* to *B* but no one agrees on the particular route. And with complexity this sort of situation proliferates because each concretization of that general desideratum leaves many of those affected with uncertain and messy anticipations.

Gridlock is only a manifestation of a larger difficulty. It may seem surprising but is nevertheless a fact of life that human development can reach, and in modern complex societies already have reached a stage in point of complexity where the prospect of finding a solution to our social problems by consensus formation on the basis of rational calculation is simply beyond us.

5. A Retrospective Reflection

The present deliberations have revolved around four significantly problematic issues: complexity escalation; obscurity of consequences and cognitive chaos; concretization quandaries; decision gridlock and immobilization. This condition of affairs obviously has substantial and significant implications for the general polity of social decision. In particular, it brings to the fore the question of how to proceed sensibly in the face of a technological progress that impels us into a sphere where the problem-field that confronts us may come to outrun the power of our cognitive capacities for problem resolution. For exactly this is the situation with which the judgmental principles of the case confronts us.

The instruments we forge for the solution of our problems—intellectual and physical—all prove effective only up to a point. And as new problems arise they will require new resources, new methods and devices. But, in the natural evolution of things the creation of ever new and more powerful instruments becomes increasingly difficult. And there is every reason to think that eventually—in the long run of things—the hurdle will be raised to a height that we simply cannot leap. Our standard resource of problem-solving—the use of process-modelling intelligence—may come to prove unavailing. A point may— and foreseeably will—be reached where the familiar role of modeling and calculation will no longer prove adequate as a problem resolving instrumentality.

Earlier in the present century, the Austrian school of economists argued that the domain of economic phenomena is inherently of so intricate and sophisticated a nature that such theorizing as it is practicable for us to manage really cannot provide an adequate grasp of the phenomena—and certainly not one powerful enough to guide our interventions in establishing effective control. Human phenomena in the domain of social affairs are inherently so complex, volatile, and variegated that the project of capturing them within the confining boundaries of universal laws is unrealizable. The complexity of the system of social processes at work in the operations of an advanced modern economy is such that there simply is no way for us to calculate the behavior of the system. No model that we devise will be adequate to handling the requisite details. As the Austrian theorists saw it, the very idea of a predictively adequate social science of human behavior is a pipe dream.[8]

We are brought back to the "bounded rationality" condition that arises in decision contexts when the complexity of a problem-situation substantially exceeds the reasoning powers of the problem-solver. And here, often as not, the best strategy is to let "matters run their course" and use the observation of its processes as a guide for the formation of our policies and programs. Where calculation based on theory is impracticable, the best we can usually do is to keep an eye on the broad tendencies of the case and let the course of experience be our guide in responding to them.

And a strong case can be made for saying that this sort of situation holds not just in economics but far more broadly throughout the social domain. For here too there are, fortunately, other ways of solving the complex problems posed by modern societies than by "figuring it out" through human artifice and calculation. One of these is to leave the solution of the problem to "the course of events" (either in nature or in a simulation-model of some sort), and then simply sit back and watch what happens. In circumstances that are incalculable for us because of excess complications, or where the requisite data cannot be had on a sufficiently timely basis, such a recourse to the practice of "watchful waiting," of simply seeing how the matters work themselves out when left to their own devices, is a variant and sometimes highly useful cognitive resource. The fact is that in situations of unmanageable complexity, practice in matters of public policy is often guided more effectively by localized experimental trial-and-error than by the theorizing resources of an intellectual technology unable to cope with the intricacy of interaction feedbacks and impredictable effects.

Notes

1. On complexity in relation to social and political issues see H. R. Kohl, *The Age of Complexity* (New York: New American Library, 1965).
2. For a good survey of the issues see Klaus Mainzer, *Thinking in Complexity: The Complex Dynamics of Matter, Mind, and Mankind* (Berlin, etc.: Springer Verlag, 1994).
3. Immanuel Kant, *Prolegomena to any Future Metaphysic* (1783), sect. 57. On the relevant issues also see the author's *Scientific Progress* (Oxford: Blackwell, 1978).
4. Adam Smith, *Inquiry into the Nature and Cause of the Wealth of Nations* (Dublin: Whitestone, 1776).
5. C. Northcote Parkinson, *Parkinson's Law* (Boston: Houghton Mifflin, 1957).
6. The dramatic failure of the U. S. Department of Internal Revenue's effort to computerize its operations is one particularly vivid example of this.
7. For a variety of vivid illustrations of the inherent vulnerability to failure of complex systems see Charles Perrow, *Normal Accidents Living with High-Risk Technologies* (New York: Basic Books, 1984).
8. See K. R. Popper, *Conjectures and Refutations: The Growth of Scientific Knowledge* (New York: Harper Torchbooks, 1965); F. A. Hayek, "The Theory of Complex Phenomena," in *Studies in Philosophy, Politics and Economics* (London: Routledge & Kegan Paul, 1967), pp. 22-420; F. A. Hayek, *The Counter-Revolution of Science: Studies on the Abuse of Reasons*, 2nd. ed. (Indianapolis, IN: The Free Press, 1979). On these issues see also Alexander Rosenberg, *Philosophy of the Sound Sciences* (New York: Westview Press, 1988; 2nd ed. 1995).

11

Complexity's Bearing on Philosophical Anthropology

(1) As limited creatures emplaced in a complex world, we cannot avoid recognizing that our aspirations must come to terms with nature's restrictive realities. The course of wisdom—and indeed our only realistic choice—is to make the best we can of a difficult situation. (2) In these circumstances, the existence of limits and limitations is itself—ironically—something of a mixed blessing. In a way, ignorance is bliss, for we are limited in such a manner that an exact knowledge of our limits and limitations is beyond us, so that there is always incentive for effort and room for hope. Accordingly, being the sorts of creatures we are, our limitedness in an unlimitedly complex world is not an unqualified tragedy for us. (3) All the same, complexity creates challenges for us throughout the range of our concerns with nature and with human artifice. (4) And this has far-reaching implications for the prospect of achieving a reasonable philosophical grasp in our place of the purport and prospects of our place in the world's scheme of things. (5) The everywhere flourishing prospect of accepting the world's complexity and devising cognitive instrumentalities for coming to grips with it is in process of giving rise to a new sensibility that renders "postmodernism" obsolete.

1. Dimensions of Finitude

As noted at the outset, a prime index of a system's complexity is the extent to which effort—intellectual and physical—is needed to come to adequate cognitive grips with it. This is exactly why complexity is a factor of such critical importance for us. For we humans

are finite creatures and the extent to which we can marshal the resources of intellectual effort—time, energy, skill, ingenuity—is also
finite and thereby imposes unavoidable limitations upon what we can
achieve in the way of complexity management. Such an inventory of
the parameters of our limitedness—however partial—indicates the complex structure of our field of incapacity. The chilling fact of our limitations confronts us both as individuals and as a species. Not only are
the naturally occurrent and humanly created environments that we
inhabit immensely complex systems, but so are we ourselves. In particular, human beings are creatures of needs and wants, and we have
more than we can ever possibly manage to be satisfied. An inescapable inability to obtain all of the things we would ideally like to have
marks us as correspondingly limited and weak. We know full well that
we cannot get our own way in this world—that we cannot obtain as
much of the things we want as we would like. We live in a complex
world where the total satisfaction of our needs and wants is totally
beyond us.

But why is this state of affairs so significant? Why should we not
rest satisfied with what we do have without concerning ourselves with
that unrealistic prospect of getting ever more?

The stark reality, alas, is that this is just not how things work. Our
human nature decrees otherwise. You are young and poor. A thousand
dollars looks to be a fortune to you. By dint of luck or effort you
manage to secure it. Are you now satisfied? Not on your life! Suddenly the securing of ten thousand dollars becomes a thing of importance. Or again—you yearn to see the Eiffel Tower, to sample the
sidewalk cafés of the left bank, to stroll on the Ile de la Cité in the
shade of Notre Dame. Finally you manage to get to Paris and savor the
objects of your dreams. Are you now satisfied? Not at all! Suddenly
Buckingham Palace, the Houses of Parliament, and the crown jewels
of the Tower of London acquire a new-found interest for you. No
matter what you master or learn or get, what you have is usually only
the start: a satisfied want is simply the initial step towards others. We
are—most of us—caught up in an inexorable escalation of demands,
once met we almost automatically raise our sights to new levels of
acquisition and attainment. Our natural disposition is such that the
limit of our desires is like a horizon that moves ever onwards to
remain frustratingly out of reach. Our needs may be finite, but our
wants are by and large insatiable. Even those who abandon the rat-

race quest for material goods incline to yearn for an ever ampler fulfillment by way of spiritual ones. Strive and succeed as we may in the pursuit of this world's goods, we cannot overcome those structurally inherent limits and limitations.

Moreover, there are various desiderata that we wish for in a comparative rather than absolute way. With us, the appeal of some goods, like money or power, does not inhere simply in their possession as such, but lies largely in our having more of them than others do. Yet it is of the very nature of such goods that we must for the most part fall short in regard to them—that most of us cannot obtain them to the extent that we would like, because it is simply impossible for *most* of us to possess them to an extent greater than people in general do.

It is, to be sure, imaginable that intelligent creatures inserted into nature by evolutionary processes might be so adjusted as to lack any wants over and above the satisfaction of their needs—of which they are wholly oblivious since they are "automatically" met in their ecological niche. This, so one must suppose, is just barely possible. But in our own case it is certainly not actual. We have numerous felt wants and wishes, and the bulk of our efforts and energies are spent in getting them satisfied—generally with very limited success. The reality of it is that our finitude is a shoe that pinches. The members of Homo sapiens are creatures of limits that have their limits, and being constituted as we psychologically are, we cannot—for the most part—avoid being rather painfully aware of them. The unwelcome lessons of finitude and incapacity are driven home to us from infancy onwards in the school of bitter experience. From the moment we enter into the world (often to the greeting of a rude slap), we discover that "we cannot have it all our way"—that we cannot satisfy our needs and wants with the amplitude and rapidity we would like. The fact that we have desires we cannot afford to fulfill, and talents and interests that we cannot develop within the time, energy, and resources at our disposal, means that life is a constant succession of choices—of compromises of one sort or another. And so, the recognition of limits is at once the course of necessity and the course of wisdom.[1]

2. Ramifications of Complexity: The Paradox of Finitude

How is one to respond to the reality of human limitation? One might, of course, simply shut one's eye to its existence, sticking one's head ostrich-like into the sand with regard to this entire issue. Yet this is neither a realistically plausible nor yet a rationally advisable course. It makes no sense to ignore our limitedness, simply pressing ahead blindly, ever striving for more and more in a willful ignorance that invites certain frustration in the end.

Nor is it sensible to adopt the course of discouraged defeatism, taking the fox and grapes approach, by telling oneself "I can't have my way—so the whole game's not worth the candle." There is no merit in failing to come to terms with the awkward realities of life; by giving up the struggle one is destined to settle for far less than is readily available.

The line of realistic acceptance is surely the only sensible course. Acknowledging the reality of limits, and recognizing that one simply cannot get all one desires of the good things of this world, one nevertheless proceeds in the conviction that it is possible to do better than one has managed so far and endeavors to effect improvements in the existing condition of things. One simply struggles along to do the best one can. Though doubtless far from ideal, this is clearly the most sensible course—the best alternative within a hard option of choices. And there is good theoretical justification for this focus on the prospect of improvement. For we are embarked on a journey that is literally endless, it is only an advancement-progress that can be achieved through our collective efforts, and not a destination-progress. We can gauge our progress only in terms of how far we have come, and not in terms of how far we have to go to reach a definite goal. Forging ahead by doing what we can is the best that we can manage. Perfection is beyond us, all we can realize is improvement. And to this, there is, to all appearances just no end—be it for better or for worse.

Not that we can obtain no aid and counsel along the way. The social realm about us is full of seeming sages. There is no shortage of political pundits who glibly assert that adopting this or that policy measure will solve various social problems, nor of financial wizards who are prepared to put the nation's economic affairs to rights. Nor in this fin-de-siècle era do we lack predictive pundits willing and eager to prognosticate the course of things in the twenty-first century.

What there is a shortage of, rather, are the spokesmen for a modest realism willing to say: "we actually don't just have a clue"; "there is just no available way of telling"; "we simply do not—and perhaps cannot—know enough to answer that sort of question." Few and far between are those who are modest—or candid—enough to insist upon facing up to the ominously problematic implications of the world's complexity. And the reason for the paucity of such voices is clear enough. Their expertise secures them a marked value of zero: they are engaged in delivering a message that nobody cares to hear.

But, of course, the unwelcome nature of the message does not mean that it is incorrect. The fact is that we live in a world where intractability and unpredictability are uneliminably rooted in a complexity of functioning. To be sure, the world is lawful. But the laws that govern its processes include laws of chance and chaos that render the details of its operations not just difficult to discern but actually impredictable. While we can answer our questions—or at least many of them—at a level of high generality and imprecision, the details will generally elude our grasp—and with them the sort of practical guidance we would ideally like to have.

In the wake of scientific and technological progress we build ourselves an ever higher tower of complexity. And so what we call progress has a darker side as well. A developmental disposition to increasing complexification is at work throughout the realm of human artifice. And there is no natural end of the road here—we can always do more and do better but perfection lies beyond us. In our practical affairs as in our theoretical endeavors we can always *compare* of performance. But we can never *perfect* it. And inherent in imperfection is the prospect of error and the risk of failure. The answer to the question of how to conduct life in a complex world is—very carefully. Caution, and whenever possible *pre*-caution, should be the order of the day.

The real world is a manifold of complexity—so intricate and intractable in its make-up (be it in its spatial, temporal, physical, and operational respects)—that its cognitive mastery in satisfying detail is somewhere between impracticable and impossible in many matters of interest and importance for us. A realm so complex that we cannot ever manage to provide a really adequate cognitive model of it is thereby also such that our cognitive control of it is bound to be imperfect. Where we cannot fully describe, neither can we fully explain or predict. And of course a realm that we cannot adequately explain and predict is for this very reason also one where our ability to control the course of things remains partial at best. Even if (contrary to fact) our *material* resources were not limited, our capacity to control nature—to bend the course of events to our will—is bound, the world being what it is, to be subject decisively to the insuperable limitations of our *cognitive* capacities.

We vaunt our scientific knowledge and our technological power because it is greater today than it was yesterday and vastly greater today than it was a century ago. But there is no way around the sobering realization that it is far, far less than what we would ideally like it to be. Many developments that matter—and matter greatly for us—will lie beyond our ken and control. The life of a limited creature in a complex world is inevitably and unavoidably a gamble. The element of risk is inescapable.

Technological progress by its very nature provides for increased sophistication in performance. But increasing performative sophistication means increasing complexification of process. And with increasing complexity comes increasing difficulty of performance. Through technical progress—cognitive progress included—we dig an ever deeper pit for ourselves. The complexity of our problem situation outruns our capacity for its management. And here we ultimately come up against the impediments that inhere in our limitations. In the eventual course of things we come upon problems whose resolution calls for a degree of complexity management that is beyond our reach.

As the setting of human interaction grows more complex, the management of affairs—be they practical and theoretical—also confronts increasing challenges. And this is true in the moral sector as well. In earlier days, the actions of people affected only those in their immediate environs, nowadays they bode potential consequences that reach even farther into the distance or into the future. In the days of the sword, the combatant could injure only those immediately at hand; in the day of the nuclear missile, the reach and impact if his actions is abroad immeasurably larger. The pace at which issues with social implications present themselves and the difficulty that their appropriate resolution presents is unquestionably increased in an era of expanding complexity.

There are two main sorts of knowledge, theoretical information and practical know-how. In a complex world both are available to us, but only on a limited basis. Practical knowledge guides us in going about getting our way in the world to secure health, wealth, happiness, and other goods. And no matter how well we do here we will generally have the feeling that we could and should be doing better. Theoretical knowledge is knowledge for its own sake—purely and simply for alleviating the discomfort of ignorance, by securing answers to our questions. But here too we always fall short in varying degrees. With every question we answer the door opens to new ones still to be resolved, and irrespective of how much more we take we will still fall into error, since merely *incomplete* information impels us into what are actually *mistaken* judgments. Much of our vaunted knowledge is not merely deficient but even defective. Our "mastery over nature," practical and cognitive alike, is decidedly limited, and we have to come to terms with the realization of an imperfect cognitive and physical control over our environment and its eventuations. Life in a complex world is no picnic. The inexhaustible complexity of the real means that this characteristic human aspiration of ours is bound to be frustrated. The world's complexity is such that we simply cannot get to the bottom of it.

We should—and do—realize full well our limited capacity in a world of restricted means, limited capacity, and finite resources. Homo sapiens may be "king of the hill" here on earth, but in the universe's larger scheme of things we are comparatively impotent, struggling to make our way with limited means to cope with the problems that confront us. Our cognitive and practical efforts may be a triumph of rationality, but they are a triumph of *bounded* rationality. The world's complexity unquestionably spells limitations that are bound to be harmful to our interests. Inevitably complexity puts a limits to the extent to which we humans can satisfy our needs—to say nothing of wants. It spells an inevitable impediment to the realization of the things that we would ideally like to realize. Our fondest wishes and our aspirations— be they intellectual or practical—are ambitions beyond any realistic hopes of more than partial realization.

But just how tragic for us is this fact of our finitude in the setting of a complex world? Fortunately, things are not quite as bad as they might be. The saving paradox of the debility of human finitude is that finitude to some extent provides its own remedy. For the important— and ironic—fact is that it is our limitedness itself that makes our limitedness easier to bear.

If we human beings were subject to no *temporal* limit, then—barring the miracle of perpetual regeneration—we would have to contemplate an unending gradual (asymptotic) decline after the bloom of youth. (Moreover the epistemic law of logarithmic returns would take an ever firmer hold with its frustrating implications for our penchant for novelty and innovation.) The limitation of time renders the limitation of our abilities easier to accept. If we have unlimited *resources*, then the limitation of talent and ability would clearly be even more painful. The ongoing struggle for our daily bread would then no longer provide a convenient smokescreen for our many other limitations. If we had no limitation of *knowledge*—if, for example, the hour of our death were a known fact rather than a matter of uncertain speculation (not to contemplate a knowledge of the real opinion that others actually have of us)—then leading one's life in the normal happy-go-lucky way we do would be very difficult indeed. In this way too ignorance is bliss.

It is a salient aspect of the human condition that we strive for the realization of our goals in the absence of any guarantee of success; we can virtually never know for sure in advance whether failure or success will attend our efforts. But because benefit by and large attaches to even merely making the effort itself—since often as not it is no less rewarding to try than to achieve—we are the better off for it. And even though taking this point of view involves the somewhat questionable course of "looking on the bright side of things," we had still better be grateful for small mercies and welcome opportunities to make the best and most of a difficult situation, realizing that the very existence of our limitedness makes those limitations themselves more bearable and helps to alleviate the burdens they impose. Being the sorts of creatures we are, the circumstance of our limitedness in a complex world is far from being an unqualified tragedy for us.

If we humans could manage to complete science and bring our cognitive struggle with nature to an end this too would simply have its tragic aspect. Research with its discovery of novelty, its advancing of "the frontiers of knowledge" must come to an end and science would become no more than a transmission of established lore in the hands of schoolmasters and encyclopedists. Such an ossification of the enterprise is clearly far from being a good thing.

Still, this line of thought affords somewhat cold comfort. Man has evolved within nature into the ecological niche of an intelligent being. In consequence, the need for understanding, for "knowing one's way about," is one of the most fundamental demands of the human condition. Man is *Homo quaerens*. The requirement for information, for cognitive orientation within our environment, is as pressing a human need as that for food itself. We are rational animals and must feed our minds even as we must feed our bodies. The discomfort of unknowing is a natural component of human sensibility. To be ignorant of what goes on about us is almost physically painful for us—no doubt because it is so dangerous from an evolutionary point of view. As William James observed, "The utility of this emotional effect of [security of] expectation is perfectly obvious; "natural selection," in fact, was bound to bring it about sooner or later. It is of the utmost practical importance to an animal that he should have provision of the qualities of the objects that surround him."[2] It is a situational imperative for us humans to acquire information about the world. We have questions and we need answers. Homo sapiens is a creature who must, by his very nature, feel cognitively at home in the world. Relief from ignorance, puzzlement, and cognitive dissonance is one of cognition's more important benefits. These benefits are both positive (pleasures of understanding) and negative (reducing intellectual discomfort through the removal of unknowing and ignorance and the diminution of cognitive dissonance). The basic human urge to make sense of things is a characteristic aspect of our make-up—we cannot rest satisfied with life in an environment we do not understand. For us, cognitive orientation is itself a practical need: cognitive disorientation is actually stressful and distressing. We deeply want and need to grasp the world in straightforward, accessible terms. And yet this is something that the complexity of that world's ways themselves preclude.

The situations is thus one that must be met with ambivalence. Evolved in a complex world we could not be what we are without the limits and limitations imposed upon us by that complexity.

3. Principles of Complexity

In closing, it is useful to pass in review the principal theses and perspectives that embody the book's overall line of argumentation. They stand as follows:

- *Complexity Holism*. In the realm of real-world phenomena, the three prime modes of complexity (compositional, structural, functional) are generally conjoined. (Chapter 1)
- *Complexity Coordination*. Complexity cannot emerge and persist without order. And since cognition is our standard instrumentality of order detection, this means that ontological complexity issues on open invitation to cognitive complexity. Conversely, the cognitive complexity of a system is our best index of its ontological complexity; in general, cognitive complexity reflects ontological complexity. (Chapter 1)

- *Complexity Potentiation.* Complex systems through their inherent mode of operation generally engender further principles of order that render the development of additional complexities both possible and likely. (Chapter 2)
- *Limitless Complexity.* The complexity of nature is limitless. There is no limit to the number of natural kinds to which any concrete particular belongs. Anything along the lines of J. M. Keynes' "principle of limited variety" must be rejected. (Chapter 2)
- *Spencer's Law of Development.* The history of human artifice—cognitive and practical alike—everywhere manifests a development from indefinite homogeneity to a more definite heterogeneity. This makes for increasing complexity throughout the course of historical development in the domain of human artifice. Human artifice is caught up in a complexity tropism. Throughout its domain—be it cognitive, technological, and social—a developmental dynamic of complexification is at work. (Chapter 3)
- *Rational Economy.* Since we cannot generally tell in advance of the fact just where and how further complexity will arise, rational people will not introduce complications except where and insofar as they are needed to accomplish the tasks in hand. (Chapter 3)
- *Cognitive Dialectic.* At any particular stage of the cognitive state of the art our limited cognitive accommodation of the world's unending complexity is inadequate. This makes for an ongoing and unavoidable destabilization—and subsequent enhanced complexification—of our scientific picture of the world. (Chapter 3)
- *Technological Escalation.* Scientific progress in a complex world requires an ever more powerful technology of observation and experimentation. In natural science, the deepening of knowledge requires the continual enhancement of technology. Natural science is involved in something of an arms race against nature. (Chapter 4).
- *Logarithmic Returns.* The world's complexity engenders a cognitive retardation effect. A vast amount of *information* has to be generated to possibilize the accession of *knowledge* (indeed our information must grow exponentially to enable our knowledge to grow linearly so as to progress at a constant pace). A law of diminishing returns accordingly obtains throughout the domain of factual inquiry. (Chapter 4)
- *Limits and Limitations.* Our knowledge of nature cannot be perfected. In this domain we have no choice but to do the best we can—to "give it our best shot"—in the full realization that in a highly complex world our best may not be good enough. (Chapter 5)
- *Question Proliferation.* Throughout the sciences, the answers to our questions always open up new questions. (Chapter 6)
- *Scientific Anthropocentrism.* Our *science* is *our* science: it is geared to our particular modes of experiential emplacement in nature's scheme of things (Chapter 7)
- *The Hydra Effect.* In the course of progress—be it cognitive or techni-

cal—problems grow faster than solutions. In consequence, our having to contend with an ever-increasing complexity in this domain pervasively complicates the management of life. (Chapter 8)

- *The Predicament of Reason.* Problem solutions developed on an imperfect basis are always vulnerable; they are themselves likely to be imperfect. And this means that in our complex world human reason is unable to issue any guarantees. (Chapter 8).
- *Perplexity Enlargement.* We confront a situation of complexity tropism. And this ongoing complexification of science and technology—and of the social systems that this progress renders both possible and unavoidable—confronts us with substantial problems of social management and decision, seeing that the successful management of our affairs becomes increasingly difficult in an environment of increasing sophistication. (Chapter 9)
- *Complexity/Risk Coordination.* Complex systems engender characteristic vulnerabilities: the more complicated a system, the greater the prospect of something going seriously wrong. Greater sophistication spells greater risks. (Chapter 9)
- *Concretization Quandaries.* With complex social systems, decision making can thus become frustrated by the fact that much of the time no concrete way of achieving a generally agreed resolution can be achieved. (Chapter 9)
- *Mixed Blessings.* The very imperfection of our knowledge is, in a way, itself a safeguard against disaster in situations of imperfect information. Our ignorance regarding just what it is that we cannot achieve provides a rationale for putting forth our best efforts. (Chapter 10)

These ideas combine to teach an overall lesson. Complexity creates difficulties for us throughout its presence in the realms of nature and artifice. The management of our affairs within a social, technological, and cognitive environment which, through our efforts, we do ourselves and must render increasingly complex is for this very reason increasingly challenging. It complicates matters by bringing in its wake vast problems of management and risks of mishap. In primitive societies, failure to understand how things work can endanger a family or at worst a clan or tribe. As man-made catastrophes on the model of Chernobyl indicate, in the modern world it can endanger millions, possibly even putting at risk the totality of human life on our planet. Life in a realm of complexity is fraught with greater risks of disaster. It deserves emphasis—and reemphasis—that the answer to the question of how to conduct life in a complex world is: very carefully. And even as our conduct of life's practical affairs must realistically gear itself to the demands of a complex world, so must our management of theoretical issues in the domain of rational inquiry accommodate itself to this perhaps unwelcome but nevertheless inexorable aspect of reality.

But what does the world's complexity mean for the moral dimension of life, seeing that morality at large is concerned with right action and that the intelligent choice of course of action is unavoidably difficult in a complex world? The answer here will depend on the sorts of moralists we are. If we are rigid utilitarians who estimate an act's rightness by its causal consequences, then heaven help us, since complex interactions will all too often be impossible to foresee. If we are statistical consequentialists who evaluate the rightness of actions via their foreseeably probable causal consequences, then matters become more manageable. Complexity is now still an obstacle to overcome, but not an insuperable one—a troublesome nuisance rather than a decisive obstacle. Finally if we are deontologists who prioritize motive and intentions in the evaluation of action, then the world's complexity becomes irrelevant; it is now the inner turmoil of personality that matters. But in any case and in any event, the cultivation of a moral life remains—as it must—a difficult project in this complex world of ours.[3] And indeed as science advances the range of effective intervention in nature's course of things these difficulties moral comportment become even more challenging. For the demands of "doing the best we can" are bound to become more challenging as the range of what we actually can do—be it for good or for evil—itself becomes enlarged in the course of scientific progress.

4. Philosophizing in a Complex World

Ever since the origination of the classical idea of a "science" in Greek antiquity, most philosophers have geared their aspirations for the discipline to the idea of a science modelled—as was the science of the Greeks—upon *mathematics*. Their goal has been to answer the questions of their field with the precision and universality characteristic of the mathematical sciences. The theories of such a "science," as classically conceived, seek to accomplish their explanatory business in terms of an unqualified universality based on what happens always and everywhere and in all circumstances. The quest for a cognitive grasp of the lawful structure of the world in terms of a deep irrefrangible necessity underlying the world's seemingly fortuitous phenomenal surface has ever been the aspiration of science. And the philosophy to which our Greek precursors aspired was to be a science in exactly this sense. (Aristotle's recourse to biologically inspired on-the-whole generalizations was soon shelved in the subsequent tradition.) Accordingly, the quest for philosophical *epistêmê*—for hard and precise mathematics-like knowledge—in philosophical matters characterized the mainstream tradition of philosophy that has come down to us from Greek antiquity. In fact, however, this aspiration is deeply problematic.

It is possible—and for various reasons desirable—to contemplate a very different, substantially more modest program for philosophical inquiry, one that proposes to proceed not in terms of *how on the basis of general principles matters must invariably stand*, but rather in terms of *how as a matter of fact (given the world's realities) matters normally do stand*. Such a less ambitious and, as it were, empirically oriented philosophy would remain satisfied with securing limited and contingent generalities rather than insisting on unrestricted and exceptionless universality. Foregoing universalistic necessitarianism, it takes a more cautious line and is willing to be guided by the teachings of our experience with the world's course of affairs, being prepared to carry on its deliberations in terms of how matters actually do stand in the world, generally and on the whole.

Such an approach carries in its wake the prospect of a more modestly conceived philosophy—one prepared to make its claims not with a view to how things must necessarily stand always and universally, but rather with a view oriented at how things generally stand in the normal, ordinary, usual course of things. In its *methodological* stance, philosophical standardism accordingly carries philosophical empiricism in its wake, seeing that the standard (normal, accustomed) is only determinable as such in a way that does—and must—be reflective of experience.[5] Through its very nature standardism underwrites an "empirical" conception of the philosophical enterprise as a process of theorizing that is inextricably interconnected with the substance of our (person-variable) experience with the issues that occupy our attention.

Philosophy is now led to take a distinctly "phenomenological" turn in becoming inextricably bound up with the world's realities as the experiential course of things presents them to us. This approach in philsophy is willing to settle the issues of the field in terms of theses that are geared to the usual or normal course of things. Its ruling maxim is: "Project your philosophical views and theories on the basis of a reasonable grasp or the customary course of things—leaving aside concern for bizarre and unusual situations that fly in the face of established patterns and normal circumstances." This variant, *standardist* mode of philosophizing based on *generalities* rather than *universalities* opens up new and far more promising prospects. It too is empirical in procedure though, to be sure, its concern with specifically philosophical issues prevents this enterprise from becoming a natural science proper.[4]

The theorist who has perhaps most emphatically stressed the standardistic aspect of philosophical conceptions was the English philosopher R. G. Collingwood. He characterized the pivotal phenomenon as "the overlap of classes." For him, philosophical generalizations of a rigidly universal sort—be it affirmative like "All *A*'s are *B*'s" (which excludes the *A*'s from the non-*B*'s) or negative like "No *A*'s are *B*'s" (which excludes the *A*'s from the *B*'s)—are always inappropriate because whenever the *A*'s and *B*'s represent philosophically germane classes or categories there will never be sharp boundaries that avert the prospect of deviant "borderline" cases: "The specific classes of a philosophical genus do not exclude one another, but overlap. This overlap is not exceptional, it is normal; and it is not negligible in extent, it may reach formidable proportions."[6] As Collingwood stressed, "imperfect" generalizations of the sort that standardism typifies are bound to play a key role in philosophical theorizing.

In any case, philosophical standardism opts for practicable modesty in a complex world. It calls for abandoning pretentions to universality and inevitability, instead shifting our attention to normal circumstances and ordinary cases. Gearing its philosophizing not to the necessities of abstract general principles, but to the actualities as our cognitive commerce with the world reveals them to us, philosophical standardism abandons the traditional a priori stance of mainstream Western philosophy in favor of one that is a posteriori and experientially oriented. It does not try to resolve issues in terms of how things must necessarily go as a matter of theoretical general principle, but rather proceeds in terms of how things do normally go as best we can determine the matter. Rather than looking to general principles of abstract necessity, it proceeds in an empirical spirit, seeking guidance in *experience*— with all its characteristic contingencies and potential incompleteness.

Viewing the issues in this light suggests that postmodern critiques of philosophy have it wrong. The shortcoming of classical philosophy that has led it into endless quarrels and perplexities is not so much an exaggerated commitment to *certainty* as one to a *precision* that is simply unavailable in philosophy's problem context, given the disparity between the complexity of the issues and the modest data at our disposal in grappling with them.[7]

5. After Postmodernism

Students of contemporary culture are given to dwelling enthusiastically on the distinction between modernism and the postmodern sensibility they themselves espouse. As they see it, the moderns, who flourished predominantly in the eighteenth and nineteenth centuries, were aficionados of what might be called the Newtonian world order of scientific lawfulness. Their outlook was that of Newton, Laplace, and Darwin with the world viewed as an orderly framework of natural law. The Kantian principle of causality standing at the forefront of their thinking and the world—natural and human alike—was seen as a cosmos where everything is orderly, lawful, intelligent, explicable. Reality was viewed as a tidy system, akin to a formal garden with orderly arrangements and tidy borders.

By contrast, the twentieth-century scene is seen as postmodern. World War I smashed the old social and political order. Einstein, Plank, Schrödinger, and company broke up the old physical order. Cantor, Gödel, Heyting, and others broke up the old mathematical order. Quantum theory issued in the breakdown of causality. Evolutionary theory now emphasized not the "survival of the fittest" but the platform of sheer randomness on which natural selection has to do its work. Existentialists stressed the arbitrary leaps of faith that marked a "death of God" ideology. Ethicists celebrated the demise of traditional morality in the setting of a Nietzschean transvaluation of values. Anthropologists and cultural relativists reduced morals to variable mores. Cognitive relativists insisted on the arbitrariness of science itself. Literary and linguistic deconstructionists dissolved a putatively coherent discourse of stable meanings into incoherent babble. On every side, the political, social, intellectual forces of disintegration have been in full cry. Everywhere the substitution of anarchy for structure contravened against the rational orderliness of the earlier modern era. Coherence is lost and anarchy rules! Or so the partisans of postmodernism maintain.[8]

But the culture critics entranced with this dialectic of the postmodern over against the modern have failed to observe a development that has been unfolding under their very eyes over the past twenty years of so. For gradually and without fanfare a new sensibility has made a gradual but inexorable transit into prominence. Unexpectedly and unheralded a new post-post-modern world-view has been emerging.

What shapes and orients the intellectual perspective of this newer style of thought is a recognition of *the self-generation of order in a universe of chance*. Fundamental to this idea is the discovery that the randomness and chance that indeed characterize nature do not make for anarchy—for unruly and incoherent lawlessness. For there is a crucial difference between anarchy (a total absence of order) and chaos, as a mode or order that can and does emerge naturally from chance and randomness. Mere chance itself engenders an order that can be analyzed by a mathematical calculus whose law of large numbers affords a pathway to lawfulness. The emergence of lawful order in a world of chance and chaos is a natural and rationally tractable phenomenon. Throughout the sciences—physics (stochastic phenomena), biology (evolutionary self-development), sociology (collective self-organization)—there is emerging a common recognition that a universe of chance and chaos is not unruly (anarchic) but merely complex, exhibiting through its natural operation the emergence of higher-order lawfulness.[9] And while formal logic has yielded its classical fixities, a new, nonclassical and many-valued (or "fuzzy") logic has risen up to take its place. Certainties have been effectively superseded by probabilities and plausibilities. We do indeed inhibit a world pervaded by chance and chaos yet such a world is not unruly (anarchic) but merely complex. What is perhaps the principal theme of late twentieth century science—and one which distinguishes it from all that has gone before—is nature's tendency to self-organization, the natural dynamic in highly complex systems of an emergence of order from disorder, lawfulness from chance, structure from chaos.

And in its own gradual way this recognition of self-organization and the natural emergence of complex order from chance and chaos has come to pervade the landscape of science. It nowadays occupies the middle ground between the modernistically oversimplification of a universe frozen into deterministic order and the postmodern vacuity of a universe viewed as anarchic, irrational, and totally unruly beyond the grasp of rational comprehensibility.

The reality of the situation is that we nowadays find unfolding throughout contemporary science a flourishing project of accepting the world's complexity and devising the cognitive instrumentalities needed to come to grips with it. On all sides the discernible indications conspire to indicate that a new intellectual sensibility is emerging that in process of rendering postmodernism obsolete.

While contemporary culture theorists almost invariably dwell lovingly on disorder, disharmony, and anarchy, recent science in every branch has been discovering and elaborating the natural mechanisms of order formation. (To be sure the "order" at issue lacks all of the neat simplicities to which modernists were attached. It is always an order which grows out of complexity and proceeds to exhibit complexities in its own right.)

We do indeed inhabit a chaotic universe of chance. But the mathematical and conceptual instruments of modern science enable us to make it possible to see such a world as the stage for the self-generation of order. In such a world order and the coherence rational intelligibility that go with it are by no means lost altogether. It only requires more powerful cognitive instrumentalities to find them. The pathway to understanding is not blocked, it only becomes more challenging to pursue.

Noting the inherent limitations of the "modern" categories of understanding and explanation, the postmoderns forsook the courage of rational conviction and viewed themselves as living in a world that is fundamentally unintelligible and inaccessible to reason. By contrast, the post-postmodern sensibility is in fact increasingly rehabilitating this rational conviction because it sees on all sides the development of intellectual tools by whose means those supposedly intractably forces of chance, contingency, and fluctuating variability permit of rational comprehension and explanation. Where the postmoderns saw incomprehensibility, their post-postmodern successors have come to see a mere complexity that is substantially tractable by new cognitive instrumentalities more powerful than those available heretofore.

How is one to account for the blindness of our contemporary culture theorists regarding to this phenomenon. Part of the explanation doubtless lies in the fact that they are so enchanted with the mystique of postmodernism that the fact that the scientific zeitgeist of the day is leaving it in the lurch is a message they do not wish to hear. But a larger part of the explanation apparently lies in the fact that they cannot hear it. For this trend is prominent in scientific culture, and their own immersion in literary culture stands in the way of their taking note of it. The best explanation accordingly resides in C. P. Snow's "two cultures" phenomenon—the distancing of literary culture from its scientific counterpart. The developments that have been taking place in physics, chemistry, biology, and mathematics are thereby substantially outside the cognitive range of our present-day culture gurus, so that the facts of life about the complex natural world in which they live are something they neither can nor wish to understand.

Notes

1. On this theological aspect of complexity see the papers assembled in *Chaos and Complexity: Scientific Perspectives on Divine Action* ed. by Robert John Russell et al. (Vatican City State: Vatican Observatory Publications, 1995).
2. William James, "The Sentiment of Rationality," in *The Will to Believe and Other Essays in Popular Philosophy* (New York and London: Longmans, Green, and Co, 1897), pp. 78-79.
3. In this regard it is well worthwhile to reflect on Emile Durkheim's challenging treatment of the division of labor in society, which serves to highlight the moral ambivalence of this ever increasing complexity. For this also serves to blunt our moral sensibilities as the enterprise of giving aid and comfort to our needy fellows increasingly becomes not the business of us all but of public institutions and their manifold specialists. See Emile Durkheim's classic *Division of Labor in Society* (1893).
4. The fact that philosophy may use the scientific facts of life for its explanatory purposes—how else, after all, would a philosophy of nature or a philosophical psychology be possible—does not make philosophy into a natural science.
5. Someone might ask, "How can a view of the customary course of matters within the framework of an experience bear on the seemingly nonempirical questions of the philosophy of mathematics or the philosophy of logic?" But this would be naive. For what is involved is not, of course, just our *sensory* experience of interaction with the physical world, but also our *conceptualizing* experience with the issues of the domain—including such abstractions as concepts, structures, numbers, etc.
6. R. G. Collingwood, *An Essay on Philosophical Method* (Oxford: The Clarendon Press, 1933), p. 3. To all appearances, Collingwood's bold generalization is problematic on its own grounds. For, "All philosophical generalizations are problematic" carries obvious consequences for this generalization itself. Here, as with many philosophical doctrines (e.g., scepticism), the table-turning argument (*peritropê*) deployed by Socrates against the Protagoras of Plato's *Theaetetus* is once again serviceable.
7. For some elaborations of this theme see the author's *Philosophical Standardism* (Pittsburgh, PA: University of Pittsburgh Press, 1994).
8. Some instances of works in which the postmodern sensibility is astir are: Jacques Derrida, *Writing and Difference* tr. by A. Bass (Chicago: University of Chicago Press, 1978); Paul de Man *The Resistance to Theory* (Minneapolis: University of

Minnesota Press, 1986); Joseph Margolis, *The Flux of History and the Flux of Science* (Berkeley: University of California Press, 1993) and *Science Without Unity: Reconciling the Human and Natural Sciences* (Oxford: Blackwell, 1987); Richard Rorty, *Consequences of Pragmatism* (Cambridge: Cambridge University Press, 1989).

9. For a vivid account of the contemporary situation in science see Klaus Mainzer, *Thinking on Complexity* (Berlin: Springer Verlag, 1994), and Ilya Prigogine and Nicolis Grégoire, *Exploring Complexity* (New York: W.H. Freeman, 1989). These writers give extensive reference to the literature

Selected Bibliography

Adams, Henry Brooks, *The Education of Henry Adams: An Autobiography* (Boston: Houghton Mifflin, 1918).

Amaldi, Edoardo, "The Unity of Physics," *Physics Today*, vol. 261, no. 9 (September 1973), pp. 23–29.

Anderson, Philip W., Kenneth J. Arrow, and David Pines, eds., *The Economy as an Evolving Complex System: Santa Fe Institute Studies in the Sciences of Complexity,* Proceedings, vol. 5 (Redwood City, CA: Addison-Wesley, 1988).

Atkins, P.W., *The Second Law* (New York: Scientific American Library, 1984).

Auger, Pierre, *Currents Trends in Scientific Research* (Paris: UNESCO Publications, 1961).

Badii, Remo and Antonio Polili, *Complexity: Hierarchical Structure and Scaling in Physics* (Cambridge: Cambridge University Press, 1997).

Barber, Bernard, *Science and the Social Order* (Westport, CT: Greenwood Press, 1952).

Barrow, John D., *Theories of Everything* (Oxford: Clarendon Press, 1991).

Barrow, John D. and Frank J. Tipler, *The Anthropic Cosmological Principle* (Oxford: Clarendon Press, 1968).

Bechtel, William, and Robert C. Richardson, *Discovering Complexity* (Princeton, NJ: Princeton University Press, 1993).

Behe, Michael J., *Darwin's Black Box: The Biochemical Challenge to Evolution* (New York: The Free Press, 1996).

Bennett, C. H., "The Thermodynamics of Computation—A Review," *International Journal of Theoretical Physics*, vol. 21 (1982), pp. 905–17.

Bohm, David, and F. David Peat, *Science, Order and Creativity* (New York: Bantam Books, 1987).

Bonner, John Tyler, *The Evolution of Complexity* (Princeton, NJ: Princeton University Press, 1988).

Brandon, Robert N., *Adaptation and Environment* (Princeton, NJ: Princeton University Press, 1990).

Bunge, Mario, *The Myth of Simplicity* (Englewood Cliffs, NJ: Prentice-Hall, 1963).

———, *The Methodological Unity of Science* (Dordrecht: Kluwer, 1973).

———*Philosophy of Physics* (Dordrecht: Kluwer, 1972).

———*Scientific Research*, 2 vols. (New York: Springer, 1967).

Cartwright, Nancy, *How the Laws of Physics Lie* (Oxford: Oxford University Press, 1983).

Casti, John L., *Searching for Certainty* (New York, Morrow, 1991; paperback: New York: Quill, 1992).

———, *Complexification* (New York: Harper Collins, 1994).

Casti, John L. and A. Karlqvist (eds.), *Complexity, Language and Life* (Berlin: Springer Verlag, 1986).

Coveny, Peter, and Roger Highfield, *Frontiers of Complexity* (New York: Fawcett Columbine, 1995).

Davies, Paul (ed.), *The New Physics* (Cambridge: Cambridge University Press, 1989).

Davies, Paul C., *The Mind of God* (New York: Simon and Schuster, 1992).

Dawkins, Richard, *The Blind Watchmaker* (New York: Norton, 1986).

Dreyfus, Hubert L., *What Computers Can't Do: A Critique of Artificial Reason* (New York: Free Press, 1986).

———, *What Computers* Still *Can't Do: A Critique of Artificial Reason* (London: MIT Press, 1993).

Dreyfus, Hubert L. and E. Dreyfus, *Mind Over Machine* (New York: Free Press, 1986).

Duprè, John, *The Disorder of Things: Metaphysical Foundations of the Disunity of Science,* (Cambridge, MA: Harvard University Press, 1993).

Eddington, Arthur S., *The Nature of the Physical World* (New York: The Macmillan Company, and Cambridge: The University Press, 1929).

Epstein, Richard A., *Simple Rules for a Complex World* (Cambridge, MA: Harvard University Press, 1995).

Flint, Robert , *Philosophy as Scientia Scientiarum: A History of Classifications of the Sciences* (Edinburgh and London: W. Blackwood and Sons, 1904).

Gleick, James, *Chaos: Making a New Science* (New York: Viking, 1987).

Godfrey-Smith, Peter, *Complexity and the Function of Mind in Nature* (Cambridge: Cambridge University Press, 1996; Cambridge Studies in the Philosophy of Biology).

Hartmanis, J., and John E. Hopcroft, "An Overview of the Theory of Computational Complexity," *Journal of the Association for Computing Machinery*, vol. 18 (1971), pp. 444–75.

Hayek, F. A., *The Counter-Revolution of Science: Studies on the Abuse of Reasons*, 2nd. ed. (Indianapolis, IN: The Free Press, 1979).

———, "The Theory of Complex Phenomena" in his *Studies in Philosophy, Politics and Economics* (London: Routledge & Kegan Paul, 1967), pp. 22–42.

Helmer, Olaf, and Nicholas Rescher, "The Epistemology of the Inexact Sciences," *Management Science*, vol. 6 (1959), pp. 25–52.

Hofstadter, Douglas, *G^del, Escher, Bach: An Eternal Golden Braid* (New York: Basic Books, 1979).

Holland, John H., *Hidden Order: How Adaptation Builds Complexity* (Reading, MA: Addison Wesley, 1995).

Horgan, John, *The End of Science* (Reading ,MA: Addison Wesley, 1996).

Hugly, Philip, and Charles Sayward, "Can a Language Have Indenumerably Many Expressions?" *History and Philosophy of Logic*, vol. 4 (1983), pp. 73–82.

Jen, Erica (ed.), 1989 *Lectures in Complex Systems* (Redwood City, CA: Addison-Wesley, 1990; Santa Fe Institute Studies in the Sciences of Complexity, Lecture Series, vol. 2).

Kauffman, Stuart, *The Origins of Order* (New York: Oxford University Press, 1993).

————, *The Origins of Order: Self-Organization and Selection in Evolution* (Oxford: Oxford University Press, 1992).

————, *At Home in the Universe: The Search for Laws of Self-Organization and Complexity* (New York and Oxford: Oxford University Press, 1995).

Kohl, H. R., *The Age of Complexity* (Westport, CT.: Greenwood Press, 1965).

Kroll, Lucian, *An Architecture of Complexity*, tr. by P. B. Jones (Cambridge, MA: MIT Press, 1987).

Lewin, Roger, *Complexity* (New York: Macmillan, 1992).

Machlup, Fritz, *The Production and Distribution of Knowledge in the United States* (Princeton, NJ: Princeton University Press, 1962).

Mainzer, Klaus, *Thinking in Complexity: The Complex Dynamics of Matter, Mind, and Mankind* (Berlin: Springer Verlag, 1994).

Mandelbrot, Benoit, *The Fractal Geometry of Nature* (San Francisco, CA: W. H. Freeman, 1977).

Margenau, Henry, *The Nature of Physical Reality* (New York: McGraw-Hill, 1950).

McIntyre, Lee C., "Complexity and Social Scientific Laws," *Synthese*, vol. 97 (1993), pp. 209–27.

Menard, H. W., *Science: Growth and Change* (Cambridge, MA: Harvard University Press, 1971).

Pagels, Heinz R., *The Dreams of Reason: The Computer and the Rise of the Sciences of Complexity* (New York: Simon & Schuster, 1988).

Parkinson, C. Northcote, *Parkinson's Law* (Boston: Houghton Mifflin, 1957).

Peirce, Charles Sanders, *Collected Papers*, 8 vols. (Cambridge, MA: Harvard University Press, 1931–58).

Penrose, Roger, *The Emperor's New Mind: Concerning Computers, Minds, and the Laws of Physics* (New York: Oxford University Press, 1989).

Perrow, Charles, *Normal Accidents : Living with High-Risk Technologies* (New York: Basic Books, 1984).

Petley, B. W., *The Fundamental Physical Constants and the Frontiers of Measurement* (Bristol and Boston: Hilger, 1985).

Pines, David, ed. *Emerging Syntheses in Science* (Redwood City, CA: Addison-Wesley, 1986; Santa Fe Institute Studies in the Sciences of Complexity, Proceedings, vol. 1).

Popper, Karl R., *The Logic of Scientific Discovery* (New York: Basic Books, 1959).

————, *Conjectures and Refutations: The Growth of Scientific Knowledge* (New York: Harper Torchbooks, 1965).

Postin, T. and I. Stuart, *Catastrophe Theory and its Applications* (London: Pittman, 1978).

Pour-El, Marion B. and J. Ian Richards, *Computibility in Analysis and Physics* (Berlin: Springer Verlag, 1989).

Price, Derek J., *Little Science, Big Science* (New York: Columbia University Press, 1963).

————, *Science Since Babylon*, 2nd ed. (New Haven, CT: Yale University Press, 1975).

Prigogine, Ilya, *From Being to Becoming* (New York: W. H. Freeman, 1980).

Prigogine, Ilya, and Isabelle Stengers, *Order out of Chaos* (New York: Bantam Books, 1984).

Prigogine, Ilya and GrÈgoire Nicolis, *Exploring Complexity: An Introduction* (New York: W. H. Freeman, 1989).

Pylyshyn, Z. W., *Computation and Cognition: Toward a Foundation for Cognitive Science* (Cambridge, MA: MIT Press, 1984).

Reichenbach, Hans, *Experience and Prediction* (Chicago: University of Chicago Press, 1938).

Rescher, Nicholas, *Scientific Progress* (Oxford: Basil Blackwell, 1978).

————, *Empirical Inquiry* (Totowa, NJ: Rowman & Littlefield, 1982).

————, *The Limits of Science* (Berkeley and Los Angeles: University of California Press, 1984).

————, *The Strife of Systems* (Pittsburgh, PA: University of Pittsburgh Press, 1985).

————, *Scientific Realism* (Dordrecht: D. Reidel, 1987).

————, *Rationality* (Oxford: Oxford University Press, 1988).

————, *Cognitive Economy* (Pittsburgh, PA: University of Pittsburgh Press, 1989).

————, *A Useful Inheritance* (Savage, MD: Rowman & Littlefield, 1990).

————, *Philosophical Standardism* (Pittsburgh, PA: University of Pittsburgh Press, 1994).

————, *Satisfying Reason* (Dordrecht: Kluwer, 1995).

————, *Priceless Knowledge?* (Lanham, MD: University Press of America, 1996).

————, *Predicting the Future* (Albany: State University of New York Press, 1997).

Richardson, Ernest Cushing, *Classification: Theoretical and Practical*, 3rd. ed. (New York: H. W. Wilson Co., 1930).

Richardson, Robert C., *Discovering Complexity* (Princeton, NJ: Princeton University Press, 1993).

Rosenberg, Alexander, *Economics—Mathematical Politics or Science of Diminishing Returns?* (Chicago, University of Chicago Press, 1992).

————, "Scientific Innovation and the Limits of Social Scientific Prediction," *Synthese*, vol. 97 (1993), pp. 161–82.

————, *Philosophy of the Social Sciences* (Boulder, CO: Westview Press, 1988; 2nd ed., 1995).

Russell, Robert John, Nancy Murphy, and Arthur R. Peacocke, *Chaos and Complexity: Scientific Perspectives or Divine Action* (Vatican City, Vatican Observatory Publications; and Berkeley California, Center for Theology and the Natural Sciences, 1995).

Salmon, Wesley C., *Four Decades of Scientific Explanation* (Minneapolis: University of Minnesota Press, 1989).

Salthe, S. N., *Evolving Hierarchical Systems* (New York: Columbia University Press, 1985).

Saunders, P. T., *An Introduction to Catastrophe Theory* (Cambridge: Cambridge University Press, 1980).

Simon, Herbert A., *The Sciences of the Artificial* (Cambridge, MA: MIT Press, 1969; 2nd ed, 1981).

Sloman, Aaron, *The Computer Revolution in Philosophy : Philosophy, Science, and Models of Mind* (Sussex, UK : Harvester Press, 1978).

Smith, John Maynard, "What Can't the Computer Do?" in the *New York Review of Books*, 15 March 1990 issue.

Spencer, Herbert, *First Principles*, 7th ed. (London: Methuen, 1889).

Stein, Daniel L. (ed.), *Lectures in the Sciences of Complexity* (Redwood City, CA: Addison-Wesley, 1989; Santa Fe Institute Studies in the Sciences of Complexity, Lecture Series, vol. 1).

Stein, Daniel L., and Lynn Nadel, eds. *1990 Lectures in Complex Systems* (Redwood City, CA: Addison-Wesley, 1991; Santa Fe Institute Studies in the Sciences of Complexity, Lecture Series, vol. 3).

Stewart, I., *Does God Play Dice?* (Oxford: Basil Blackwell, 1989).

Ulam, Stanislaw M., *Adventures of a Mathematician* (New York: Scribner, 1976).

Vaughan, Diane, *The Challenger Launch Decision* (Chicago: University of Chicago Press, 1996).

Waldrop, M. Mitchell, *Complexity* (New York: Simon and Schuster, 1992).

Weaver, Warran, "Science and Complexity,"*American Scientist*, vol. 36 (1948), pp. 536–48.

Weinberg, Steven, *Dreams of a Final Theory* (New York: Pantheon, 1992).

————"Impact of Large-Scale Science on the United States," *Science*, vol. 134 (1961; 21 July issue), pp. 161–64.

Weizs‰cker, C. F. von, "The Unity of Physics" in Ted Bastin (ed.), *Quantum Theory and Beyond*, (Cambridge: Cambridge University Press, 1971).

Wheeler, John, *At Home in the Universe* (New York: American Institute of Physics Press, 1994).

Wigner, E. P., "The Limits of Science," *Proceedings of the American Philosophical Society*, vol. 93 (1949), pp. 521–26.

————, "The Unreasonable Effectiveness of Mathematics in the Natural Sciences, " *Communications in Pure and Applied Mathematics*, vol. 13 (1960), pp. 1–14.

Winston, P. H., *Artificial Intelligence* (Reading, MD: Addison Wesley, 1977).

Zurek, W. H. (ed.), *Complexity, Entropy, and the Physics of Information* (New York: Addison Wesley, 1990; Santa Fe Institute Studies in the Sciences of Complexity, Proceedings, vol. 8).

Index of Names